W9-DHF-694

UNTAPPED GOOD

The Rehabilitation of School Dropouts

UNTAPPED GOOD

The Rehabilitation of School Dropouts

By

NORMAN M. CHANSKY, Ph.D.

Professor of Educational Psychology
School of Education
Temple University
Philadelphia, Pennsylvania
Formerly Associate Professor of Psychology and Educational Research
North Carolina State University
Raleigh, North Carolina

CHARLES C THOMAS · PUBLISHER
Springfield · Illinois · U.S.A.

Published and Distributed Throughout the World by

CHARLES C THOMAS • PUBLISHER
BANNERSTONE HOUSE
301-327 East Lawrence Avenue, Springfield, Illinois, U.S.A.
NATCHEZ PLANTATION HOUSE
735 North Atlantic Boulevard, Fort Lauderdale, Florida, U.S.A.

Library of Congress Catalog Card Number: 66-21420

Printed in the United States of America
C-1

This study is dedicated to

The Honorable Terry Sanford

whose love for and understanding of the people of North Carolina moved him to seek educational programs which would benefit the retarded and the gifted, the young and the old, the college bound and the dropout. Only through ennobling the human mind can great men live in a Great Society.

INTRODUCTION

OPERATION Second Chance (OSC) was North Carolina's manpower training scion ingrafted to the imaginative educational programs of former Governor Terry Sanford. Its aim was to raise the general educational and technical thresholds of hard core unemployables, but most especially the school dropout. Funded by the Office of Manpower, Automation and Training of the United States Department of Labor (OMAT) and the Area Redevelopment Administration (ARA), it was poised to instill a life purpose to the diffident dropout and to make available trained manpower for the local community and State labor markets. To plan such a program, the governor appointed to a state advisory committee representatives of several state agencies: Labor, Employment Security, Welfare, and Education. At the helm was a succession of supervisors from the Education and Employment Security arms of the state government. James Ellerbe of the Department of Community Colleges was the fourth and final chairman of a floundering committee. In retrospect, it must be confessed, that little is truly known about the selection and retraining of dropouts. Not only that, but even less is known about the peculiar traits of character which have earned them a special title. Thus, the OSC leadership was destined to be drawn from a limited pool of government servants who had a monopoly on a limited reserve of fragmentary and occasionally ambiguous information about the rehabilitation of school dropouts.

A faith that *education* could catalyze the betterment of North Carolina and its citizens was the faith shared by the members of the state advisory committee. Ill reputed dropouts, the committee was confident, could redeem themselves by learning a trade. Well known to the group were the views that the dropout was a moral leper and a parasitic teenager who sucked the teats of the Welfare and Employment Security agencies. Some members of the committee held these same suspicions. Confronting them, in addition, was the evidence of the high rate of failure on the Selective Service examinations. Often such failure was linked to functional illiteracy.

After its initial ramblings the attention of the committee shifted from the dropout being orphaned by the schools to finding the trades which he could learn so he might fit into society. Irrespective of what dropouts are or what they might be, the committee voiced enthusiastic endorsement for any educational program which extended hope to the many economically distressed communities.

The purpose of OSC was noble. It was to give youngsters limping through life a chance to walk upright. They could achieve dignity through labor. To accomplish this, interagency cooperation was essential. The Employment Security Commission was assigned the responsibility for identifying the training needs of an applicant and to place the graduate in a job after the Department of Community Colleges provided a trainee with a suitable curriculum.

In each community in which OSC programs were active, a Local Advisory Board was established. Local educators, clergymen, industrialists and politicians pooled their efforts to sell early school leavers the idea of vocational training. By and large this was accomplished through the office of the local project coordinator. After he received the names and addresses of school dropouts between the ages of sixteen and one-half and twenty-two, he contacted them by mail or in person. Local newspapers carried stories about OSC; television stations made spot announcements about it.

After recruitment, applicants were assigned to ARA approved training programs. Upon graduation, many students actively sought work. The kinds of jobs they received were classified as training related and training unrelated. Some graduates, however, sought but did not find employment. Others never looked. These were the unemployed graduates. This report is the story of the subsequently employed and unemployed trainees who were granted a second chance to learn a skill. Could the program outcomes have either been predicted prior to training or surmised during training? The record which follows is penumbral. This partially lighted area might have been much larger had not the history of the dropout problem urged upon us the very set of questions which eclipse enlightenment.

At this point, it is necessary to define the role of the writer. Newspapers have referred to OSC as an experiment. In its strictest sense "experiment" denotes introduction of some novel techniques or operations to determine their effects on some known behavioral outcomes, often in studies like the present one, placement and job adjustment. The word "experiment" connotes, moreover, a high degree of control over all forces other than the experimental technique which might influence the outcome. Such influences would only obscure the role of the experimental technique in producing the outcome. Since no "new" techniques were studied under highly controlled laboratory conditions, it would be more appropriate to refer to this investigation as an assessment of a demonstration project. This would put the investigation in its proper context. The program was a pioneering attempt to revitalize communities by retraining their burdensome dropouts. The writer's mandate, it would be appropriate to say, was to define the several phases of the program and to determine their effects. As outcomes of so few of these phases were anticipated, only these could be evaluated statistically for testing the few hypotheses formulated. As is well known, when one evaluates he refers his observations to some set of criteria, standards, or stated outcomes. Due in part to the exigencies of the moment and the widely disparate views of those held knowledgeable in this field, the aims of the program if spelled out at all were often so vague and inarticulate as to deprive them of precise definition. As such they were useless for generalized hypotheses testing.

Hypotheses concerning ability, interest, and personality were formulated. They are widely believed to be linked to progress in training. Therefore, part of this study was concerned with testing assumptions about training. Part of it was exploratory. The observations to follow, it is hoped, will contribute to a more precise perception of the dropout and training him to fit into our economy. With no theory as a guide it became necessary to fish for answers. After an intensive search of one phase of the program, it was the writer's experience to reel in a larger set of more appropriate questions. The overwhelming number of uncertainties and assumptions concerning the capabilities of the dropout as well as the generally unfavorable image of the dropout led the writer to examine available research reports on the dropout. These reports are summarized in Chapter I to provide a frame of reference to view the results of the OSC program.

The terminology in this report is an admixture of the metalanguage of science so necessary for giving organization to one's view and vernacular English so necessary for giving flesh to the skeleton. This writing style was intentional. Laymen, educators, economists, and sociologists have all shown interest in OSC. The problem of communicating to them the views of a psychologist armed with a vocabulary unknown to the readers had to be faced. The writer, therefore, endeavored to present his research findings in words familiar to both specialists and to nonprofessionals without compromising scientific rigor.

It would be improper for the reader to regard the narrative which follows as anything but untouched snapshots of school dropouts being retrained. Favorable outcomes of the program are reported where trainees become fully functioning, productive, working citizens. There were many trainees who were not elevated to this station in life. Much will be learned from these trainees, too. Why might an adolescent give up sixteen weeks of his life, receive training, and never look for a job? This student is not an oddity to be found in North Carolina. Neither is the student who fully utilized every moment of his training to become a model American.

Communities throughout the country have their "good" and "bad seeds." Training the hard to reach student is not solely dependent on the "seed." Some communities provided abundant sunshine and photosynthesize the latent energies of its people; others wilt in darkness.

ACKNOWLEDGMENTS

THE writer wishes to thank the many people who cooperated in both the research and training programs. For most OSC personnel, an eight hour day was often viewed as a luxury. Roger Moss and James B. Jones, graduate students at North Carolina State University were popular figures to the trainees. It was not uncommon for them to locate elusive trainees in pool rooms and soda shops and then to test or interview them in unheated, unlighted storage rooms any hour of the day, 7:30 AM or 10:00 PM. The OSC teachers, too, had little leisure during the visits of the OSC research staff. Faculty meetings often ended at 2:00 AM. But to the trainees the writer is most deeply indebted. Without their unhesitating loyalty and cooperation this report could never have been written. This narrative of their anguish, joys, hopes, achievements, plans, disappointments and excitements etched in the writer's mind what is mankind. My greatest sorrow is that John F. Kennedy did not live to see the fruits of his hopes and plans for society's stepchildren. He extended hope for a better life to the neglected and rejected before his own was so tragically taken.

My work on the rehabilitation of school dropouts was an effort to understand enigmatic educational, sociological, economic and psychological phenomena linked with the worker who is inadequately prepared to cope with the demands of the world of work. Many insights were developed by culling from the wisdom reported in published and unpublished forms. The writer extends his appreciation to the following agencies and persons who consented to quoting and paraphrasing from their works:

Abrahams Magazine Service, D. Allen, C. Aller, Allyn and Bacon, Inc., American Sociological Association, American Council on Education, *American Economic Review,* Atlanta Public Schools, Arizona Migrant and Indian Ministry, H. J. Battle, H. Bienstock, J. C. Bledsoe, P. H. Bowman, *British Journal of Educational Psychology,* California State Department of Education, Calipatria Unified School District, The Clearing House, E. S. Cook, Jr., J. Davie, A. Davis, J. Deck, Dade County Public Schools, Everett, Massachusetts Chamber of Commerce, Greensboro City Schools, Harper and Brothers, *Harvard Educational Review,* Harvard University Press, R. J. Havighurst, State of Hawaii Department of Education, Her Majesty's Stationery Office, Idaho Department of Education, Illinois Office of Public Instruction, Illinois Education, Indianapolis Club of Western Electric Employees, International Bureau of Education, *Journal of Educational Research,* Journal Press, Kentucky Department of Education, Macmillan and Company, Maryland State Department of Education, D. Merachnik, Michigan State Department of Public Instruction, *High Points,* H. P. Miller, L. Miller, Morgan School, Clinton, Connecticut, National Association of Secondary School Principals, National Child Labor Committee, National Education Association, National Society for the Study of Education, Board of Education of the City of New York, University of the State of New York, Bureau of Guidance, North Carolina Department of Administration, North Carolina Department of Public Instruction, North Carolina Employment Security Commission, Oregon Department of Education, Pennsylvania Department of Public Instruction, Pasadena Public Schools, *Personnel and Guidance Journal,* Pennsylvania State Employment Service, Philadelphia Public Schools, *Rural Sociology,* Saint Paul Public Schools, Science Research Associates, Board of Education of the City of St. Louis, Jewish Employment and Vocational Service of St. Louis, South Carolina Department of Education, E. Sibley, Tacoma, Washington Public Schools, Teachers College Columbia University Bureau of Publications, Tennessee State Department of Education, H. Teuber, Tucson Community Council, UNESCO, Vermont State Department of Education, *Vocational Guidance Quarterly,* Virginia State Department of Education, West Virginia State Department of Education, Wyoming Department of Education, P. B. Wilson, L. A. Van Dyke, Winston-Salem Public Schools, John Wiley and Sons.

This study was made possible by a grant to the North Carolina Department of Administration from the Office of Manpower, Automation, and Training.

N.M.C.

CONTENTS

Page

Introduction vii
Acknowledgments xi
List of Tables xvii

PART I

FINDINGS

Chapter

I. Dropout: Phenomenon or Epiphenomenon 5
Economics and Dropping Out 10
Prevalence of the Problem 16
Holding Power of Schools 23
The Withdrawal Decision 31
Counseling and the Dropout 38
Work-study Programs 41
Life After School 47
Post-school Work Study Programs 50

II. Operation Second Chance 59
Sample 62
Procedure 64
Training Programs 66
Some Characteristics of the Trainees 69
Achievement 69
Intelligence 73
Personality 78

III. Results 81
Intelligence Changes 81
Achievement Changes 83
Predictability of Outcomes 86
Pretraining Histories 91

Chapter		*Page*
	Trainee's Estimation of OSC During Training	94
	Follow-up	99
	Regional Differences	102
	Summary	104
IV.	VIEWS OF THE TRAINING PROGRAM	105
	Trainees	105
	Faculty	106
	Coordinators	108
	Impressions of Employers	113
	Local Advisory Board	115
	Other Educators	117
	Community	117
V.	SUMMARY, CONCLUSIONS, RECOMMENDATIONS	123
	Overview	123
	The Helm	128
	The Employment Service	131
	Local Advisory Board	133
	Program Staff	135
	Midwife to the Dropout's Rebirth	137
	Curriculum Theory	139
	Ability	139
	Personality	140
	Occupational Information	141
	Curriculum Planning	142
	Generalist Training	143
	Equipment	144
	Recruitment	144
	Incentives to Learning	145
	Program	146
	Self	146
	Feeling of Accomplishment	147
	Familiar	148
	Choosing Incentives	148
	The Self in Career	149
	Recommendations from Trainee Views of Program	150

PART II
CASE STUDIES

(Norman M. Chansky and James B. Jones)

Introduction 159
Unemployed at the Time of Follow-up Interview 163
Conclusions 253

Appendix
A. 259
B. 259

Author Index 263

Subject Index . . . .

TABLES

Table		Page
I.	Rankings of Causes for Dropping Out	37
II.	Grade Completed and Occupational Pursuits	48
III.	Essential Economic and Educational Data on Three OSC Training Areas	63
IV.	Typical Teacher Evaluations of Students in Two OSC Centers	70
V.	Comparison of the Intelligence Quotients of Two Samples of Dropouts	74
VI.	Tests of Significance Between Aptitudes and Achievements of Two Samples	74
VII.	Intercorrelations Among WAIS, GATB and WRAT for Both Samples	77
VIII.	Typical Personality Ratings of Two Samples of Dropouts	78
IX.	Changes in Intelligence Quotients During OSC Training	82
X.	Changes in Achievement Scores During OSC Training	84
XI.	Pre-training Correlates of Post-training Intelligence and Achievement Scores	87
XII.	Pre-test Intelligence, Achievement, and Personality Scores of the Employed and Unemployed Graduates	89
XIII.	Pre-training Histories of OSC Graduates: Typical Observations	92
XIV.	Typical Training Replies Distinguishing Between the Three Groups of Graduates	95
XV.	Percentages of Ratings Received by Trainees	96
XVI.	Teacher Estimate of Work Habits and Attitudes	99
XVII.	Agency for Obtaining Employment: Percentage Reply	100
XVIII.	Typical Follow-up Observations	101
XIX.	Regional Differences in Response to Interviews	102
XX.	Citizen Views of OSC	118
XXI.	Employment Status of OSC Graduates in the Three Regions	127

XXII. Average Pre-training Achievement Test Scores of Trainees 254
XXIII. Average Achievement Scores of Intelligence Groups . . 254
XXIV. Frequency of Pre-training Persistence-drive-conformity Ratings 255
XXV. Frequency of Post-training Persistence-drive-conformity Ratings 256

UNTAPPED GOOD

The Rehabilitation of School Dropouts

PART I

FINDINGS

Chapter I

DROPOUT: PHENOMENON OR EPIPHENOMENON

THE stereotype of the dropout commands us to look back. What might we see? He was in school almost ten years before he left on his sixteenth birthday. He could hardly read. Certainly in ten years he should have learned his times tables but he did not. In third grade he was a hell-raiser. By the time he was thirteen he was damned defiant. If he had gotten a demerit everytime he was caught smoking in the lavatory he would have been kicked out when he was twelve years old. As for his language, it was vivid, provocative, but embarrassing.

Now the stereotype tells us to look around. Who was caught breaking and entering? Who was too illiterate to be drafted? Who in the poolroom has a bottle of beer in one hand and a girl in the other? Who never works but collects unemployment checks? Who spreads his semen among the willing and the unwilling?

Look ahead, the stereotype urges us. In this decade, seven and one-half million adolescents will leave school before graduation day. Automated devices will do much of the work that both unskilled and some skilled workers used to do. The young inexperienced worker does not have much chance to win in any competition with the more dependable automated machines and the older skilled workers. As for the dropout, he is not dependable at all. When the likes of him are dislocated by magnetic tape and IBM cards, he won't be missed.

It is no wonder that the word "dropout" makes us think of trouble. He was in it, he is in it, and he is expected to be in it. Now that this image is indelibly engraved on our psyches, often with the help of sensationalist newspapers, we have no difficulty believing that the girl was raped by a dropout, that the bank was robbed by a dropout, that the school windows were broken by a dropout and that our flag was defiled by a dropout. Apart from being a convenient scapegoat for our social ills, his alleged stupidity provides a convenient frame of reference for comedians. "Did you hear the one about the dropout who . . ." sets the audience up for a good laugh. Updating of the old moron jokes is a dependable source of the funny.

In a highly competitive society like our own, it is inevitable that some of us will fail while others succeed. Even among those who succeed what often keeps them going is a feeling of inadequacy. They produce abundantly in order to palliate their anxiety temporarily. Each day is spent in removing self doubts. Each new task accomplished furnishes them with evidence that they have some value. Confidence does not suffuse their every action, though; therefore, knowing that one is superior to the dropout, a morally degenerate, stupid social leper, is an illusion that remedies psychic ills. This knowledge somehow metamorphoses otherwise frightened mice into lions.

Early school leavers are not new to the American educational scene. It was not until recently that more students graduated from the high schools of North Carolina than dropped out. Statistics indicate, however, that today *smaller* percentages of students are leaving school prior to graduation than ever before. The dropout phenomenon is not new. What is new is the problem of fitting the job applicant without a high school diploma into existing jobs.

A careful reading of statistics will reveal that the act of dropping out is incidental to this problem. The symptom is easily recognized as leaving school prior to graduation. Its causes are illusive. Both the causes and the problems are imbedded in inefficient economic and educational systems.

The profit motive has led to the production of goods at a fraction of its previous cost. To facilitate this production, human power has been replaced by electronic brains controlling robot-like responsive machinery. The replacing of the simple, perhaps monotonous, task requiring little intellectual acuity, has virtually closed down a job market formerly open to the young and unskilled workers. Formerly such jobs were niches in which dropouts could easily fit. Available now are jobs which can be filled only by workers who on the job will *think, solve problems, use their aptitudes and push themselves to succeed.* Overproductivity results. Often, however, there is no receptive market for many products. Advertising agencies have been indispensable aids to industry. For it is they who contrive human needs and create markets for inferior goods with built in obsolescence. The morality of such economics notwithstanding, a cold fact of life which we must face is that only as *workers* will adults find a place in the sun.

Few early school leavers seem to fit these stringent intellectual and motivational requirements. This is in part due to the insistence of schools that students perform obediently and ritualistically many a perfunctory assignment. Discipline is maintained through school marks to ensure that students perform the prescribed mental exercises in the ordained way. The fact that some communities do not allocate funds to provide the best developmental and remedial teaching for the growing and retarded students sets the stage for early school leaving. It is also partly due to the teacher preference for tractable and verbal students. The student who is articulate is preferred to the verbally awkward one, even though his verbalizations may be nothing more than vapid platitudes. Some students know life primarily through books and through talk, others know it by living it. There is a difference between youngsters who know about food by growing it, about shelter by repairing holes in the roof, about money by its scarcity, and about law by being arrested and those who know of it from their social studies text. To the dropout, the school is like a spider's web. It is an environment in which he can neither adapt nor out of which he may easily escape. Only time weakens the web. Life in school has little in common with life in the street.

Nor are these all of the issues. "Individual differences" has long been a phrase on educators' lips. How to organize a school program that truly teaches the slow-learning child how to read, how to write, how to appreciate beauty, how to understand numbers, however, has been a dream unrealized. Rather than construct such programs, teachers give up on the slow learners and spend more time with the faster ones. In this way they cripple the independence incentives of the faster learners and exclude the slow learners altogether. There are teachers who boast that they are able to identify in the first grade those students who will drop out in high school. In fact, dropouts in this study were differentiated from graduates in their community from the earliest of teacher evaluations. Why should not such early identification of learning problems betoken early solutions?

The probable dropout then may be expected to acquire information which he will never use and learn how to act in a way in which perhaps is foreign or even alien to his family. Time was when he "served his sentence" in school and could look forward to achieving importance through dignified work. Today, this can happen rarely. Some of the reasons for this are valid, namely the increase in automation, displacing the unskilled and creating a market for the technologically adept. More important, though of questionable validity, is that today's job applicants are required to hold a high school diploma. Now *this certificate* accredits one for the achieving of status through dignified work. It is not so much that a high school graduate need be any more educated than the dropout, it is only that he must bear the parchment which symbolizes respectability. The educational significance of the diploma has become inflated. Merely scoffing at its symbolic value does not, however, render it less important as a social document. The graduate with the diploma is not only entitled to the right to a well-paying job but to bank credit, to civil treatment in all phases of community life and what is more important to the adolescent, invitations to teenage dances and parties. This diploma initiates one into the dominant society. It is, without any question, highly coveted by dropouts who have been denied access to life's riches.

If one could imagine society as the mother of us all then the dropout is a waif. The school, mother's handmaiden, has not fed him a diet of ideas that he could digest. It has been too acidic. The dropout develops mental ulcers. The false importance assigned to the diploma has squeezed him out of the labor market which might have both paid him decent wages and opened up social and cultural opportunities. Industry, mother's servant, has found that electronic devices can outperform mortal men and has forced the stray into a labor market which pays him substandard wages. The umbilical cord is severed, and no fresh blood can circulate from society to child. The dropout wanders aimlessly and is unattached.

Shut off from the dominant society, the dropout is alone. Yet he is hungry like everyone else. Like others, he is warm and cold. Also, like others he has sexual feelings. He, too, quite normally yearns for companionship. He, perhaps as much if not more than others, seeks safety, seeks love, seeks self esteem. But this separation from society is definite; the gulf is obvious. Being mortal, he creates his own devices to meet his needs. From the avoidance of the dominant class, he senses he has little worth in the eyes of the community. His plan then becomes one of satisfying mortal needs through subterfuge. Soon he finds others who, like himself, are rejected and lonely. Shut off from mother's benevolent life-giving substances, who knows by what toxins he will now be poisoned?

Dropouts are frequently viewed as alienated youth. To be sure, they do behave in ways foreign to and often misunderstood by the prevailing class. Anomie and lawlessness appear to be their mode of life. This view that dropouts have no standards may be due to the fact that the prevailing class is estranged from the underclass. The unfriendly feelings between the classes are mutual. Each class sees the other as consisting of pariahs. Given, then, is the condition in which the ways of each class are neither known nor understood by the other. There is, moreover, one outcome that cannot be denied. Neither the dropouts nor the prevailing class will work out the solutions on its own. To expect this is being irrationally idealistic. Yet bridges have to be built so that the several classes will not only be cognizant of the other but will also communicate with one another. These must be language bridges. It is through exchange of ideas and experiences that the goals of each class will become known to one another, then, perhaps, the poverty, ignorance, despair, destructiveness cycle may be destroyed.

Class differences are strong, yet members of the underclass are due respect merely because they are human beings. If rejection is continued, if the basic necessities are denied them, they will become frantic. When hope for personal improvement fails, mental disturbance sets in. Life, itself, loses value. People become absorbed in fantasy. Some become suicides; others murderers; others become disintegrated personalities. An investigation of a recent plane crash revealed that a frenzied young adult with no hope of improvement in his life situation shot the pilot and co-pilot of the plane he boarded, thus plunging to death all passengers, none of whom were known to him. To ensure that suspicion does not replace trust, viable social intercourse must take place. This involves grasping the meaning of each word and gesture another person uses. The price we have to pay for estrangement is high. Vengeance and retribution may be directed against anyone symbolizing the dominant class. Solutions to human problems, especially those which divide man from his fellow are not simple, yet to restore dignity to all men and to insure the maintenance and regeneration of our democracy, a beginning has to be made by trying to understand the world from the dropouts' point of view. Only when the dropout is understood may the dominant class begin to adjust its ways to live harmoniously with the underclass. Let us begin by heeding the words of the wise Edwin Markham who suggested we must consider all mankind a part of ourselves.

> He drew a circle that shut me out
> Heretic rebel a thing to flout
> But love and I had the wit to win
> We drew a circle that took him in.

ECONOMICS AND DROPPING OUT

The job opportunities for high school dropouts are indeed few. Not only that but the few jobs available are low salaried. As of March, 1962, Bienstalk[1] reported 22 per cent of the white collar workers had not completed their high school education but 65 per cent of the blue collar workers were without diplomas. A United States Department of Labor reporter estimated that no more than five per cent of all available jobs between 1960 and 1970 will be of the unskilled variety.[2] While it is true that many blue collar workers are skilled, the job outlook for the dropout is not very promising. The young dropout of years ago tended upon entering the labor force to take a job requiring little skill.

---

[1] Bienstalk, H.: Realities of the job market for the high school dropout. In Schreiber, D. (ed.): *Guidance and the School Dropout*. Washington, D. C., The National Education Association, 1964, 84-108.

[2] U. S. Department of Labor, Bureau of Labor Statistics: *Manpower Challenge of the 1960's*. Washington, D. C., Superintendent of Documents, GPO, 1960.

With employment barriers up, what is to happen to the 7.5 million adolescents expected to drop out of school during this decade? The underachievements in language, arithmetic, and science, characteristic of most dropouts bar them from the few but available skilled and white collar job. It is not surprising, then, that the unemployment rate cited by Bienstalk is higher for the dropout than it was for the graduate. They were 8.1 and 5.1 per cent, respectively. By October, 1963, the unemployment rate of all young workers was twice that of the national average. There were 730,000 persons under twenty-two who were looking for work.[3] There is little doubt that if he had to choose between a dropout and a graduate, an employer would choose an applicant with a high school diploma.

Statistics on the average earnings of dropouts appear to be commensurate with the job opportunities open to them. In 1958, according to Miller,[4] the average annual income of adult males twenty-five years of age and older who had graduated college was $9,200. Those who had graduated high school, $5,600; and those who had less than eight years of formal education, $2,500. Compare the $2,500 per year of the adult with elementary school education with the $4,600 of the adult with a high school education but no diploma. Negroes, moreover, with the same education as Caucasians had significantly less earning power. In 1939, 5.4 per cent of Caucasians who had grade school education were earning $2,500 or more. According to the 1940 census[5] fewer than four per cent of the Negro college graduates earned that much. The relationship between years of schooling and annual income is close. Workers with little education are unable to carry out the tasks considered of greatest importance to employers and, therefore, are paid low salaries. In addition, preferences for certain ethnic groups affect the labor market. Katz[6] pointed out that the

---

[3] Perrella, V. C.: Employment of high school graduates and dropouts in 1963. *Monthly Labor Review,* 1964, 87, 522-527.

[4] Miller, H.: Education and average annual income in relation to education. *American Economic Review,* 1960, 50, 5.

[5] 1940 Census Population: Special reports, Series P-46, No. 5, June 18, 1946.

[6] Katz, A.: Educational attainment of workers, 1959. *Monthly Labor Review,* 1960, 83, 113-122.

income of city men without a diploma decreased $18 per year between 1956 and 1958; graduates increased $139 per year during this time. The labor market clearly favors the graduate.

Evidence is mounting concerning this education-earnings relationship. Cantoni[7] studied a class of 468 boys and girls who attended school in Flint, Michigan between 1939 and 1943. In general, all students were observed to have better positions than their fathers; the fathers had less schooling. The 55 per cent of the students who graduated tended to be classified as "skilled" or "managerial" workers; the 45 per cent of those who dropped out were employed largely as "unskilled" or "semiskilled" workers. Might one ask if a student stayed in school longer that he would necessarily have a better paying job? It is quite tempting to answer "yes" to the question, yet there are contingencies which must be considered before a thorough understanding of the education-salary relationship could be grasped.

The ranks of the dropouts are filled by adolescents whose parents enjoy few social and economic advantages. Davie[8] observed that only 13 per cent of the dropouts came from the upper social classes; 72 per cent came from the lower classes. Hollingshead[9] determined class position according to the way the family lived, its income, possessions, educational achievements, standing in the community, and participation in community activities. Not only did he find that 89 per cent of those from the lower classes dropped out of school but that some 70 per cent left before their sixteenth birthday. Social class in and of itself does not explain early school leaving. Intelligence is clearly a factor.

Sibley,[10] examined the records of 5,677 boys who in 1926 were enrolled in grade six in Pennsylvania. Although most of the boys with intelligence quotients of 100 or above reached the first year of high school irrespective of the occupational status of the father, the boys graduating had high IQ's and were from higher social

---

[7] Cantoni, L. J.: Stay-ins get better jobs. *Personnel and Guidance Journal,* 1955, 33, 531-533.

[8] Davie, J.: Social class factors and school attendance. *Harvard Educational Review,* 1953, 22, 175-185.

[9] Hollingshead, A. B.: *Elmstown's Youth.* New York, John Wiley and Sons, 1949.

[10] Sibley, E.: Some demographic clues to stratification. *The American Sociological Review,* 1942, 7, 322-330.

classes. Havighurst and Neugarten, moreover, in studying male and female dropouts found that 63 per cent of the boys in River City were from the lower classes but 88 per cent of the dropouts came from this class. Similarly, 63 per cent of the girls were from the lower classes but 84 per cent of the dropouts were from this class. With respect to intelligence, 53 per cent of the boys and 47 per cent of the girls had low IQ's, but 74 per cent of the boys and 78 per cent of the girls who dropped out had low IQ's. The relationships between intelligence and education as well as between social status and education are well known. Now, perhaps, the education-salary relationship makes more sense. Members of the lower social and intelligence groups leave school early and are destined to receive low salaries. Stated another way, the economically disadvantaged and mentally retarded receive insufficient education to qualify them for anything but the low paying, mentally undemanding jobs.

Havighurst and Neugarten[11] commented that the areas of high dropout rate contain the unbroken cycles of low education, low income, poor health, low aspirations, cultural mediocrity, and civic apathy. In some city slums as many as 70 per cent of the youth between sixteen and twenty-one are out of school and unemployed. The changing scene in agriculture, moreover, has caused more socially dislocated adolescents to swell the slums of the already overburdened city. The slums of a city are not, however, the only high dropout areas. Wilson and Buck[12] studied 1,900 sophomores from seventy-four rural high schools in Pennsylvania. Those who remained in school were distinguished from dropouts in several ways. The stayins lived in villages rather than isolated rural areas; they were interested in science; they preferred white collar work; they had high IQ's; they were from smaller families; and they had better personality adjustments.

The figure of the dropout cut from those studies is that he lives in physical and cultural isolation; he does not strive for entry or advancement in high prestige occupations; he has modest intellec-

[11] Havighurst, R. J., and Neugarten, B. L.: *Society and Education*. Boston, Allyn and Bacon, 1962.

[12] Wilson, P. B., and Buck, R. C.: The educational ladder. *Rural Sociology,* 1960, 25, 404-413.

tual abilities which manifest themselves in low scholastic achievement; and he has inadequate personality adjustment. Despite the apparent accord reached by many research workers in the United States, a study carried out in New Zealand says that this image is not cast from a universal die. Havighurst and others[14] found the number of years students remained in school was neither significantly related to their intelligence nor to their achievement. Cross cultural differences, then, exist among dropouts.

The characteristic ways of behaving, the values, mores and traditions of a social group have effects on scholastic achievement, early school leaving, and employment. In his Inglis lectures, Davis[15] described the lower class slum people as fearing starvation. The reason being their having an uncertain food supply. In addition, they fear eviction from their shelters. Light is so inadequate that they worry about it. To them life is an alternating cycle of depression and recovery. One may note that in times of prosperity, lower class members buy the foods (steaks) and automobiles (Cadillacs) which symbolize prestige in the middle class. Otherwise they subsist on a low protein, high carbohydrate diet. The image the lower class youngster must develop for himself is that of one who is unsurpassed in *fighting* and in *swearing*. Though such self images are alien to the middle class, they are realistic and adaptive in the slums.

The low self esteem, the personal and social disorganization, the apathy, the disregard for those values cherished by the dominant society are routed in utter economic deprivation and in psychological disenfranchisement. Such is the legacy of the lower class. It is absorbed by the child from his parents who in turn learn those adaptive measures in order to survive. Many a slum resident refers to his community as a "human garbage dump." The waste of talent at a time when our nation is in dire need of

---

[14] Havighurst, R. J., Somerset, H., Archer, E., Borrie, C., and Morrison, W.: Factors involved in the age of school leaving in two New Zealand communities. In Havighurst, R. J.: *Studies of Children and Society in New Zealand.* Christchurch, Canterbury University College, Dept. of Ed., 1954.

[15] Davis, A.: *Social Class Influences Upon Learning.* Cambridge, Harvard University Press, 1948.

social regeneration is dreadful. Davis[16] explained the situation in the following manner:

> Children in the families of the lowest economic level are regarded as a drain upon the community and nation, rather than as a storehouse of ability and human capital. Children of this submerged third of the population, a bottom economic level, are truly the voiceless and forgotten human beings in America. . . . the child's subordinate place in society in the subordinate place of his parents, friends, and neighbors tends to weaken his self esteem. The self depreciation typical of all low status children is the result of their social subordination in most of their relationships with dominant groups, such as teachers. Not only do they acquire a poor self image, but often actual self contempt is hidden beneath a mask of resentment and hostility.

Davis suggested that the school can help eradicate the problem. He admitted that it is easy to abandon those students who manifest displeasing and offensive behaviors which originated in low economic surroundings. He urged that faith be developed in these children. The true impact of the school in such children cannot be assessed until years after they leave school. Many do raise themselves to higher social and economic levels. They become teachers, nurses, owners of businesses. Yet their ways which were conditioned and constantly reinforced by economic and social deprivation are highly resistant to change. The starting point, according to Davis, is changing the attitudes held by the dominant society that these young citizens are social lepers.

"To overcome this problem of high school dropouts," concluded Jerre Nelson, a winner of the Tennessee Dropout Essay Contest, "everyone will have to give a little of himself.[17] Undoubtedly, these programs of improvement will add a large expense to the cost of the operation of schools. But, the cost of unemployment, juvenile delinquency, crime, and human lives that have been wasted is much greater."

[16] Davis, A.: *The Education of Culturally Deprived Children*. Los Angeles School Districts. May 11, 1962. Unpublished.

[17] Tennessee Dropout Essay Contest. Tennessee Attendance Teachers' Study Council, Nashville, Tennessee, 1963.

The problems of the dropout are exaggerations of typical teenage problems. Silberman[18] asserted that the decline in manufacturing employment for teenagers is only in part due to automation. Household conveniences and appliances have created leisure time for housewives. These wives now vie with teenagers for early entry jobs. The textile industry employed some 165,000 teenagers in 1930. By 1960 this number was reduced to 15,000. Rigid enforcement of child labor laws, the growing proportion of adolescents remaining in school, the minimum wage law, the growth of trade unions, the migration of mills to the South from New England, known for its tradition of child labor, are several explanations for the decline in teenage employment. It is apparent to the writer that the labor market shift has created a need to change the public school training which was sufficient for an earlier era in our history. The schools, today, are not feeding the labor market with workers who have the competencies demanded by today's industries.

IN SUMMARY, the dropout is a caricature of today's adolescent. He is apt to have less mental ability than most youngsters. Coming from a low social class which abounds in cultural disadvantage, poverty, and disease, he cuts an unattractive figure to an employer who can select from a large supply of better bred adolescents also hunting jobs. Is the problem that of the culture of poverty or one of the poverty of culture?

PREVALENCE OF THE PROBLEM

Records on early school leavers have been kept in each state for many decades. Included among these records are computations of dropout rates. It is regrettable that these dropout rates are not determined by the same definition. In some states the dropout rate is defined as the percentage of first graders who do not graduate twelve years later; in others, it is the percentage of ninth graders who do not graduate three years later. Confounding any interpretation of the prevalence of the problem are the nonstan-

[18] Silberman, C.: Let's talk about the real world. Manpower Policies for Youth Symposium. N.C.E.Y. of the National Child Labor Committee. Washington, D. C., Sept. 23-25, 1964.

dard definitions of dropout rates, the lack of distinction between dropouts and transfers, the lack of distinction between dropouts and exclusions, and finally, the less than perfect accuracy of record-keeping by school personnel. In reading the statistics to be presented here, the absence of a commonly agreed-upon operational definition of dropouts should be borne in mind.

Compulsory education ranges from none in Indonesia to ten years in Tasmania, so reported a UNESCO publication.[19]

Education is free in all the countries studied except in Holland and in Jordan. Whereas 95 per cent of children in the United States enter high school, only 50 to 60 per cent do so in Canada. The United States high schools, moreover, graduate some 70 per cent; the Canadian, 30 per cent. Dropout rates in different countries are not strictly comparable because compulsory education laws differ. Yet some guides to the prevalence of the problem are available.

Within the United States where the school holding power approaches 70 per cent, there not only exists wide differences between states but within states as well. Also, the currently high holding power of the schools is in sharp contrast to the three per cent retention rate of 1899-1900.[20] This is considerable progress.

As of May, 1963, the states with the lowest dropout rates were Hawaii, 17 per cent; California, 17 per cent; Wisconsin, 18 per cent, and Washington, 20 per cent.[21] American Samoa had a rate of 22 per cent.[22] Most of the students there leave for mainland United States, however.

Even in Hawaii where there is the lowest dropout rate in the country, vast differences were found in these rates among the islands.[23] On Oahu there were 1,110 withdrawals, 508 being

---

[19] Fourteenth International Congress on Public Education: *Compulsory Education and Its Prolongation.* Paris: UNESCO, 1951.

[20] *Biennial Survey of Education in the United States,* 1952-1954. U. S. Office of Education, 1957.

[21] Miller, L.: *The Dropout.* U. S. Dept. of Health, Education and Welfare, Washington, G.P.O., 1963.

[22] Senter, M. J.: Personal communication, October 8, 1963.

[23] Chang, T. M. C.: *Statistical Report of the Administrative Actions Taken on Pupil Behavior for 1962-1963.* Dept. of Education: Division of Guidance, Health and Special Education, Honolulu, Hawaii, 1963. Unpublished.

voluntary. On Hawaii where there were eighty-seven withdrawals, fifty-nine were voluntary; on Maui of twenty-five withdrawals, fourteen were voluntary; and on Kauai, thirty-two of the thirty-four withdrawals were voluntary. The grade level of voluntary withdrawals differs, too. On Oahu, boys leave in grade eleven; girls in grade ten. On Hawaii, most of the boys leave in grade ten; most of the girls, in grade twelve. On Maui, girls leave in grades ten and twelve; very few boys leave at all.

In Wyoming, 40 per cent of the first graders do not complete high school. Twenty per cent of the first graders do not enter the ninth grade. Twenty-five per cent of the eighth graders do not complete high school. It is estimated, however, that if the present annual increases in school holding power continues, that by 1993, every child entering grade one will graduate 12 years later.[24] One should, however, be wary of such projections. They assume no change in anything but the former retention rates. The conditions which produce these things may not exist in 1993, hence, it is possible to reach 100 per cent retention earlier. It is also possible not to reach it at all.

Some states have much higher dropout rates than others. Even within the same geographic region, the percentages of early leavers vary. According to the U. S. Office of Education:[25] Utah graduated 77.4 per cent; Colorado, 70.7 per cent; Arizona, 65.8 per cent; New Mexico, 59.0 per cent; and Nevada, 63.2 per cent. These western states contain a large Indian and Spanish speaking population. Physical barriers such as mountains are present. Migrant farm work is an established job opportunity for many rural and underclassed youth.

A terrain with a similar economy and with a large rural underclass has been called Appalachia. Among some of the neighboring states there is less variability than among the Colorado Basin. West Virginia graduated 59.9 per cent of their ninth graders; North Carolina 59.1 per cent; and South Carolina, 60.0 per cent. These data are quite limited because they are based on 100 per cent of

[24] *Wyoming's Wasted Resources—Those Who Leave Early*. Cheyenne, Department of Education, 1963.

[25] Miller, L., *op. cit.*

the ninth grade enrollment. A large percentage of the students in these states leave prior to the ninth grade. In West Virginia,[26] 41 per cent of the dropouts had left school prior to grade ten. Using grade *one* rather than the U. S. Office of Education grade *nine* criterion, 68 per cent of the students in South Carolina are known to drop out of school whereas 54 per cent in North Carolina do so.[27]

Within the state of North Carolina, the percentage of dropouts varies markedly. For the academic year 1962-1963[28] Lincolnton had the highest percentage of students dropping out, namely, 3.8; Elkin had the lowest, namely .7 per cent. Neither community is large. Mere size of the student body appears to have little bearing on percentage of dropouts. One clue to how many students will leave before graduation comes from a study in Oregon.[29] Lowest dropout incidence was in *residential* areas, namely 23.5 per cent. A somewhat higher incidence was for *industrial residential* areas, namely 25.2 per cent. *Rural* area losses were 33.7 per cent and *rural industrial,* 40.1 per cent. Lincolnton is a rural town in the hinterland of textile and furniture manufacturing centers of North Carolina. The high dropout rate may be linked to its distance from urban culture.

Statistics on school holding power indicate at least two dimensions to the dropout problem. One is the urban-rural dimension; the other, the industrial-agrarian dimension. Transcending those are poverty-wealth and learning-ignorance dimensions.

It should be pointed out, however, that the statistics must be interpreted with caution. Repeating the reason for this, each state has its own method for determining holding power. In some states the base line is grade one, in others grade five, and in still others grade nine. Many state accounting systems do not distinguish between dropouts and exclusions. Some cities account for

---

[26] *Student Dropouts in West Virginia, Secondary Schools.* Mimeographed, 1963.

[27] *Dropouts in South Carolina.* State Department of Education. Columbia, S. C., 1963.

[28] *School Dropouts: A Waste We Cannot Afford.* Raleigh, N. C. State Department of Public Instruction, Feb., 1964.

[29] *High School Pupil Loss in Oregon by Community Types.* State Dept. of Ed., 1962.

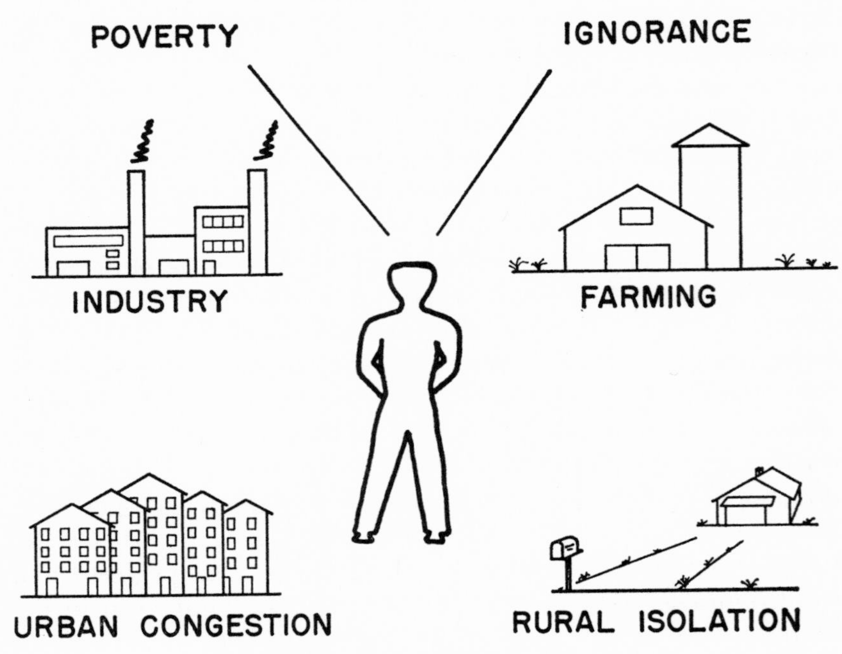

Figure 1. Forces affecting the dropout.

dropouts who returned to graduate; others do not. Without knowing the formula for determining percentage and rates of voluntary school withdrawals, precise understanding of the magnitude of the dropout phenomenon is not possible. Therefore, comparative statements concerning the incidence of dropouts is quite risky. Some standardized formula to be used by all school systems is a preliminary step to defining the problem as it exists in the thousands of communities throughout the country. As it stands now, one community using a grade five criterion would certainly appear to have a higher percentage of dropouts than one using a grade nine criterion. One such formula which deserves attention is that proposed by Segal and Schwarn.[30] This formula permits the calculation of the percentages of students for any year corrected for increases and decreases in the school population. Per-

[30] Segal, D., and Schwarn, O. J.: *Retention in High Schools in Large Cities.* Bulletin No. 15. U. S. Dept. of Health, Education and Welfare, Washington, G.P.O., 1957.

centages of voluntary withdrawals, involuntary withdrawals, and transfers are determined separately.

A common belief is that students withdraw from school when they reach their sixteenth birthday. This is the minimum legal age for terminating attendance in school. Miller's[31] summary of dropout studies indicated this was the case too infrequently to permit such a generalization. In the Dillon study,[32] 54 per cent of the students withdrew at the age of sixteen; 10 per cent, prior to age sixteen. In the California study,[33] 58 per cent withdrew at sixteen; 16 per cent earlier. In Syracuse,[34] 43 per cent left at age sixteen. In Rochester,[35] the largest number of dropouts left at seventeen. This was also observed in Tacoma, Washington.[36] While a large number of students withdraw at age sixteen, in many cities more than half of the students who do drop out persevere well beyond this age. Age is certainly connected with early withdrawal from school. Data from Tucson, Arizona suggested that this age of withdrawal from school is linked with a student's economic status.[37] The city was divided up into census tracts; those from tract one spent 8.4 years in school; from tract three, 11.8 years; and from tract five, 12.6. The greatest percentage of deteriorated housing and the lowest income group was in tract one. The smallest percentage of graduates, 37, was in tract one; the largest, 90, in tract five. Very similar results were obtained by Bledsoe[38] in his study of dropouts from a small high school in Georgia. The ratio of dropouts for the several occupational groups varied with occupational status of the parents.

The grade at which the majority of dropouts occur nationally is

---

[31] Miller, L., *op. cit.*

[32] Dillon, H. J.: *Early School Leavers.* New York, National Child Labor Committee, 1949.

[33] McCreary, W. H., and Kitch, D. E.: *Now Hear Youth.* Bulletin of the Calif. State Dept. of Ed., Sacramento, Oct., 1953.

[34] Miller, L., *op. cit.*

[35] *Ibid.*

[36] Tacoma-Pierce County study of education. *These Left Before Graduation.* Tacoma, Wash., May, 1958.

[37] Tucson's dropout problem—report of a study with recommendations by The Youth and Work Committee. Tucson's Community Council, Tucson, Arizona, 1962.

[38] Bledsoe, J. C.: An investigation into six correlates of student withdrawal from high school. *Journal of Educational Research,* 1959, 53 (1), 3-6.

grade ten.[39] This was found in Los Angeles[40] and Dade County.[41] Plunkett and Riches[42] found that 40 per cent of the dropouts in their sample completed tenth grade. Grittner[43] pinpointed the exodus of students in St. Paul, however, to be after grade ten and before the completion of grade eleven. He found 69 per cent of the loss of students occurred at this time. Similarly, in Kentucky[44] the largest percentage of withdrawals, 26.9, occurred after grade ten. Regional and perhaps local factors influence the grade at which students withdraw. In school systems where the tradition is to retain inadequate achievers, the grade at which students leave may be lower than in school systems like St. Paul where the school policy is to keep students with their age-mates.

Promotion practices alone do not explain the grade at which students will withdraw. Wolfle[45] found that in the IQ group, 95-104, 85 per cent enter high school but 61 per cent graduate. An even more dramatic contrast is observed in the IQ group 85-94. Seventy per cent enter, but only 38 per cent graduate. Therefore, both promotion practices and intelligence level of the students have determining influences on the highest grade attained by students. The nature of the curriculum seems to have some bearing on the dropout rate. In Los Angeles,[46] the largest percentage of dropouts were from special schools. While school holding power continues to grow for the special schools, the percentage of drop-

---

[39] Nelson, L.: The dropout problem—a growing educational concern today. *National Assn. of Secondary School Principals,* 1961, 45, 275-277.

[40] *Transfers, Entrants and Dropouts in Los Angeles Secondary Schools, 1962-1963.* Research Report No. 258. Evaluation and Research Section. Los Angeles City School Districts, 1964.

[41] *Dropout Study: Two Year Report*—Dept. of Research and Information. Dade County Public Schools, Miami, Fla., 1963.

[42] Plunkett, M., and Riches, N.: *Schools and Early Employment Experience of Youth—A Report on Seven Communities, 1952-1957.* Bureau of Labor Statistics Bulletin No. 1227. Washington, D. C., 1960.

[43] Grittner, K. F.: *The Dropout Studies: A Critical Analysis.* Office of Secondary and Vocational Education, St. Paul Public Schools, St. Paul, Minnesota, 1962.

[44] *Initial Tabulation*—Kentucky statewide dropout study. State Department of Education. Frankfurt, Kentucky, 1963.

[45] Wolfle, D.: *American Resources of Specialized Talent.* New York, Harper and Bros., 1954.

[46] *Transfers, Entrance, and Dropouts in Los Angeles Secondary Schools, 1962-1963, op. cit.*

outs increased from 24.8 per cent in 1959 to 35.8 per cent in 1963. Students tend to leave school in September and in January.[47] Many students who considered dropping out during the summer give school another chance. Often they still find it unpleasant and leave permanently. The high incidence in January probably coincides with failures on semester examinations.

IN SUMMARY, dropout rates vary among geographic regions. Among the factors which influence the records of holding power of a school system are (1) the base year with which subsequent losses are compared; (2) the demographic region in which the school is located, promotion practices of a system, and the aptitude of the students.

HOLDING POWER OF SCHOOLS

Schools today are graduating a greater percentage of students than ever before. One might only speculate what the reasons are for this trend. In the first place, the public has become more education conscious. In addition, some schools are providing attractive programs which interest the would-be dropout. The least flattering reason, though probably the most important one, is that there are *few jobs for teenagers.*

In the past, adolescents who left school had jobs waiting for them. One should not infer, however, that they left school for economic reasons. Rather, the availability of a job seemed to have been more enticing than continuing education. Dillon[48] interviewed many, many hundred school dropouts in the late 1940's. Thirty-six per cent said they preferred work to school; only 15 per cent needed the money to buy clothes and to help their families financially.

Lately, Nienstedt[49] reported that 67 per cent of the dropouts in Connecticut leave to enter employment; only seven per cent leave because of financial necessity. The high rate of unemployment for teenagers is a deterrent to school withdrawal. Rather than have to

---

[47] *Reducing the School Dropout Rate.* A report on the holding power project. Univ. of the State of New York, Bureau of Guidance, Albany, 1963.

[48] Dillon, H. J., *op. cit.*

[49] Nienstedt, C.: *A Report to the Council on Higher Education.* Connecticut State Dept. of Ed., 1963. (Mimeographed.)

endure the monotony and isolation of joblessness, many potential dropouts remain in school. To be sure, there are still many youngsters who find their self esteem so debased that they abandon further schooling. Others leave for no plain reason. It is certain that they regret leaving. Dillon[50] found almost 50 per cent of the dropouts he surveyed were sorry they left school. They do not return to school because they fear being out of place with a younger social set.

Holding power of a school is related to the type of secondary school it is. In Los Angeles[51] in 1959, the percentages of dropouts were 1.1 for the junior high schools, 10.5 for the three year senior high schools, 5.2 for the six year high schools and 24.8 for the special high school. In 1963-1964, the corresponding percentages for each type of school were 0.6, 9.2, 4.7 and 35.8. All secondary schools except the special high schools declined. In fact, the percentage of dropouts increased in the welfare and continuation schools. A U. S. Department of Commerce report[52] indicated that the lowest percentage of dropouts come from college preparatory high schools, the highest from those offering general curricula. The specific dropout percentages were 4.1 for college preparatory; 12.7 for commercial and vocational; and 18.3 for the general high school. Not all high schools, then, have improved in holding power.

Several structural factors are related to higher school retention rates. In 1954,[53] New York State began a study of school holding power. Schools with fewer than 100 and more than 200 enrollees retained proportionately more students than those with 100 to 200 students. Neighboring Vermont[54] revealed a somewhat different trend. Schools with fewer than 100 students reported 31.2 per cent

---

[50] Dillon, H. J., *op. cit.*

[51] *Transfers, Entrance and Dropouts in Los Angeles Secondary Schools, 1962-1963, op. cit.*

[52] U. S. Dept. of Commerce, Bureau of Defense, and the U. S. Dept. of Agriculture, Economic Research Service: Factors related to college attendance of farm and nonfarm high school graduates. 1960 Series, Census ERS-P27, No. 32, Washington, D. C., Bureau of the Census, June 15, 1962.

[53] *Reducing the School Dropout Rate, op. cit.*

[54] A status study of Vermont school dropouts: *Study Group of Dropouts.* State Dept. of Ed., May 16, 1963.

of their students dropped out. Those with 100 to 249 students reported 27.8 per cent quit. The smallest percentage of drop-outs, 27.8, were found in schools accommodating 250 students or more. In New York, the distribution of dropouts as a function of their students dropped out. Those with 100 to 249 students smaller schools had the fewest dropouts. In Vermont, the drop-out incidence was a decreasing monotonic function of school size. In Connecticut where schools with populations under 1,000 had a dropout rate of 3.3 per cent and those 3,000 and over one of six per cent, the dropout incidence was an increasing monotonic function of school size.

School size is a clue to the enigma of holding power. It is obvious, though, that within any one region, its relationships to holding power are not the same. Geopolitical factors were found in New York to be linked to dropout rates. Small rural communities and large cities had higher rates than school districts of intermediate size. One of the most important observations made in this study was that the kind of people living in the school district influence educational outcomes. High school seniors from the high holding power schools valued education more than those from the low holding power schools.

The counselors in this New York study asked the potential dropouts why they were leaving. The majority of the students, they found, did not get along with their teachers. Sixty-two per cent of the dropouts left because they preferred money to education. Half of this group went to work; half entered the service. Students from the high holding power schools more so than those from high dropout schools wanted to avail themselves of many educational opportunities. Several planned to enter professions. The parents of the dropouts had shown considerably less interest in the education of their children.

A Maryland study[55] dramatically demonstrated how important school size may be. At age sixteen, 50 per cent of the quitters were from schools with a census of 500 or less; 45 per cent, from schools with 1,500 or more students. At age seventeen, 19 per cent of them

---

[55] Maryland State Department of Education: *Our Dropouts*. Baltimore, Maryland, 1963.

were from schools of 500 or less; 39 per cent from schools of 500 or less; 39 per cent from schools of 1,500 or more. At age eighteen, eight per cent were from schools of 500 or less; 12 per cent, from schools of 1,500 or more. Size of school is a rough index of the age at which a student will withdraw. Of considerable importance are certain instructional and placement policies of the schools. These are, however, rarely isolated for study.

School size and curriculum are related to the incidence of dropouts. The relationship is not causal. Rather it appears that small schools located in rural areas and large schools located in large cities include in their census many disadvantaged youth who can ill afford to value prolonged schooling when their immediate needs for clothing, food, and shelter are in jeopardy.

Fine[56] described a program to increase holding power in the Fontana, California schools. Conferences are held with parents of potential dropouts. Programs are mapped out for the student. This includes parent-counselor contact and student-counselor interviews. The nonpromoted student is assured that if he improves his work he will be placed in the grade with others who are of his age. Flexible promotion practices such as this one have spread to other schools with very promising results. According to the New York study,[57] being overage for the grade is especially a factor favoring junior high school dropping out. Offering the failing student a plan whereby he is assured to join his age-mates when academically ready prevented early school withdrawal in those Fontana students whose motivation for school has slackened. The academically slower 15-year-old adolescent is saved the embarrassment of sitting in class with 13-year-old prepubescents.

Holding power was investigated in Illinois, too.[58] Schools with more books per student, a large offering of extracurricular activities, and larger assessed valuations per student had lower dropout rates. In addition to these factors, judges examined certain personal characteristics of students in an effort to predict early school

[56] Fine, T. W.: Student retention in junior high school. *Bulletin of the National Association of Secondary School Principals,* 1961, 45, 84-85.

[57] *Reducing the School Dropout Rate, op. cit.*

[58] State of Illinois: *Procedures for the Identification of Potential High School Dropouts.* Office of Public Instruction, 1962.

leaving. Among the factors considered were (1) the number of years a child was retarded, (2) what courses of study he selected, (3) how often he was absent, (4) how low his aptitude and achievement test scores were, (5) how low in class rank he was, (6) how little he participated in extracurricular activities, (7) how low in occupational status his father was, and (8) how little education his father had. In eighty-three cases out of 100, when all eight symptoms were present the judges correctly identified the dropouts. This leaves almost one-fifth of the dropouts misjudged.

Teachers are often hard put to decide who are the potential dropouts and which of these should be referred to the counseling agency. Several of the following signals should alert the teacher to the possibility of early withdrawal. Among these are frequent absenteeism, frequent failure in school subjects, hostile attitude toward school, lack of participation in extracurricular activities, and inadequate reading ability.[59]

Family status, community factors, attendance habits, ability, and extracurricular involvements are signs of the gathering clouds of early school withdrawal. The State of Michigan Department of Public Instruction[60] has listed some 20 signs, many of which Dresher[61] had previously observed. These were as follows:

(1) consistent failure to achieve in regular school work;

(2) grade level placement two or more years below average age for grade;

(3) irregular attendance;

(4) active antagonism to teachers and principals;

(5) marked disinterest in school with feeling of not belonging;

(6) low scholastic aptitude;

(7) low reading ability;

(8) frequent changes of schools;

(9) nonacceptance by school staff;

(10) nonacceptance by schoolmates;

---

[59] Craigo, R. T.: Reducing the number of dropouts. *Personnel and Guidance Journal,* 1957, 35, 331.

[60] Michigan State Department of Public Instruction. Quickie kit on school holding power. Lansing, Michigan, 1963.

[61] Dresher, R. S.: Factors in voluntary dropouts in the public schools of Detroit, Michigan. *Personnel and Guidance Journal,* 1954, 32, 287-289.

(11) friends much younger or older;

(12) unhappy family situation;

(13) marked differences from school mates with regard to size, interest, physique, social classes, nationality, dress, personality;

(14) inability to afford the normal expenditures of schoolmates;

(15) nonparticipation in extracurricular activities;

(16) inability to compete with or ashamed of brothers and sisters;

(17) performance consistently lower than potential;

(18) serious physical or emotional handicap;

(19) being a disciplinary case; and

(20) a record of delinquency.

These signs which recur on the many lists published by local and state education agencies should be interpreted in the same manner firemen respond to an alarm box signal. Occasionally the presence of one of these symptoms of early school withdrawal may merely be a false alarm. But we can ill afford to ignore the signal. In New York,[62] each of these signals was studied to determine its bearing on school withdrawal. Among the highest coefficients observed were for grade retardation, learning rate, pupil interest, and school marks. Not one of these coefficients was above .40. Generally, a coefficient *above* .40 indicates a modest relationship. Each of the commonly accepted symptoms of school withdrawal, then, when examined in and of itself merely hints at school withdrawal. When as many as eight of these symptoms appear together, a prognosis of school withdrawal is more reliable. Yet even these cannot be trusted in every case.

Both graduates and dropouts manifest a few of the many symptoms observed to be linked with early school withdrawal. Supportive counseling may give the potential dropout the self confidence to continue in his scholastic endeavors. Counseling alone is not enough. Instruction adjusted to a student's level of reading ability, financial aid, opportunities to earn money, classes on marriage and home economics are important, too.[63]

---

[62] School to Employment Program: *Second Annual Report*. N. Y. State Education Department. Division of Pupil Personnel Services, Albany, 1963.

[63] Wills, C. C.: Program to decrease the number of early school leavers. *Bulletin of the National Association of Secondary School Principals,* 1957, 40, 93-97.

Free public education, moreover, is a misnomer. The "price tag" for public secondary education was determined in Illinois. Direct costs in the form of book and athletic fees escalate the unattractiveness of schools to the disadvantaged. The indirect costs such as those for proms, clothes, and dates are incalculable. Quite often the prevailing social groups in schools are underpinned by family wealth. The cost of fitting in or surviving in the adolescent peerage is too great for the economically disadvantaged to bear. Opportunities to earn while they learn would hold many would-be dropouts. More than that, however, teachers and administrators must take more active roles in regulating social activities. More than the economically disadvantaged will benefit from this intercession. Mutual understanding among students cannot take place without interplay.

While there is no one to one relationship between financial independence and holding power, the two do go hand in hand.[64] Dropout statistics, moreover, are often misleading. They suggest that there is a far greater loss to schools than is actually the case. Many dropouts return to day school, others go to technical training schools, but many attend evening classes. Savitzky[65] noted that 44 per cent of the 11,000 students enrolled in evening high school had been dropouts. Many early leavers, then, do continue their education. They feel that during late adolescence and early adulthood they must earn and learn. Observations such as these force us to reconsider the view that dropouts are disinterested in learning.

The results of President Kennedy's 1963 campaign to bring dropouts back into the school fold amply demonstrates this last point. Sixty-three communities in twenty-three states participated in this campaign. School counselors contacted more than 59,000 dropouts, more than half of whom returned to school in September. As of November 1,[66] 92 per cent remained in school.

Students returning were greeted with a variety of remedial reading and arithmetic programs, cultural programs such as field

[64] Dillon, *op. cit.*

[65] Savitzky, C.: Dropouts and holding power. *The Clearing House,* 1963, 89-92.

[66] Miller, L. M., and Smith, H.: Doors were opened. A commentary on the 1963 dropout campaign. *School Life,* 1964, Jan.-Feb., 8-10.

trips to zoos, libraries, concerts, and museums as well as more intensive counseling. The reason most often given for returning and staying in school was that someone thought him important enough to contact.

Singled out for special mention is the campaign endeavor of the city of Atlanta.[67] Of the 1962-63 dropouts, 1,733 (75.2 per cent) were contacted. Special counseling and testing sessions were set up. School principals made curricular adjustments, service organizations cooperated. The American Legion approved a $4,000 Scholarship Fund to be used for needy students who might otherwise drop out of school. The principals made special allowances for several students. A half-day attendance program was arranged for thirty-one students who had to work part time. Late afternoon and evening programs were arranged for 151 students who worked during the day. Vocational courses were begun for fifty-three students. The remaining 156 were enrolled in the regular academic program.

Changing school policies is easy enough. Correlating the newer school practices with the newer policies meets, however, with several obstacles. Practices once established tend through inertia to maintain themselves. Mentally the teachers reconcile their old ways with the newer policies. They change the label of their activities to be in keeping with the new policy. They do not, however, change the activity itself. This is especially true for those school factors which predispose a student to drop out. In 1954, a study of dropouts in St. Paul, Minnesota was undertaken. In the final report, the following were recommended: better identification of reasons for dropping out, improvement of follow-up procedures, flexibility of curriculum, and employing a full time social worker. It was believed that keeping students with their age mates and marking according to ability would reduce the number of dropouts. Grittner[68] surveyed the 1959 class and found no difference in the incidence and time of dropping out. Not only that, but at the time of leaving, 65 per cent of the 1954 dropouts had no failing marks; in 1959, 37 per cent had no failing marks. The

[67] Summary of the report of the 1963 dropout program. City of Atlanta and Fulton Public Schools. Oct. 30, 1963.

[68] Grittner, K. F., *op. cit.*

recommendations of the 1954 study clearly had not been implemented.

IN SUMMARY, where the holding power of the schools has increased, it may be in part due to the fact that potential leavers anticipate unemployment. They view boredom as intolerable. To be sure, schools have been slowly developing programs to increase their holding power, but these programs do not merely provide professional guidance services. They teach the students salable skills. This development was recently given impetus by the late President Kennedy's return to school campaign. The central emphases of such programs were to involve the student in personally gratifying school activities and to develop marketable employment skills. Greater participation makes the would-be dropout feel he is a part of the school and the school is part of him. Follow-up studies reveal that suggestions to increase holding power in schools were not always implemented. Every measure should be taken to prevent the student from thinking that he is a stranger.

THE WITHDRAWAL DECISION

To reduce the number of dropouts, recent research and thinking advises the schools to provide and improve prevocational educational offerings. This has not always been the emphasis. The earliest studies of dropouts focused on the characteristics which made them different from other people. Many educators supposed the dropouts were maladjusted. Because many dropouts were disabled readers, it was believed low reading and, perhaps, it was reasoned further, mental ability *caused* voluntary withdrawal.

It is difficult to build up any case for any particular indication as the cause of early leaving. Most information about the dropout is acquired after he has decided to leave. The prime reason he resolved to give up school may no longer exist nor be remembered. Any speculation about the decision, is furthermore, after the fact. What are available for study are the attendant combinations of traits and circumstances which are conjoined to the dropout decision. Many of these traits alleged to cause early withdrawal are really epiphenomena, events which are contiguous in time but have no bearing on the decision. In addition, school promotion policies and curricular offerings vary widely. School "A" has rigid promotion practices. Overage students often leave school because the social stimulation they receive is immature. They do not want to emulate youngsters; their heroes are adults. Slower students in school "B" are placed in courses adjusted to their reading ability and geared to fascinate them. They continue until they graduate. Had they been in school "A," might they have withdrawn?

The point to remember is that there are observable behavioral signs which the teacher, counselor and principal may detect very early. Prognosis of early withdrawal does not, however hinge solely upon these behavioral signs. Rather, circumstances in an adolescent's private world, such as his family economic conditions, what the school offers him, what the values of his peer group are, and changes in his body image will steer the vulnerable student out of school.

Are personality problems prognostic of the early withdrawal decision? Matthews[69] reported a study in which a group of early school leavers was matched with a control group on the basis of sex, intelligence, and social status. As early as grade one the personal and social adjustments of the future dropouts were found to be different from the future graduates. In the same series of studies on the Quincy, Illinois sample, Bowman and Matthews[70] observed the personal values of dropouts were different from that of stay-ins. This was especially noted for the concepts of *self, father, school,* and *competition.* The dropouts tended to rate *self* and *school* as "inactive" and "lacking in industriousness." *Competition* was rated as "less active." Female dropouts especially viewed their fathers negatively.

The State of Maryland's[71] study of dropouts revealed that 1.3 per cent of the students left school because of social maladjustment. The majority of dropouts were not considered behavior

---

[69] Matthews, C. V.: The serious problem of the school dropout. *Illinois Education,* 1962, 50 (5), 209-212.

[70] Bowman, P. H., and Matthews, C. V.: Motivations of youth for leaving school. *Cooperative Research Project No. 200.* U. S. Office of Health, Education and Welfare, 1960.

[71] Maryland State Department of Education, *op. cit.*

problems by either school counselors or principals. Twenty-one per cent of the sample were judged behavior problems. It is possible to infer from other data in this study that parents have an important influence on the educational aspirations of students. Assume that students model their behavior after the parents. Approximately 81 per cent of the students were living with their parents. Sixty-three per cent of the parents themselves had left school prior to grade nine. In addition, 46 per cent of the parents were engaged in unskilled and 29 per cent in skilled occupations. Six per cent were unemployed. The parents, then, had received limited education. Were these dropouts being inspired to receive limited educations, too?

Occupational status of parents appears in the educational horizon as paramount. In Oklahoma City, 649 dropouts from grades nine through eleven were compared with a control group. Allen[72] found the occupational status of the dropout fathers to be significantly lower than that of the fathers of stay-ins. In a small high school in Georgia, Bledsoe[73] studied 247 dropouts. He calculated the "chance" proportion of dropouts. Then he compared *chance* with the "actual" incidence of dropouts. The ratio of observed dropouts to the chance expectations for professional-managerial parents was .09; for the agricultural parents, .65; for homemaking, .92; for sales personnel, .39; for clerical, .06; for skilled labor, 1.02; for unskilled labor, 2.64; and for the unemployed, 3.49. Again, parents with jobs demanding little education had children who left school early. A comparison between low ability dropouts and low ability stay-ins revealed that the parents of their dropouts earned less money and were engaged in unskilled occupations.[74]

An occupation in one part of the country, however, may not have the prestige value it has in another. In Idaho, for example, dropouts were found to live in districts whose economy is based

[72] Allen, D.: A study of dropouts from the Public Secondary Schools of Oklahoma City. *Dissertation Abstracts,* 1957, 17, 3, 1703-1704.

[73] Bledsoe, J. C., *op. cit.*

[74] Sorenson, M. A.: Low ability dropouts versus low ability graduates. *Personnel and Guidance Journal,* 1960, 39, 144-145.

primarily on industry, mining, or lumbering. Dropout rates in agricultural areas, though, were low.[75] In Dade County, 35 per cent of the dropouts came from families which were below average in socioeconomic status.[76]

Observations from British studies parallel those undertaken in the United States. Collins[77] found a high percentage of children of unskilled workers leaving school early. In the modern school the percentages were somewhat lower than for the grammar school. In another study, 25 per cent of the children of unskilled workers were adjudged capable of doing sixth form work only 6.7 per cent were receiving it. Forty per cent of the early school leavers, moreover, were from this group. Though capable, fewer children of unskilled workers used to advantage the educational opportunities available to them.[78] Persistence in school is lower for children of lesser skilled workers in the United States, too.[79]

Piecing these fragments of information together let us assume the position that the environment in which the dropout finds himself teaches him certain practical values but maladaptive attitudes about education and about work. The parent after whom he models his life is often modestly educated and employed in an occupation requiring a minimum of mental problem solving. Schooling involves taking part in a set of strenuous tasks, the completion of which entitles one to pass into adult society. When schooling ceases to be related to the adult role the youngster envisions for himself, he decides to leave school. Study after study reveals that students do not find schooling interesting.[80, 81, 82, 83, 84, 85, 86, 87]

---

[75] Jeffries, A. P., and DeLaurier, E.: What About Idaho's High School Dropouts? 1962.

[76] Gillingham, J.: *A Study of Dropouts.* Dade County, Florida Public Schools, Miami, Florida, 1964.

[77] Collins, M.: Causes of premature leaving from grammar school. *British Journal of Educational Psychology,* 1954, 24, 129-142.

[78] Ministry of Education: *Early Leaving.* London, Her Majesty's Stationery Office, 1954.

[79] Van Dyke, L. A., and Hoyt, K. B.: *The Dropout Problem in Iowa High Schools.* Des Moines, Iowa, Department of Public Instruction, 1958.

[80] Gillingham, J., *op. cit.*

[81] Transfers, Entrants, and Dropouts in Los Angeles City Secondary Schools, 1962-1963, *op. cit.*

The schooling they receive conflicts with their beliefs about education. What they are exposed to is irrelevant to them; what educational experiences are truly relevant to them is not what they are exposed to.

This theory implies that the dropout does not fit in the typical school environment. Both teachers and pupils exclude him. Teachers are known to judge as poor achievers those students whose values are not the same as their own.[88] Bowman and Matthews,[89] moreover, assert that dropouts are seen by their peer group and their teachers as no person to choose as a friend and no person whose lead to follow. In addition, they are viewed as "withdrawn."

Only occasionally are they judged "rebellious." When the adolescent does leave school, he might use much stronger language to describe the reasons for his leaving. Most dropouts prefer to sever their academic ties peacefully. This is also predictable. They have learned from their parents to cause no trouble in school. "Give the teachers answers they like to hear," they have been warned. A readiness to respond inoffensively but not necessarily truthfully to the questions put to them by teachers and counselors is observable at the concluding interview with the dropout. This set to respond is a barrier to the scientist who seeks causes for withdrawal. It is, however, highly adaptive for the dropouts. It is the vehicle in which he drives out of school.

Some proof that this is indeed the case is suggested from Wolfbein's work.[90] The school records of the dropouts surveyed

---

[82] Dillon, H. J., *op. cit.*

[83] Plunkett, M., and Riches, N.: School and early employment experience of youth. Bulletin No. 1277, U. S. Dept. of Labor, 1960.

[84] Cook, E. S., Jr.: An analysis of factors related to withdrawal from high school prior to graduation. *Journal of Educational Research,* 1956, 50, 191-196.

[85] Initial tabulation, Kentucky statewide dropout study. Frankfort, The Dept. of Education, 1963.

[86] Johnson, E. S., and Legg, C. E.: Why young people leave school. *Bulletin of National Association of Secondary School Principals,* 1948, 32, 14-24.

[87] *Report on School Leavers.* Greensboro City Schools, Greensboro, N. C., 1962.

[88] Battle, H. J.: Application of inverted analysis in study of the relation between values and achievement of high school pupils. Unpublished Doctoral Dissertation. University of Chicago, 1954.

[89] Bowman and Matthews, *op. cit.*

[90] Wolfbein, S. L.: Transition from school to work; a study of the school leaver. *Personnel and Guidance Journal,* 1959, 38, 98-105.

indicated 19 per cent of the boys said they left because they reached age sixteen; 17 per cent of the girls were reported as giving this reason. Later contacts with these dropouts reveals six per cent of the boys and four per cent of the girls left for this reason. In addition the school records indicated that 24 per cent of the boys and 21 per cent of the girls left because of adverse school experiences. The followup contact revealed that 38 per cent of the boys and 31 per cent of the girls left for this reason. In Los Angeles, 12 per cent of the early school leavers gave as their reason: "financial." On the followup questionnaire 26 per cent gave this reason. Four per cent originally said they were not interested in school; upon follow up, 22 per cent gave this reason. In still another study, this one of Negroes in Maryland, school records revealed three basic reasons for dropping out: (1) over compulsory attendance age; (2) fourteen years old and unable to do high school work, and (3) physical incapacity. The dropouts themselves listed the following as reasons: (1) pregnancy (two per cent); (2) work (17 per cent), and (3) dislike for or disinterest in school (13 per cent).[91]

Formulated here is a theoretical guide to the behavior of the individual who decides to withdraw from school. The models he emulates do not consider prolonged schooling essential. Rather, they emphasize concrete or easily manipulable ideas or tools. The absence of relevance of learning to the potential dropout's aspirations sets the stage for him to become a nonparticipant in school. The withdrawal is spurred on by student and teacher rejection of him. Because he does not feel a part of the school body, we find he reads below grade level,[92] he fails many subjects,[93] he achieves little relative to ability,[94] and participates little in extracurricular activities.[95, 96, 97]

---

[91] Moore, P. L.: Factors determining elimination in the Negro secondary school. *Bulletin of the National Association of Secondary School Principals,* 1954, 38, 42-48.

[92] Penty, R. C.: *Reading Ability and High School Dropouts.* New York, Bureau of Publications, Teachers College, Columbia University, 1956, p. 93.

[93] Gillingham, J., *op. cit.*

[94] Maryland State Department of Education, *op. cit.*

[95] Bowman and Matthews, *op. cit.*

[96] Greensboro City Schools, *op. cit.*

[97] "Dropout Study of the Winston-Salem, North Carolina Public Schools." Paper presented, N. C. Personnel and Guidance Association, Durham, 1964.

TABLE I

RANKINGS OF CAUSES FOR DROPPING OUT

Cause	*Pupil*	*Teacher*	*Parent*	*Prin-cipals*	*Attend-ance Officer*	*Laymen*
Financial	1	3	1	3	2	3
Inadequate curriculum	2	6	2	6	5	6
Early marriage	3	7	7	7	7	8
Poor health	4	8	5	8	8	7
Inadequate guidance	5	1	3	1	1	1
Poor interpretation of school program	6	4	4	4	4	4
Too many fees	7	10	6	10	10	10
Low mentality	8	2	9	2	3	2
Frequent change of schools	9	9	10	9	9	9
Poor discipline	10	5	8	5	6	5
Correlation with pupil rankings:	—	.41[1]	.81[2]	.14[1]	.33[1]	.13[1]

[1] Little agreement.
[2] High agreement.

The dropout has been greeted with hostility. Pity has been extended him, too. Without any question, however, he is not understood. His view of the reasons and causes for early school leaving is quite different from that of his teachers, parents and principals. This is dramatically shown in a study by the Tennessee Attendance Teacher Study Council.[98] Presented in Table I below are the relative importance to pupils, parents, school personnel and laymen of reasons for early school withdrawal.

Clearly, with the exception of parents, no group viewed the withdrawal decision the way the students themselvs did. What are important contributors to the withdrawal decision from a student's point of view are not from the points of view of school personnel. This table is instructive in that it not only notifies the readers that there are points of disagreement, but exactly where they are. According to the pupils, the three most important reasons for leaving school are money, intrinsic attractiveness of the curriculum, and heterosexual relationships. Doubtlessly the only adults understanding dropouts are the parents.

IN SUMMARY, the school behavior of the dropout is explainable.

[98] Tennessee Attendance Teacher Study Council, Vol. 2. Murfreesboro, Tennessee State Dept. of Ed., April, 1962.

The dropout does not belong. His feeling of not belonging is, moreover, existential. It may be noted in such responsible activities as serving in the armed forces and working for a living. In South Carolina, the state with the highest number of draft rejectees, the school records of those accepted into and refused from the service were examined. Those who passed the mental test had completed 10.8 grades of school; those who failed, 8.6 grades. The average number of grades completed by mothers of those accepted was 9.21; of those rejected, 5.47. Fathers of those accepted had completed 8.15 grades; fathers of those rejected, 5.06 grades. Both those who passed and those who failed believed the purpose of school was to prepare one for a job. Finally, and of considerable importance, is that counties with better educated citizens had a higher percentage of youth accepted into the service; counties in which the per pupil allotment was low had a high number of rejectees.[99] It is only after he leaves school that the tragic saga of the dropout unfolds.

COUNSELING AND THE DROPOUT

In an ever changing technology, economic roles and habits become altered, too. Family roles are remodeled. These, in turn, render obsolete traditional ways for adolescents to cope with their everyday problems. How to satisfy their ever pressing needs is not altogether clear to the adolescent. Some youth are strong and enterprising and strike a salutory solution in meeting their needs at school. Others are less adept at compromise and find they cannot fit themselves into the existing social or academic framework of the school.

Some students are shy. They, perhaps, know what to say to other students but hesitate to try conciliatory efforts with other students. Others, however, do not know what to do when they meet the normal frustrations which confront them in school.

The school counselor may help the youth face the unpleasant and speak about their fears. This would clear the way for the youngster to develop more realistic aspirations for himself, to de-

[99] Mitchell, five N. P.: *Factors Contributing to Selective Service Examination Failure in South Carolina During 1962.* Columbia, State of South Carolina, 1963.

vise alternative paths to attaining his goals and removing frustrations, and behave harmoniously with others.

There is some evidence that schools with better counseling services have lower dropout rates.[100, 101] Rothney and Roens warned, however, that the incidence of dropouts in "guided" youth is about the same as for those without guidance.[102]

Too often guidance programs have been assumed to influence youth to change. Systematic studies of the guidance process are rare. One of the few controlled studies was conducted between the years 1937 and 1945.[103] The aim of the program was to prevent delinquency in underprivileged boys by counseling them. Two groups of 325 boys each were matched for age, IQ, school grade, delinquency rating and ethnic background. The boys were between the ages of six to ten. A coin toss determined which of the members of the pair would receive the counseling. A follow-up of the boys suggested that counseling had no effect on subsequent delinquency. Ninety-six treated boys and ninety-two control boys made court appearances. The counseled boys had 264 charges against them; the untreated boys 218. Furthermore, a study of the counselor-client relationships indicated that the therapists had completely misunderstood the attitudes and feeling of the boys. It was these counselors, moreover, who felt that they had indeed changed the boys.

Clients conducted themselves in a manner to please the counselor. The trained counselor should be prepared for this. Also he should be prepared for counter-transference, or volleys of aggression aimed at what he represents. In both situations he should not confuse a client's words with the spirit in which he speaks them.

There are several potential values to counseling programs. *Stu-*

---

[100] Gill, G. E., and Morrow, R. O.: Guidance and the dropout rate in 19 southeastern Ohio schools. *Vocational Guidance Quarterly,* 1957, 5, 153-155.

[101] Young, J. M.: Can counseling reduce dropouts? *The Clearing House,* 1955, 30, 22-23.

[102] Rothney, J. W. M., and Roens, V. A.: *Guidance of American Youth.* Cambridge, Harvard University Press, 1950.

[103] Teuber, N. L., and Powers, E.: Evaluating therapy in a delinquency prevention program. *Proc. Assn. Res. Nerv. Ment. Dis.,* 1954, 31, 138-147.

dents will experience catharsis. Frequently, this release of bottled up tension is sufficient to allow him to see his problems more clearly as well as to bring up alternative solutions. *Counseling may be supportive.* Students have worked out solutions to their problems but are encouraged to actualize them after they have first checked with an interested adult. *Counseling may be informative.* Career guidance, occupational information, and self study were observed in Calipatria[104] to turn negative attitudes toward school into positive ones. *Counseling may be rehabilitative.* Not only will the dropout experience catharsis but he will reorganize his plan of behavior.

A monumental study of rehabilitative counseling was undertaken by Lichter *et al.* One hundred and five boy and girl potential dropouts participated. Most had been truant and were not achieving satisfactorily. All were above ninety in IQ. Parents were interviewed as well. The therapists isolated five psychodynamic causes of school difficulty.[105] These were (1) unsuccessful handling of impulses; (2) maladaptive supervising of work; (3) acting out in school of problems caused elsewhere; (4) general personality problems, and (5) existential frustrations.

The clients in the study were mostly underachievers. Many had academic problems in elementary school. Several were disciplinary problems. More than half of the students had record of truancy. After counseling the potential dropouts, the writers concluded that their clients were difficult to treat. Many terminated the counseling sessions shortly after they got underway. The type of problems boys presented were different from those of girls. Boys created problems by their inactivity; girls, by their activity. Boys' problems started in elementary school; girls' in secondary school. Although the authors' criteria for improvement were highly subjective, they noted six of the seventeen girls who remained in treatment improved; sixteen out of twenty-three boys improved. The theme running through the life stories of most of these clients was the fear of being unsuccessful.

---

[104] Calipatria Unified School District, Calipatria, California. *Report of Project Under Title V-A, NDEA, 1963.* Unpublished.

[105] Lichter, S. O., Rapien, E. B., Seibert, F. M., and Sklansky, M. A.: *The Dropouts.* Glencoe, Free Press, 1962.

IN SUMMARY, counseling is no cure-all. Alone, it may help the potential dropout face life with greater equanimity. Together with changes in the school environment, it may be even more useful. No other technique permits the unearthing of the unique and irrational motivations which make the dropout behave as he does. Despite its limitations it is an approach to be experimented with. It should be noted that Secretary of Labor Wirtz[106] has endorsed it as one of the many ways to meet the manpower problems created by the 7.5 million youth who will in this decade leave school before graduation. In addition to counseling, communities need to train their youth for jobs which exist.

WORK-STUDY PROGRAMS

Technological changes in industry with its subsequent displacement of young workers has demanded that youth become highly qualified for the jobs they will hold. Educators are meeting this challenge. Two types of training programs exist. One is developmental and an integral part of the vocational education programs of a public school system. The other is remedial and is only occasionally sponsored by the public school system. Its purpose is to retrain unskilled workers in the labor force as well as the unemployed. The developmental program has among its objectives the improvement of school holding power and the provision for preparing youth for the manpower requirements of a community. The remedial program has among its objectives: training the unskilled, upgrading the competencies of the unskilled and elevating disadvantaged workers to a higher level of dignity.

Forward looking school systems have been operating work release programs for several years. There were, moreover, several varieties of programs from which to choose. In his book, Burchill[107] brought together samples of several of these programs. Few educational programs have met with as much optimism and enthusiasm as these. In Flint, Michigan, through the public schools, a program was inaugurated to help school dropouts become self-supporting

[106] Wirtz, W. W.: The Challenge of Jobless Youth. President's Committee on Youth Employment. Washington, D. C., Government Printing Office, 1963.

[107] Burchill, G. W.: *Work-study Programs for Alienated Youth; A Casebook.* Chicago, Science Research Associates, 1962.

workers. An enrollee in this program went to class daily for basic educational improvement. Often individual instruction and counseling for many youth were provided. After class, the students received on-the-job training in part-time work assignments. The development of good work habits was stressed. School personnel continued to visit students during the critical transition period from training to work. The cooperation between understanding supervisors and attentive counselors and teachers soothed the pains of adjustment to adult responsibility. Flint is a transitional community with its share of delinquency and unemployment. The community believes, however, that education is *a part of* and not *apart from* life. Through education, the board of education has asserted the individual may unravel his own problems and may help settle community crises.

Burchill cited a program in New York City organized along slightly different lines but, like Flint, whose purpose it was to combat juvenile delinquency. In 1955, boys enrolled in certain high schools were invited to participate in a program requiring them to study basic school subjects in the morning and to work in private industry on official afternoon school time. Teachers visited the boys at work. During the academic year 1959-1960, 30 per cent of the boys returned to regular class, another 30 per cent enrolled for one more year of the work experience program, and 24 per cent entered the labor force or the armed services.

This is by no means the only work experience program undertaken by New York City schools. Slotkin and Forlano[108] describe several others. Among these were an evening school program for school dropouts and a preemployment work orientation program. The evening school program included a counselor who screened the students and discussed their problems with them several times a year. The evening school dropouts were matched for ability with students registered in the continuation school program. Students in the experimental group were required to take at least two high school subjects. Several differences between the two groups were

[108] Slotkin, H., and Forlano, G.: *New Programs for Dropouts in New York City*. Office of Research and Education, Board of Education of the City of New York, December, 1962.

noted at the end of the year. Employers of the experimental students rated them significantly better workers than did employers of control students. In addition, parents and students found the experimental program more helpful than the traditional continuation school program. Also, the vocational goals of the dropouts were more realistic than those of the control group.

The preemployment job placement program was for 16-year-old dropouts with no serious court record. Another requirement of the program was that students be at least low average in intelligence. The program lasted twenty days. It included testing interests, aptitudes, and skills; guidance, developing job getting skills in any one or more of the following occupational areas: clerical, retailing, merchandising. Control group students once again came from a continuation school and did not differ at the outset from the dropouts. At the end of the month, it was noted that in contrast to the control group, the dropouts in training attended school more often, received higher ratings of personal and social characteristics, reenrolled in school at a higher rate, and had lower unemployment rates during this period.

Other large cities have developed similar programs. In the Chicago schools,[109] there is a program for unemployed youth aged sixteen to twenty-one. Dropouts who are retarded in grade level qualify for the program. Curricular units on participation in government through voting are offered. In addition, a reading clinic was established. Typing, auto service station mechanic, wood products assembly were among the preemployment vocational skills taught. An afternoon vocationally oriented industrial training program was set up. Each shop produces a marketable article not manufactured by local industries. Many of the students, a followup report indicated, found jobs. Some trainees earned as much as $125 per week.

In this same conference, Koontz described an educational program for unwed mothers in Washington, D. C. It served forty girls who left school because of pregnancy. Retired teachers and com-

[109] Programs for the educationally disadvantaged. A conference on teaching youth and children. U. S. Department of Health, Education and Welfare, Bulletin No. 17, Washington, D. C., Government Printing Office, 1963.

petent housewives were recruited by the Urban Corps to instruct the girls in basic education. Studies of home economics were offered. Instruction was either at home or at the school administration building. After the birth of their children, many girls returned to school to pick up the threads lest they fray. Motivation for learning was sustained and precious human resource talents were preserved here.

In St. Louis,[110] two groups of students equal in intelligence, age, and history of failing marks in school were studied. One group was given normal school services; the other the normal school services plus counseling. During the first year of operation, the uncounseled group had a 57 per cent higher dropout rate than the counseled. During the second year services to the experimental group were decreased. The uncounseled group still had a higher dropout rate, but the difference was only 4.4 per cent. Case studies indicated, moreover, that some students benefitted from vocational counseling to the extent that they envisioned new vocational aspirations. One student entered a teacher training college.

In 1959, a Youth Conservation Corps was established by the Department of Public Welfare of Philadelphia.[111] Work projects were set up in public parks and institutions where the boys, aged fourteen to seventeen, would work under close supervision. The boys did a real job and were paid for it. The school system dismissed the boys early so that they could go to work. The boys worked twenty hours per week during the academic year and forty hours per week during the summer. The junior high school students responded especially well to the program. In 1961, 49 per cent of the work experience group improved in school and 44 per cent made no change. In 1963, 72 per cent had improved but 26 per cent had not changed at all. Teachers were of the opinion that the money received made a big difference in a student re-evaluating his attitudes toward school. Many would-be school problems, other teachers averred, were prevented.

---

[110] School and community work-related education program of St. Louis Public Schools. St. Louis, Missouri Public Schools, 1962.

[111] School District of Philadelphia, Department of Superintendents, Division of Commercial and Distributive Education: *Survey of Students of School Work Programs Serving in Youth Conservation*. February, 1963.

Project HOPE in Pasadena, California[112] is still another program. Parent-student conferences with teachers and guidance personnel were arranged for the faltering student. The reading teacher grouped the students according to age, social needs and ability. One phase of the program was directed at the nonverbal chronic low achiever. A team teaching approach was used with 100 such potential dropouts. Courses in science, social studies, and English were offered to all. Those academic skills necessary for gainful employment were stressed. What the program did was bring pupils and teachers closer together, reduce the number of disciplinary referrals, and reduce the number of dropouts. So successful was the program, that Pasadena doubled its efforts the next year.

In Union County, New Jersey,[113] similar endeavors were undertaken. With parents' consent, low ability students were accepted into the training program for a one year trial. Slow learners were grouped for special academic remedial and vocational offerings. In grades nine and ten, instruction is in basic school subjects, citizenship education, and vocational exploration. In addition, shop and home economics were taught. In grade eleven, English, social studies and health education were taught while the students were enrolled in courses in occupations, record keeping, sales and consumer economics and work adjustment training, e.g., units in plumbing, carpentry, welding, etc. In grade twelve, the English, social studies and health courses were continued. The student took these in the morning and went to work in the afternoon. A follow-up study of twenty-eight graduates indicated that 92 per cent of them were offered employment by the employer who trained them; 75 per cent accepted such jobs. These graduates entered the labor force as shipping clerks, screw machine operators, waitresses, assembly workers, receptionists, nurses' aides, plastic machine operators and electronics assemblers.

The Morgan School[114] Program is still another variation. Students were selected to take on a work day corresponding to that of

---

[112] Project HOPE: *Pasadena Schools in Action,* Vol. 6, No. 2. October, 1963.

[113] Merachnik, P.: *The Slow Learner in the Secondary School: Report of a Program.* Union County Regional High School, Berkeley Heights, New Jersey, 1963.

[114] *Morgan School Work Experience Program.* Clinton, Connecticut Public Schools, 1960. Unpublished.

employees in local businesses. Students were required to have grades of *80* in English, shorthand, bookkeeping and office practice. For nine days, students went to school to take the required English course. Then they were dismissed to observe and participate in work functions of the local sponsoring business. They returned to school at 2:40 PM. After the first nine day period, the students returned to school for two days. They exchanged experiences and learned more about worker-employer relationships. Stressed at this time was the application for a job. The student went out into the world of work again. This time, she introduced herself to the new employer. Again, she spent nine days observing the company. The participating companies rated each trainee. It was interesting to note that the girls rated themselves lower as workers than did the company officials who supervised them. The sponsors felt the program should be continued and extended. Most participants felt they would not have learned to "break the ice" had it not been for the program.

Programs such as these bridge the gap between school and work. Too often the connection between the two is frayed by a bad experience in school or lack of knowledge of what are the demands of work. Work experience programs provide continuity between school and work. Occasionally, community organizations take over this connecting function. One such example is the Everett Prep Club.[115] A voluntary youth center program is provided for boys and girls of high school age. Industrial firms like Monsanto Chemical Company support the programs. Through films, discussion, readings, and role play the youth learn about the American business system, they endeavor to establish personal and realistic vocational goals, and they have a good exercise in youth self government.

Large scale work experiences have been started in several states, notably New York and North Carolina. A summary of the School to Employment Program[116] in New York indicated that after one year of half day work, 27 per cent of the students returned to normal school programs; 11 per cent entered full time employment,

---

[115] The Everett Prep Club Youth Program: *Preparation for Employment*. Everett, Massachusetts, Chamber of Commerce, March 16, 1963.

[116] School to Employment Program, Second Annual Report 1962-1963, *op. cit.*

44 per cent completed the program; and 18 per cent left the program either voluntarily or involuntarily. In contrast to a control group, more STEP students were in full time employment or doing satisfactory work in school. The students in the program heartily endorsed it.

IN SUMMARY, opportunities to learn and apply knowledge and skills taught in school make schooling a personally meaningful experience. Not only that but "earn because you learn" is a powerful incentive to continue in school. A survey of the earnings of students enrolled in work experience programs in Pennsylvania[117] revealed that most students were paid attractive wages. While 112 pupils earned nothing; 199 earned less than $1.00 per hour; 854 between $1.00 and $1.24 per hour; 468 $1.25 to $1.49 per hour and 47 $1.50 and over per hour. Their work experiences were, moreover, quite varied. Data processing, agriculture, construction, food services, printing, electricity, and office work were but a few areas in which the high school students were working.

LIFE AFTER SCHOOL

Most male dropouts look for and find work within several months after leaving school. Dillon[118] found that 85 per cent went to work immediately. Half of the early leavers shopped around for a job; approximately half found their jobs through friends. Plunkett and Riches[119] found 84 per cent of male dropouts found a regular job within four weeks of leaving school. This was the same percentage as for graduates. The remaining 16 per cent of the dropouts, however, did not get jobs for many months. Many more dropouts than graduates were found to be in the labor force but unemployed or not in the labor force at all.

Forty-nine per cent of the male graduates got jobs in semi-skilled manufacturing or nonmanufacturing; 36 per cent of the male dropouts get such jobs. Eighteen per cent of the male graduates were in unskilled occupations; 35 per cent of the dropouts

---

[117] Report relative general work experience programs in the public secondary schools of the Commonwealth of Pennsylvania for the 1962-1963 school term. Harrisburg, Department of Public Instruction, 1963.

[118] Dillon, H. J., *op. cit.*

[119] Plunkett, M., and Riches, N., *op. cit.*

TABLE II

GRADE COMPLETED AND OCCUPATIONAL PURSUITS

Grades Completed	*Professional; Technical; Skilled Per Cent*	*Semiskilled Unskilled Per Cent*
Five	1.3	94.2
Six	6.5	86.8
Nine	25.3	55.9
Eleventh	29.9	59.4
Twelfth	52.9	39.4

were so employed. Most female graduates were engaged in office work; most female dropouts in unskilled work.[120]

Dillon[121] found 24 per cent of the dropouts were in sales occupations, 20 per cent in manufacturing occupations; and 56 per cent were scattered among 25 other types of work. The Dillon study was undertaken more than a decade before the Plunkett and Riches. A contrast between the two indicated that the more recent trend is toward employing early school leavers in unskilled occupations.

The relationship between grades completed and occupational pursuits is seen in the table below adapted from Bell.[122]

Students who live in the city tend to stay in school longer than those who live in the country. In 1940, the average number of school years completed by city students was 8.7; in 1950 it was 10.0. On the other hand, the average number of grades completed by rural students in 1940 was 7.7; in 1950 it was 8.4.[123]

One impression of the dropout is that his meager high school education is terminal. In a follow-up study of high school graduates and early school leavers,[124] the State Board of Education in Virginia found 5.5 per cent of the dropouts had gone to college, 4.1 per cent to business school; 9.5 per cent trade school and 6.5

---

[120] *Ibid.*

[121] Dillon, H. J., *op. cit.*

[122] Bell, H. M.: *Youth Tell Their Story*. Washington, D. C., American Council on Education, 1938.

[123] U. S. Department of Commerce, Bureau of the Census: 1950 Census of Population, Preliminary Report. May 3, 1952 Series Pc-7, No. 6.

[124] Virginia's high school graduates and dropouts of 1939-1940. *Bulletin,* State Board of Education, 1951, Vol. 33, No. 8. State Dept. of Ed., Richmond, Virginia.

per cent had apprentice training. These statistics are to be considered as approximations because only 1,720 dropouts or 25 per cent of those surveyed responded to the questionnaire.

There is other evidence, however, that many dropouts do continue their education. Savitzky[125] reported that in 1960-1961, 14.2 per cent of the students in the evening academic and 16.7 per cent of those in the evening vocational high had left high school prior to graduation. Similarly, in Los Angeles[126] it was found that 13 per cent of the dropouts who had graduated from the adult high schools had gone to trade or business schools after they withdrew from the day high school. Of considerable interest here, moreover, is that more than 94 per cent of the dropouts who later attended adult high school had achieved average or above average marks in the last semester of night school. In addition, of the dropouts who later returned to the adult high school, 45 per cent planned to enroll in a junior college and nine per cent planned to take courses at a trade school.

Given the opportunity, many dropouts will learn. Not only that, but their motivation for learning increases. Perhaps the reason dropouts in many communities appear to be disinterested in continuing their education is that opportunities to do so are meager. What cannot be denied is that they have the appetite for learning.

A notable example of motivation for a high school education blossoming later in life is the Indianapolis Club of Western Electric Employees. This club was organized in 1911.[127] Two years later it incorporated its own evening school. The school operated on a joint effort of the Western Electric Club, the Western Electric Company, and the public school system. The club publicized the program and arranged the classes; the company furnished classroom space within the plant; and the Indianapolis public school system staffed the school, arranged for transfer of credit, and

---

[125] Savitzky, C.: The dropout problem in New York City: fact and fancy. *High Points.* October, 1963, 45, 11-18.

[126] The dropout who returns to graduate from adult high school. Evaluation and Research Section. Research Report No. 253. Los Angeles City School Districts, April, 1963.

[127] The Indianapolis Club of Western Electric Employees: *Memorandum of Record of In-plant High School.* Nov. 12, 1963.

granted high school diplomas to those who have earned them. The cost to the employee who is not a high school graduate was $1.00 per twenty week semester. Classes were arranged for three hours per day and conducted on each of the three shifts. Those Western Electric employees who attended the programs did so because they were conveniently located, the teachers were interested in helping adults, and because they wanted to become better models for their children. The company, moreover, rewarded the high school graduate by making him eligible for its college tuition refund plan.

In summary, schooling is attractive to an early school leaver when seen by him as relevant to his immediate life circumstances, when made easily accessible, and when promoted by significant individuals who truly care about him. Not all industries provide training programs; nor do all communities provide in-school work training programs. Personnel policies have been tightened up. The better educated and trained are preferred to the dropout. The advice to dropouts has been that they come to the employment office better equipped before they will be considered for jobs. Who will give them the job experience? Where can the dropouts, many of whom are destitute, find the money to get trained?

POST-SCHOOL WORK STUDY PROGRAMS

For many years now, the federal government has supported local and state vocational education programs. In the twentieth century alone the federal government has reached new heights in helping local educational units meet its obligations to prepare youth for employment. In 1913, vocational agriculture programs were instituted. A Federal Board of Vocational Education was established. In 1931, the Board extended its policies to permit reimbursement to local communities for part time work experience programs. The depressing economic outlook of the early thirties was a source of despair for many communities whose adolescents became despondent about their futures as working men and women. Hope glimmered on the educational horizon in 1936 when the seventy-fourth Congress passed P. L. 673, the George-Dean Act. For the first time, federal funds were used especially to support cooperative training with industry. Industrial Cooperative Training Programs in North Carolina has grown from the solo program in Wilmington in 1936 to the thirty-four in 1959 and the sixty-one in 1963.

While this progress is remarkable, it is obvious that there is now and has been for many years a multitude of unserved youth. They were unprepared for their displacement by electronic thinking machines and electrically generated labor replacement devices in the mines, on the farms, and in the factories. The more recent crop of dropouts are on the threshold of work, face to face with the door to employment. But this door has no handle to grasp, push or pull. Nor do they have the right complement of skills to get this door open, even a crack. The labor force is becoming restricted in age to those between twenty and fifty. Desperately they pound on the door. The feeling of despair of the willing workers under twenty and over fifty makes for unhealthy personal and social adjustments and the premature burial of our most precious natural resource, people.

To meet many of these exigencies the Office of Manpower, Automation, and Training (OMAT) was set up to fund the training of unemployed and underemployed members of the labor force for occupations in which there is a reasonable expectation of employment. The urgency which preceded these programs and the speed with which they were set up precluded elaborate planning. Many programs were meant to be bootstrap operations. They were to demonstrate to other parts of the country what could be done for the unemployed. Yet the problems of the unemployed dropout and the displaced unskilled older workers are still with us. What might the educational and employment agencies learn from the results of the recently funded manpower programs to prevent further proliferation of unemployment ills? The remedial vocational education programs have built a stronger democracy by teaching workers marketable skills.

Aller[128] pointed out that the experimental demonstration project, one of OMAT's vocational endeavors, will succeed if it is accepted as part of the "social subsystem with which it deals." The objective of such a program is to reshape the styles of life of the trainees. Although this is a respectable undertaking, it is

[128] Aller, C.: *Summary Report,* OMAT Training Conference. Airlie House, Warrenton, Virginia, Aug. 6-8, 1964. Unpublished.

an enormous one. Yet it cannot take place without first identifying what are the current styles of life, the environments which reinforce these styles, the aspects of the styles most susceptible to change, and the features of the new environments which will reshape and maintain these changed styles.

Judging from reports of experimental demonstration projects, several of them financed by OMAT, the attempts to actualize Dr. Aller's philosophy have met with varying degrees of success. Surprise inheres in each project; discovery results from each. Only in recent years have we developed a better understanding of the OUTS: left-outs, dropouts, kick-outs, push-outs, seduced-outs, and kept-outs. Programs like those sponsored by OMAT have contributed in large measure to our knowledge. Available to us today is a large reserve of information concerning the forces which shape and maintain the behavior of dropouts and, more important, the incentives and practices which will change his behavior.

One indisputable fact is that the OUTS are rarely understood in school. They do not speak the same language of their teachers or those who are *in*. Certainly they are affected by the prevailing values in the schools but they often do not have the economic resources, experience background, or social values to join them. They set up a verbal facade which becomes difficult to penetrate. This facade is adaptive because it permits them to maintain themselves in a basically unfriendly society. As was pointed out earlier, this facade operates as a buffer zone. Those social scientists who truly want to help the OUTS are rarely capable of doing so. The reason for this is undoubtedly their fear that such strangers asking for highly confidential information may harm them.

There are a few recent instances in which leaders of programs for the OUTS have gained the confidence of the trainees and were permitted access to a goldmine of information about the motivations and behaviors of socially and economically dislocated youth. James Deck,[129] a tireless and dedicated educator, suspected that the dropouts in his retraining program were uttering verbal platitudes about the reason they left school. He visited the homes of the dropouts, got acquainted with their parents, and learned

[129] Deck, J.: *The bold new venture report*. Mercer County, West Virginia Schools, 1963, Unpublished.

what were their aspirations. The trainees knew he was sympathetic and sincerely interested in their future. When they went astray he was there to help them out. His trainees did not disguise their attitudes about school. One trainee wrote Mr. Deck:

> The reason I left school was I don't like no one fussing at me because I done something wrong. I would rather take a spanking. I like spelling and shop best. I don't like science, math and geography. What I would like to do is repair furniture and build furniture. I had polio when I was seven years old and I'm not very strong.

The way the youth looks at himself determines in large measure what activities he will value. In schools, teachers rarely respond to anything but a child's surface behavior. That there is deep significance to even the most basic of a child's responses is generally not appreciated. This comes through clearly in another letter Mr. Deck received:

> I was raised in a poor family; Dad got cut off about six years ago and I never did have very much. I have not got very good clothes. My dad is not making very much on the state road so we don't have very much. That is why I don't like to go to school. Because I don't have very good clothes. I like to do math, spelling and science. I like most of the teachers but I was in trouble most of the time. I didn't make very good grades in school and that is why I don't like school very much. If you try to do the work to pass they would say that you are not trying.

The boys for Deck's program were recruited from dropout rolls of the local schools. Classes in auto mechanics, welding, building trades, and electronics were offered them. On the first day of class the boys were ready for action, they wanted to work on projects. They were looking for tangible and immediate evidence of success. The instructors were ready, however, to talk to them and to give them directions and warnings. The boys had itchy fingers to work; the teachers, lessons in morality. The first day was a disappointment to all. Rapport with the boys was established eventually, but not until the boys proved to themselves that they could weld a bead, test radio tubes, or replace car generators. The program was beset with many problems. Toilets were defaced; equipment and tools were stolen or broken; one teacher came to class intoxicated.

There were 149 trainees in the program; 114 completed it. After the program was over, twelve returned to school, fourteen got jobs; nine went into the service and seventy-nine unemployed. The program lasted but three months, an insufficient amount of time for a trainee to become truly competent. In addition, most trainees were not even seventeen years old when the program came to an end. They were too young to get jobs. The program started with good intentions, namely rehabilitating dropouts in an economically depressed area. What was learned from this study is the truly unique character of the individual dropouts. The importance of this study, though, lay in the fact that understanding of the dropout is not enough. It is equally important to recognize that 16-year-olds cannot develop sufficient competence in three months to become employable in the highly competitive labor market of economically depressed areas.

Altro Work Shops, Inc.,[130] has a reputation for rehabilitating people with physical and emotional handicaps. In February, 1963, Altro undertook a retraining program for dropouts. They were to provide training in the garment industry toward the goals of employment and improved social adjustment. Forty-six of the eighty-seven referrals to the program were admitted. One year later, nineteen remained in the program. Medical assessments indicated that 65 per cent of the trainees had some medical problem. Among the disorders observed were asthma, epilepsy, narcolepsy, syphilis, and enuresis. Emotional problems were observed in 88 per cent of the trainees. Fifty-four per cent of the trainees tested were in the borderline intelligence category. Mrs. Benney questioned the validity of the test findings, however. She suggested that the widespread reading problems might have lowered the intelligence test scores.

Shortly after the program got under way, the trainees were observed to roam around the shops and congregate in the rest rooms. Production personnel at the training site were not amused by this. Morale among workers was at a low. Altro handled these

---

[130] Benney, C., Altro Work Shops, Inc.: *Report on MDTA Project,* New York Special Youth, Number 1, 1964. Unpublished.

problems in two ways. A case worker was assigned to the shop every day to talk over problems with the staff and trainees. Also, the manager met with the professional staff and decided that nonproductive time should not be paid. Should it be the responsibility of the foreman to take time out to look for an absentee trainee? It was suggested that trainee cliques be broken up and individuals be spread out among several foremen. This would then weaken the bonds of affiliation with their nonproductive buddies and permit the formation of closer ties with the more experienced and more dependable workers.

Mrs. Benney doubted that all trainees would find jobs in the garment industry. She did feel, however, that the training in personal adjustment for work was a good exercise. In her judgment, student handicaps in basic arithmetic and reading mitigated against the trainees making the most of on-the-job training.

Basic training in academic subjects, general occupational orientation and improvement of social skills have been recognized by many project planners as indispensable requirements for a training program. Los Angeles[131] incorporated these areas in their youth training program. This was done in one of two OMAT projects in Philadelphia.[132] Low achieving dropouts were given a remedial communications program. They increased 1.83 grades in reading speed and .75 grades in comprehension. The problems experienced in Philadelphia were quite similar to those in other project areas. There were delays of three to five months in locating a suitable workshop site; materials were delivered late or where unsatisfactory recruitment time was inadequate, work contracts for the work adjustment center were hard to obtain, and business competition was high. Noted also was a lack of community involvement. While St. Louis[133] experienced much the same travail, it had more openings than trainees.

---

[131] "Youth Employability." A Project of the Youth Opportunities Board of Greater Los Angeles under the Manpower Development and Training Act of 1962. Unpublished.

[132] *Two Projects for Dropout Youth*. Philadelphia Council for Community Advancement. Jewish Employment and Vocational Service, Pennsylvania State Employment Service, July 1, 1964.

[133] *The Youth Training Project: A Demonstration Program*. Jewish Employment and Vocational Service. St. Louis, Missouri, 1965. Unpublished.

Notable contributions of both the Philadelphia and St. Louis programs were the training-testing work sampling for broad occupation categories such as small parts assembly, packaging, sewing, building, maintenance, clerical, electronic and auto parts repair. Observations of how the trainee performs with and without pressure yielded indications of the trainee's proclivities.

In the Philadelphia study, trainees were paid minimal wages with automatic increments. Some students responded to the wages by increasing productivity; others worked at the same pace irrespective of the wages. Later, when trainees were paid according to their production record, their performances improved. Incentive rates were more powerful than the guaranteed shop rate in improving job performance. Of utmost significance to the research worker and personnel counselor was the finding that sex, age, highest grade attained in school, reading ability, and presence of vocational handicaps had no bearing on post-training employment.

What confronts those of us involved in the training of disadvantaged youth is the devastating realization that we know too little to develop a recipe for action that will work with the wide variety of peoples classified under the one category *disadvantaged.* We are learning, though.

One discomforting fact that we discovered has been that our assumptions about the behavior of dropouts were not viable. Not only that, they were hopelessly inadequate and often wrong. We learned also that we could not rely completely on standard psychometric tests of abilities and interests to guide us in selecting who would profit from training. There is a hint in most studies that open-door admission policies are not at all impractical. Most applicants may be trained for a wide variety of jobs. The most judicious use of research time is to study the individual trainee with his many attributes in the context of the outstanding features of the training program and of the local economic community.

A start toward this was made in El Mirage, Arizona.[134] One hundred and fifty persons, age seventeen to fifty-five were selected as prospective trainees. They were rural, migrant, unskilled, and

---

[134] Experimental and Demonstration Project, MDTA Project, El Mirage, Arizona. Phoenix, The Arizona Migrant and Indian Ministry, 1964.

functionally illiterate. Many trainees could only plan for the immediate future. Their health habits were poor. They were neither neat nor clean. The odor from their mouths was offensive. Recruitment was almost on a door to door basis. Interviews were to be held at the project site but the building was usurped by a well baby clinic. Interviews, therefore, were held in the park amid barking dogs and shouting children. Later, the project moved into a schoolhouse. On the first day, the floor collapsed.

When training did begin, only forty-eight of the seventy-five recruits showed up. Some selected trainees said they would go only if their friends went. Particularly discouraging to the trainees was that the $32 per week allowance could not be given them for two weeks after the beginning of training. The program consisted of literacy training plus vocational training in farming or laundering.

To prevent a rising tide of dropouts from the program due to failing health, a fund raising effort by the project realized $2,400. This money was distributed to needy trainees. Medical doctors donated their services; pharmacies gave discounts; surplus commodities were distributed.

Study halls, music, sports, reading, vocational training, and budget preparation gave the trainees a well balanced program. Post-training followup indicated that of thirty who completed the farm hand training, sixteen were in training-related jobs, one training-unrelated, one unemployed, ten underemployed and two moved out. In the laundry training group only one was in a training-related job, five were in training-unrelated jobs and twelve unemployed. The conditions which the trainees met at the laundries were so poor that most preferred not to work.

Now we must raise a vital question: How realistic is it to prepare workers for jobs with little which will engage their interests for the present; and even less for the future?

Unintentionally, Operation Second Chance in North Carolina blundered. The interviewing conditions were no better than in El Mirage. The testing did not differ much from that undertaken in most other projects. The training was as good as elsewhere. Several endeavors we undertook we found it advisable to discard. But OSC was to be a community effort. Training cannot be divorced from the community in which it takes place. The trainee-community relationships that we discovered are what we are eager to share with the different readers of this report, be they officials of OMAT, state chairmen of educational enterprises, guidance counselors, teachers, dropouts, graduates and citizens seeking enlightenment.

Here is our story.

Chapter II

OPERATION SECOND CHANCE

THE central purpose of Operation Second Chance (OSC) was to train school dropouts for employment. It was the hope of OSC to teach jobless adolescents a trade and to increase the level of technical competence of the underemployed. The subsequent employment of trainees in trades for which they were trained was the conviction upon which OSC rested.

What if the trainees did not get related jobs? What if they entered the labor force in training-unrelated jobs? Was it not conceivable that some would get no jobs at all? In light of the employment statistics on adolescents, and especially on school dropouts, these were not unreasonable expectations. Certainly training-related employment could be viewed as an outcome of OSC. But training-unrelated employment as well as unemployment, events which also take place when a training program is completed, must be similarly viewed as outcomes. Because so many circumstances surround both the training and employment, what ever it is that *causes* the latter is frequently masked. Many more treatment and control groups than were available would be needed to determine causation.

It is not sufficient to know, moreover, how many trainees were and were not placed. What the circumstances are loading upon placement is a question whose answers would serve as guidelines for future training programs anywhere in the United States. In answering this question, the employment sequence was studied as follows. (See Figure 2.)

A trainee with an individualized arrangement of skills, abilities, values, and personality traits receives instruction in one of several vocational training programs. At the threshold of employment, he is confronted with an employment situation which itself varies in many qualities, namely, positions available, wage and fringe benefits, job permanence, and personal characteristics of the workers.

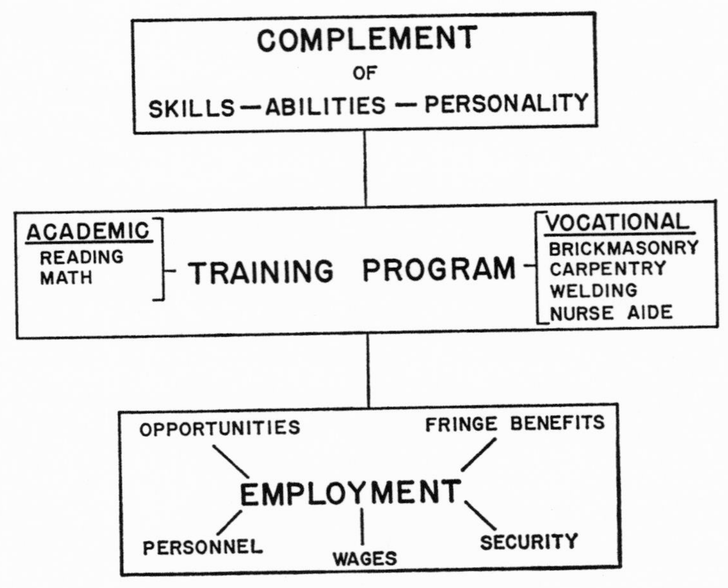

Figure 2. Employment sequence.

Employment status, it is hypothesized, does not happen by chance. Rather, it is a logical outcome of training. The kind of training program and the degree of competence of the trainee, it is assumed, definitely affect employment. But employment as well as training may be related to personal attributes of the trainee. The more able might be expected to perform tasks demanding more mental ability better than the less able. The more cooperative worker might be expected to work better at tasks like those in brick masonry than the less cooperative. Stated another way, a trainee brings his individual *attribute mix* into the training situation. Elements within this "mix" are related to success in training. These elements plus success in training have a bearing on employment. Employment, however, hinges upon factors like job opportunities, personnel practices, and wage incentives, all of which are extrinsic to training.

To be even more specific, this investigation was concerned with the effects of general mental ability; specific aptitudes like numerical, spatial and verbal; achievement in reading, arithmetic, and spelling; personality attributes including perceptual organization, interests, and temperament on employment.

But training itself is related to employment. Therefore, it is also necessary to study the relationship between these same mental and emotional characteristics with training outcomes. The position taken by the OSC planning committee was that a skilled tradesman must know more than manipulative skills to be an effective worker. Underpinning effective workmanship in a trade are reading and arithmetic accomplishments. These allow the worker to make precise mental judgments which he couples with refined eye-hand coordination in executing vocational tasks. Subjecting a trainee to vocational and basic programs will, it is therefore hypothesized, increase his achievement in reading and arithmetic. It will also prepare him for the trade he will enter. Mental ability, achievement, and personality attributes, it is further hypothesized, have bearing on the different degrees of improvement in reading, arithmetic and language achieved during the program.

Several well known research projects have indicated that with increasing age, there is a decrease in scores made on tests of mental ability. Asher[1] found the average IQ of Kentucky mountain children age six to be in the 80's; age twelve, in the high 60's; age fifteen, below 60. Measuring intelligence of Tennessee mountain children in 1930 and again in 1940, Wheeler[2] found the curves to decelerate from age six through 16. In 1940, the average IQ at age six was above 100; at age sixteen, in the low 80's. Similar declines for underprivileged urban children were observed by Skeels and Fillmore.[3]

---

[1] Asher, E. J.: The inadequacy of current intelligence tests for testing Kentucky mountain children. *J. Genet. Psychol.*, 1935, 46, 480-486.

[2] Wheeler, L. R.: A comparative study of the intelligence of East Tennessee mountain children, *J. Educ. Psychol.*, 1942, 33, 321-334.

[3] Skeels, H. M., and Fillmore, E. A.: The mental development of children from underprivileged homes. *Pedogogical Seminar and J. Genet. Psych.*, 1937, 50, 427-439.

There is some evidence,[4] however, that mental ability scores improve as a function of improved and stimulating environments. Intelligence involves the making of refined judgments. The Operation Second Chance training through its mental and motor exercises designed to awaken the senses and sharpen motor and muscular responses, it is further hypothesized, will increase intelligence test scores.

SAMPLE

Three areas in North Carolina were selected to serve as experimental and demonstration project centers. It was believed that one project center in each of the three main regions of the State would gain the attention of the local citizenry as well as those in the adjacent communities. They would see what could be done for dropouts, and, in turn, would set up programs of their own.

Selection of project sites were determined by several criteria. Among these were low school holding power, proximity of the community to an area industrial education center and to an office of the Employment Security Commission, and approval by the Area Redevelopment Administration of the Overall Economic Development Program submitted to it by the Community Planning Board.

The three centers chosen were Mitchell, Avery, and Yancey Counties in the West; Lincoln County in the Piedmont; and Washington and Tyrell Counties in the East. Table III reveals what are the basic economics of the three areas, the percentage of unemployed insured workers, the annual average weekly earnings, and the percentage of dropouts in the year in which OSC trainees were recruited. The unemployment rates are all above the state average. As few as four out of 100 workers were unemployed in Washington County; as many as twenty-three out of 100 in Mitchell. The average weekly earnings were below the State average of $76.36 in all counties but Washington. It should be pointed out, however, that in 1962, the year in which OSC was begun, Wash-

---

[4] Freeman, F. N., Holzinger, K. V., and Mitchell, B. C.: The influence of environment on the intelligence, school achievement and conduct of foster children. *Twenty-seventh Yearbook.* National Society for the Study of Education. 1928, Part I, 103-217.

TABLE III

ESSENTIAL ECONOMIC AND EDUCATIONAL DATA OF THREE OSC TRAINING AREAS

Project Centers	*1963* *Insured†* *Unemployed*	*1963* *Annual Average Weekly Earnings*	*1962* *Percentage of Dropouts‡*	*Major Sources of Employment*	*Other Data**
Western Counties					
Mitchell	22.8	$60.18	.49	Manufacturing	Mineral resoures, tourist
Avery	10.5	56.86	.56	Stone, Clay, glass processing	area, welfare. Payments to more people than any other area in
Yancey	12.3	65.03	.57	Retail trade	the State; 62 per cent of recruitable workers unskilled; 11 per cent out migration in past decade.
Piedmont County					
Lincoln	10.0	$61.64	.50	Manufacturing, retail trade, farming	Some mineral deposits; large number of male unemployed; out migration high among adolescents.
Eastern Counties					
Washington .	3.9	$91.12	.46	Farming, lumber, wood processing, Gov't services	Primarily unskilled recruitables; some tourism; major forestry area
Tyrrell	7.2	47.94	.54	Farming, lumber, wood processing, Gov't services	Plan to improve agricultural economy
State	3.7	$76.36	.48		

* O.E.D.P. Submitted to ARA.

† North Carolina Labor Force Estimates by Labor Market Area. 1964. Employment Security Commission, Raleigh, N. C.

‡ Statistical report on dropouts North Carolina Public Schools, W. W. Peek. State Department of the Public Instruction. Fifth grade enrollment is the base year.

ington County had an unemployment rate of 8.8. Also, the average family income was $42.02; for the non-white population it was $26.42.[5] The percentage of youngsters dropping out of school was above the North Carolina average in all counties but Washington. The recruits, then, were drawn from counties where most families were destitute, where school holding power was low, and where the percentage of insured unemployed was quite high.

PROCEDURE

In each center, the OSC administrative structure was essentially the same. A local advisory board was formed. It was composed of key community figures who were most familiar with the problems and assets of an area. In addition, they took their responsibilities as citizens seriously. Welfare, health, education and industry were represented in this body. Liaison between the community and the State Advisory Committee as well as liaison between trainee and community were regarded as their most vital duties.

Recruitment for the training program also followed essentially the same pattern in each center. The OSC program was announced in local newspapers, television shows and radio programs. The local project coordinator, upon the recommendation of the local advisory board was appointed by James Ellerbe, State Chairman of OSC. It was the responsibility of the local coordinator to contact each school dropout between the ages of sixteen and a half and twenty-two. Each dropout received a letter announcing the program. Often, especially when the coordinator suspected illiteracy in the family, he visited the homes of county school dropouts to explain the program to them.

After a recruit agreed to enroll in the training program, he registered at the local employment office. The intake interview and testing procedures of ESC then followed. All recruits received the General Aptitude Test Battery (GATB). After the GATB was scored, recruits returned to the ESC office for an interview. The purpose of this interview was to assess the vocational interests of

---

[5] North Carolina Labor Force Estimates by Labor Market Areas. Raleigh, Employment Security Commission, 1963.

trainees. Next, the research staff administered their battery of tests. This included, (1) the Wechsler Adult Intelligence Scale (WAIS), an individual test of intelligence requiring no writing or reading; (2) the Benton Visual Retention Test (BVRT), another non-verbal measure of intelligence; (3) the Wide Range Achievement Test (WRAT), measuring achievement in reading, language and arithmetic from first grade through college, and (4) the Structured Objective Rorschach Test (SORT), a measure of personality attributes. The majority of the testing was given individually. This was to make certain that applicants would give the most truthful answers. In group testing, they may have been tempted to cheat or to fill in the IBM sheet without regard for the questions.

The course offerings were based on the judgment of what were (1) the employment opportunities in an area, (2) which of the dropouts with different ability patterns might best profit from them, and (3) which of these courses would receive the approval of ARA. After courses were approved in Washington, the vocational and academic training began. During the instructional period, members of the research staff visited each training site. There were three visits. Each visit coincided with completion of specific phases of the program. Trainees were interviewed individually for approximately thirty to forty-five minutes. Their opinions about the course, opinions of self as a worker, and vocational plans were discussed.

At the conclusion of the course, the research staff readministered its battery of tests. This time including the (1) Wechsler-Bellevue II, an alternate form of the individual test of intelligence; (2) Benton Visual Retention Test; (3) the Wide Range Achievement Test, and (4) the Structured Objective Rorschach Test.

One month after the completion of training, the research staff returned to the training sites to interview the graduates. During this follow-up interview, inquiries were made about employment status, vocational plans, the good and poor features of the program.

Contacts with many trainees were maintained beyond the one month follow-up, primarily with trainees who felt the interviewers were their friends. The terminal point in collecting the data, however, was the one month follow-up interview.

TRAINING PROGRAMS

Training programs were for entry occupations. *Pre-apprentice bricklayer* was one such program. Its objectives were (1) to develop the necessary skills, technical information, and job judgment that is required for employment as an advanced learner in the brick masonry trade; (2) to provide the experience necessary to perform jobs using clay, stone, and cement; (3) to develop safe, orderly and reliable work habits; (4) to develop occupational competence and high standards of workmanship, and (5) to develop an appreciation and understanding of the work done by other crafts and how this work fits into the total building process. Among the topics considered were blueprint-reading and mathematics, bonding, constructing pilasters, constructing brick steps, facing tile, and maintaining clay masonry structures.

Another program was *upholstery* cutting and sewing training. Its objectives were (1) to familiarize the student with different types of fabric; (2) to learn to consider the multiple uses of remnants in cutting fabric; (3) to learn to measure frames and make patterns correctly; (4) to learn to operate a power sewing machine; (5) to learn to sew material in order to have proper fitting of patterns, and (6) to learn to match fabric. Among the tasks practiced were cutting with shears, drawing patterns on upholstery material from predrawn patterns, cutting striped and figured material to match, and cutting loose cushions.

The *apprenticeship welder* course had among its objectives: (1) that the student learn to make proper electrode selection; (2) that he learn to judge which is appropriate current; (3) that he learn to maintain a proper arc; (4) that the trainee learn to butt weld, to lap weld, and to fillet weld; and (5) that he learn to make welds of different thickness. The welding circuit, groove welding and fillet welding were emphasized. Welding practice was given in horizontal, vertical and overhead positions.

The role of the carpenter in the construction industry was discussed first in the *pre-apprentice carpentry* course. The grades, sizes and uses of woods were considered next. Shop mathematics and graphics were introduced early since the carpentry concepts cannot be taught without these basics. Among the activities of the carpentry class were (1) foundation form work; (2) wall and floor framing; (3) roof framing; (4) exterior finishing, and (5) interior finishing. Also introduced were activities designed to shape buying habits of carpenters. Practice was given in estimating and ordering materials.

Familiarizing the student with the fundamentals of all component automotive units was the first objective of the *automobile service station mechanic.* Another objective was to teach the students the practical applications of identifying defective parts. In addition, how to make minor adjustments and motor tune-ups were studied. The safe use of tools and machines was correlated with the use of testing equipment. Among the activities stressed were using wrenches, hacksaws, portable power tools, reading automotive drawings, and the application of mathematics to auto repair. Taught also were fundamentals of the gasoline engine, automobile chassis, automotive electrical system, ignition system, cooling system, lubrications system, and steering system.

The purpose of the *nurses' aide* course was to teach the trainees the duties to be performed by them in the hospital. The aides were taught what is the organization of the hospital. Lines of authority were described next. Hospital terminology, such as "abdomen," "resuscitate," "plasma," were taught also. Personal care of the patient, his skin, hair, teeth, hands, weight, and posture were discussed. The optimum ward environment was described. The focal point of this unit was the patient's signal. How to admit a patient was detailed briefly. Practical experience with obstetrics, pediatrics, genitourinary and gastrointestinal patients rounded out the program.

In addition to six hours of vocational training, all trainees were required to take two hours of academic training daily. One-half hour was to be spent in reading; another, in arithmetic; another, in language; and the last, free choice between any one of the above plus general science, geography, history and civics. Because students varied widely in initial achievement, programmed instruction in each of these subject areas were given the students at the level at which he was capable of achieving satisfactorily, be it first grade or college.

Programmed instruction is a recent innovation in the educational field. The basic idea is quite simple. The program does the teaching. Although there are variations in programming format, each will be composed of frames or instructional units. The frame will make a statement or pose a question. The trainee will construct his own reply. This reply is then checked against the correct answer which appears close by in linear programs or adjacent to no particular frame in branching programs.

For example,

Linear Program

Frame 1. **-fy** at the end of a word means "to make." "Magni-" means large. What does magnify mean?________________
Frame 2. To enlarge or make larger. **-ificent** at the end of a word means "that which is made." What does "magnificent" mean?

Branching Program

Frame 1. **-fy** at the end of a word means "to make." "Magni" means large. What does magnify mean?__________ The correct answer appears to the left of frame 46.
Frame 46. If you said "to enlarge" or "make larger" go on to Frame 21. If you said "something great," you have not learned that **-fy** means "to make." Go back to Frame 1.
Frame 21. **-ificent** at the end of a word means "That which is made." What does magnificent mean? __________ The correct answer appears to the left of Frame 13.

Adjusting instruction to a level at which each and every trainee could learn the maximum amount within his potential was the target of the programming approach. It was a practical solution to the problem of accommodating instruction to a wide range of talent. This approach also freed the student from teacher domination. Like it or not, he was on his own. Each instructional unit, moreover, is at the most fundamental level possible. The student who checks his constructed reply to the question in the frame learns what is the correct answer but, more important, that he has the ability to solve mental problems.

Among the materials used were *Reading for Understanding,* Science Research Associates; *McCall-Crabbs Tests Exercises in Reading Books A-E,* Bureau of Publications, Columbia University; Spelling Rules TT 101, First Steps in Reading, General Science, Grollier; *Steps to Better Reading,* Harcourt Brace; *How to Measure Board Feet Program 1003,* B. K. Donald Publishing Co.; *Vocabulary Building 1 and 2,* Cenco; Language C-D; Language E-F;

Reading E-F; Arithmetic C, Arithmetic D, Arithmetic E-F, California Test Bureau; Basic Math, Seventh Grade Math; Algebra I, Plane Geometry I, Solid Geometry I, Temac; *Tutor Test Fractions,* Doubleday; *Blueprint Reading,* McGraw-Hill; History 4016, 4017 and Geography 4013 and 4014, Universal Electronic Lab. Corp.; *Constitution,* Ginn and Company; and *Medical Terminology,* John Wiley and Sons.

SOME CHARACTERISTICS OF THE TRAINEES

Research on the characteristics of dropouts has burst forth at an unprecedented pace. Generally, the image issuing from such studies is that of the chronic underachiever, of the destitute young breadwinner, and of the scholastically apathetic adolescent. Rarely is the dropout favorably perceived. It is even more rare when he is seen as at all normal.

Too often we allow our passions to dictate our beliefs. Should the dropout be pitied or should he be made to "toe the line?" Should the OSC teachers be permissive with trainees or should they be dominating? Should the trainees be expected to pull themselves toward self improvement or should they be pushed? Even with the unfavorable image he does have, how to manage dropout trainees in a retraining program was not known.

These questions, all of which were raised by OSC teachers, had no readily available solutions. The writer took the position that before functional classroom management procedures could be developed, the often cited stereotype of the dropout had to be vindicated. Since the questions of the OSC instructors all dealt with achievement, ability, and personality traits, these features were investigated.

ACHIEVEMENT

School records of applicants to the program were secured from the local school files. Regrettably, records were not available for all trainees. A sufficient number were secured, however, to be considered representative of the dropouts in each of two centers where ample records were available. One OSC instructor raised the question of how valuable these records would be if the achievement of the "normal" (i.e., graduates) were not known. Each rec-

TABLE IV

TYPICAL TEACHER EVALUATIONS OF STUDENTS IN TWO OSC CENTERS

Behavior Grades	*Lincoln County*		*Avery-Mitchell-Yancey Counties*	
	Dropouts	*Stayins*	*Dropouts*	*Stayins*
Arithmetic				
1-3	B	B*	B	A*
4-6	C	B*	C	B*
7-9	C	B*	D	B*
Language				
1-3	B	B*	B	B
4-6	C	B*	B	B*
7-9	C	B*	C	B*
Reading				
1-3	B	B*	B	B*
4-6	B	B*	B	B*
7-9	C	B*	C	B*
Cooperation				
1-3	Ave.†	Above ave.*	Ave.	Ave.*
4-6	Ave.	Above ave.*	Ave.	Ave.
7-9	Ave.	Above ave.	Ave.	Above ave.
Courtesy				
1-3	Ave.	Above ave.*	Ave.	Ave.
4-6	Ave.	Above ave.*	Ave.	Ave.
7-9	Ave.	Above ave.	Ave.	Above ave.*
Dependability				
1-3	Ave.	Above ave.*	Ave.	Ave.*
4-6	Ave.	Above ave.*	Ave.	Above ave.*
7-9	Ave.	Ave.	Ave.	Above ave.*
Industriousness				
1-3	Ave.	Above ave.*	Ave.	Ave.*
4-6	Below ave.	Above ave.*	Below ave.	Above ave.*
7-9	Below ave.	Above ave.*	Below ave.	Ave.
Initiative				
1-3	Below ave.	Ave.*	Ave.	Ave.*
4-6	Below ave.	Ave.*	Below ave.	Ave.*
7-9	Below ave.	Ave.	Below ave.	Ave.*
Leadership				
1-3	Below ave.	Ave.*	Ave.	Ave.*
4-6	Below ave.	Ave.*	Ave.	Ave.*
7-9	Below ave.	Ave.*	Ave.	Ave.*
Maturity				
1-3	Ave.	Ave.*	Ave.	Ave.*
4-6	Ave.	Ave.*	Ave.	Ave.*
7-9	Ave.	Above ave.*	Ave.	Ave.*

Behavior Grades	*Lincoln County*		*Avery-Mitchell-Yancey Counties*	
	Dropouts	*Stayins*	*Dropouts*	*Stayins*
Appearance				
1-3	Ave.	Above ave.*	Ave.	Ave.
4-6	Ave.	Above ave.*	Ave.	Above ave.*
7-9	Ave.	Above ave.*	Ave.	Ave.*
Self-Control				
1-3	Ave.	Ave.*	Ave.	Ave.
4-6	Ave.	Above ave.*	Ave.	Ave.*
7-9	Ave.	Above ave.*	Ave.	Ave.*

* The distributions of ratings for dropouts and stayins were compared. Chi square, a statistical test assessing differences between distributions, was applied and found to be of such magnitude that the distributions were unlikely to be similar. The specific chi squares values appear in a paper, "School Histories of Dropouts and Stayins." No asterisk signifies the teachers did not differ in their ratings of dropouts and stayins.

† Ave. is used in the table above as an abbreviation of the word *average*.

ord of the OSC trainees was matched with that of a graduate on the bases of chronological age and date of entrance into school. In Table IV are the typical teacher evaluations for students in Lincoln and in Avery-Mitchell-Yancey Counties. Too few dropouts were enrolled in the eastern North Carolina project to make a similar analysis possible.

The most common rating is technically called "the mode." In both OSC training centers the modal ratings in the academic subjects for the primary grades is the same for dropouts and stayins, namely, *B*. The asterisk following each row of rated characteristics, however, indicates that as early as the primary grades, the *distribution* of marks for the subsequent dropouts differed significantly from those of the stayins. The observed frequencies of A's, B's, C's, etc., for dropouts deviated beyond chance expectations from those of the graduates. Thereafter, the differences between dropouts and stayins are quite apparent.

It is easier for the reader to see that a distribution of ratings with a "Below Average" mode is different from one with an "Above Average" mode (initiative ratings, Lincolnton, grades seven to nine). More difficult to apprehend are those instances in which the modes are the same, yet the distributions are significant-

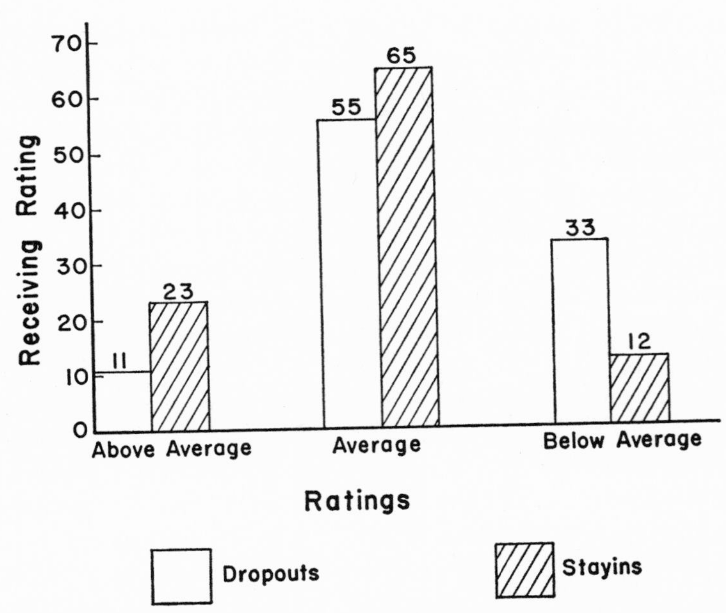

Figure 3. Percentage of grade five leadership ratings of dropouts and stayins in the tri-county site.

ly different. The illustration in Figure 3 is typical of this situation. For all distributions of teacher ratings examined, fewer dropouts received high ratings and fewer stayins than dropouts received low ratings. Other comparisons in Table IV in which the typical score of the dropouts is the same as the stayins and yet the distributions are significantly different, may be similarly viewed. Dropouts receive fewer high and more low ratings than stayins.

Table IV indicates that in both OSC regions, dropouts received lower ratings than stayins. Yet the average dropout received average ratings. In his early academic history, he received better than average marks. While the ratings of stayins tend to be stable through the grades, always *B;* those of the dropouts tended to decline. The student who later dropped out was an average and often a good student in elementary school. He had demonstrated reading, spelling, and arithmetic achievements. Although his marks in junior high school were somewhat lower, they were, nevertheless, *average*. The ratings of personal and social assets clustered around *average* for both dropouts and stayins. Quite clearly, stayins received higher ratings but the typical ratings dropouts received for *cooperation, courtesy, dependability, maturity, appearance,* and *self control* paints no gloomy portrait of dropouts. The only consistently unfavorable ratings the dropouts received were for *industriousness* and *initiative*. Close scrutiny of this table reveals that the marks and ratings received by mountain dropouts were higher than those from Lincoln County. The characteristics which constitute a dropout in one location were not those which made for one elsewhere.

The imposing correlation of decline in ratings with increasing years in school may appear to the reader a justification for the view that poor achievement *causes* early school leaving. While this may be true, alternative explanations are offered to temper any hasty conclusion from the figures in Table IV. In the first place, the assumptions that the teacher's judgment of a student's achievement are valid, infallible, and precise have never been substantiated. If any position is assumed from the voluminous research literature on marking practices, it is that teacher judgment of achievement is neither valid nor consistent. The designs of the studies are simple to compare teacher judgment of achievement with scores on a standardized achievement test and with their own judgment of test papers rescored some weeks after the initial marking. In the second place, it is possible to support the view that the teacher's low evaluations of a student's work precipitated early school withdrawal by informing the student that if he wanted to escape personal devaluation he had better leave.

INTELLIGENCE

Another characteristic difference between the samples was with regard to their mental abilities. In Table V are the distributions of intelligence quotients for the Piedmont and the West. Two tests had been administered individually; the Wechsler and the Benton. Scores on the Benton were lower. The table points out also that the incidence of below normal IQ's was quite high. Significantly lower IQ's were reported for the mountain group. This

TABLE V

COMPARISON OF THE INTELLIGENCE QUOTIENTS OF TWO SAMPLES OF DROPOUTS

Category	*Wechsler Adult Intelligence Test*		*Category*	*Benton Visual Retention Test*	
	Piedmont	West		Piedmont	West
Below 74	18	34	Below 70	39	91
75-91	51	103	70-79	22	31
92-108	39	36	80-94	20	28
109-123	2	0	95-104	21	10
			104+	6	11
Chi Square	8.44*			17.74*	

* The difference in distributions in intelligence between the Piedmont and Western sample will not occur by chance more than two times in one hundred.

TABLE VI

TESTS OF SIGNIFICANCE BETWEEN APTITUDES AND ACHIEVEMENTS OF TWO SAMPLES

Test	*Piedmont: N = 110* *Mean*	*Standard Deviation*	*West: N = 179* *Mean*	*Standard Deviation*	*t*
GATB					
G—Intelligence	80.7	17.9	79.2	13.6	—
V—Verbal	80.2	13.3	81.4	10.7	—
N—Numerical	78.1	18.5	73.4	17.8	2.14*
S—Spatial	87.9	21.5	85.5	17.6	—
P—Form perc.	87.8	21.1	87.4	18.9	—
Q—Clerical perc.	86.0	13.3	86.2	12.1	—
K—Motor coordin.	84.2	22.1	88.1	18.8	—
F—Finger dext.	83.2	22.5	83.6	18.5	—
M—Manual dext.	85.9	22.6	85.8	20.3	—
WAIS					
Verbal IQ	86.6	12.4	84.5	9.9	—
Performance IQ	86.6	12.8	83.6	10.1	2.07*
Full Scale IQ	85.7	12.4	82.7	9.6	2.14*
Wide Range Achievement					
Reading grade	6.2	2.9	6.0	2.5	—
Spelling grade	5.6	2.5	5.2	1.8	—
Arithmetic grade	5.7	1.8	4.8	1.9	4.09†

* Significant beyond $p \leqslant .05$ with 287 df.
† Significant beyond $p \leqslant .001$ with 287 df.

might seem strange to the reader who might have anticipated higher IQ's in this group of dropouts who received higher marks in school.

A more refined summary of the intelligence and achievement scores is presented in Table VI. The majority of aptitude scores of both samples of dropouts lies close to eighty-five. Approximately 16 per cent of the scores were normal intelligence or better. The average reading scores in the Piedmont were at the grade six level. Spelling and arithmetic averages were at grade five. The reading and spelling test scores for the mountain sample were the same as for the Piedmont. Arithmetic scores, however, were significantly below those of the mountain group. Regional differences were in favor of the Piedmont. Though the two samples were located no more than fifty miles apart, the aptitude and achievement differences crushed any hope of generalizing about North Carolina's dropouts. If economically disadvantaged dropouts living in the same state and exposed to similar curricular offerings are so prominent, one would expect differences between dropouts in several states to be even more extreme.

The standard deviation is a statistic which defines the variability in a sample. It denotes the sampling fluctuation from the average score. Thirty-four per cent of the sample has scores between this average and plus one standard deviation; another 34 per cent has scores between the average and minus one standard deviation. If the average Piedmont full scale WAIS IQ is 86 and the standard deviation is 12, then 34 per cent of the sample has IQ's between 74 and 86; 34 per cent, 86-98. Sixteen per cent, moreover, will have IQ's lower than 74; 16 per cent, higher than 98.

Now if the intrasample variability, i.e., standard deviation, is examined, one is compelled to conclude that within any one region dropouts differ considerably from one another in aptitude and in achievement. The middle range of reading scores in the Piedmont circumscribe almost six grades; in the mountains, five. The boundaries defining the average scores were hardly proximate. How then is an unequivocal view of the dropout justifiable?

In science, we endeavor to explain one trait in terms of others. One statistical technique used is to correlate any two or more traits. Once the degree of association is expressed as a correlation coefficient, it may be squared. This new statistic, the coefficient of determination will reveal how much of a score to attribute to some other score. For instance, in Table VII below, the correlation between verbal IQ and spelling achievement in the Piedmont is .68. Squaring this number, we find that 46 per cent of the reading achievement may be attributed to verbal IQ; but the correlation is .45 between these same scores in the West. There the verbal IQ explains but 20 per cent of spelling achievement. In Figure 4, this is graphically presented.

The difference in the degree to which verbal IQ explains spelling in each region is especially noteworthy since the regional averages for verbal IQ and spelling achievement were quite similar. This observation opens the door to the understanding of dropouts even further. Even where dropouts are similar in some characteristics, they may differ markedly with respect to how much they use this ability to prosper in a scholastic environment. The notion that endowment is *the* vital determinant of learning does not always ring true. The considerable differences of aptitude and achievement correlations between the regions entice us to ask

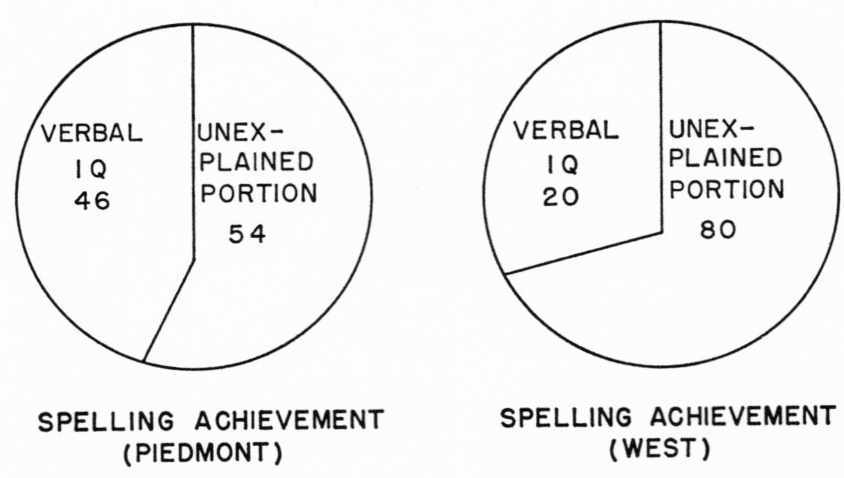

SPELLING ACHIEVEMENT (PIEDMONT)

SPELLING ACHIEVEMENT (WEST)

Figure 4. Spelling achievement attributed to verbal intelligence in the Piedmont and the western North Carolina samples.

TABLE VII

INTERCORRELATIONS AMONG WAIS, GATB, AND WRAT FOR BOTH SAMPLES

		WAIS		WRAT			GATB								
		Perf	*Full*	*R*	*S*	*A*	*G*	*V*	*N*	*S*	*P*	*Q*	*K*	*F*	*M*
WAIS															
Verbal	P	70	95	71	68	72	78	69	72	64	65	48	52	45	48
	W	59	92	55	45*	62	68	74	56	43*	41*	45	31*	32	17*
Performance .	P		87	49	52	60	76	48	67	74	70	47	52	54	52
	W		86	33	24*	44*	59*	48	50*	51*	59	39	41	40	30*
Full Scale ...	P			68	67	74	84	67	76	74	73	53	58	53	57
	W			51*	41*	61*	72*	70	60*	52*	54*	48	39*	39	25*
Wide Range															
Reading	P				93	59	66	78	64	33	51	55	52	28	$\overline{03}$
	W				77*	38*	43*	65*	35*	19	25*	50	24*	06	39*
Spelling	P					62	68	73	69	37	56	57	52	32	39
	W					48	43*	58*	43*	22	19*	48	24*	06*	$\overline{05}$*
Arithmetic ...	P						82	67	85	58	70	59	60	54	56
	W						59*	52*	63*	33*	48*	53	28*	34*	19*

* Results of Z tests indicated that the differences between the correlations in the two samples are significantly different beyond $p \leqslant .05$ level.

A negative correlation is indicated by a line above a number (i.e., $\overline{03}$).

why a student from the Piedmont need not utilize as much ability in order to learn.

To be specific, significant difference between correlations obtained in the two regions were observed for verbal IQ with spelling achievement and GATB: space, form perception, motor coordination; performance IQ with spelling and arithmetic achievements and GATB; general intelligence, number, space, manual dexterity; and full scale IQ with all achievement scores and GATB; general intelligence, number, space, form perception, motor coordination and manual dexterity. In addition, differences were noted among scholastic achievements and between scholastic achievement with most of the aptitudes measured by the GATB. The importance of these findings for education and guidance are considerable. Since it is commonly believed that a characteristic like IQ may be manipulated to effect changes in achievement, clearly the same manipulation in one geographic region will not result in the same result in another.

PERSONALITY

There are several approaches to the measurement of personality. One is the simple scoring, objective type measures; the other, the more difficult to interpret idiosyncratic response measures. The personality test used in OSC, the Structured Objective Rorschach

TABLE VIII

TYPICAL PERSONALITY RATINGS OF TWO SAMPLES OF DROPOUTS

Attribute	*Piedmont N = 110*	*West N = 179*	*Chi Square Value*
Theoretical	Low	Low*	32.41
Practical	Average	Average*	70.36
Pedantic	High	Average*	134.81
Induction	Average	Average*	45.46
Deduction	Average	Average	29.13
Rigidity	Average	Average*	54.53
Structuring	Average	Average*	39.37
Concentration	Average	Average*	26.92
Interest range	Average	Average*	28.40
Human interests	Average	Average*	166.89
Popular responsiveness	Low	Average*	141.91
Original responsiveness	Below ave.†	Average*	121.58
Aggressiveness	Average	High*	85.80
Social responsibility	Average	Low*	147.68
Cooperation	Average	Average*	79.43
Tact	Average	Average*	23.06
Confidence	Average	Average*	25.69
Consistency	Above ave.	Average*	35.04
Anxiety	Average	Average*	28.29
Moodiness	Average	Average*	34.85
Activity potential	Average	Below ave.*	126.55
Impulsiveness	Average	High*	242.33
Flexibility	Average	Above ave.*	25.75
Conformity	Low	Low*	24.73

* For chi squares higher than 18.46 the differences between the distributions of personality traits of the two samples of dropouts will occur by chance fewer than one time in a thousand. As the chi square value increases, the likelihood that these are chance observations becomes even slimmer. The raw data appear in a paper "Some Psychological Characteristics of School Dropouts." Southeastern Psychological Association Convention, April 2, 1964, Gatlinburg, Tennessee.

† Ave. is used as an abbreviation of the word *average*.

Test, combines the best features of both approaches. A testee is presented with a series of inkblots which he organizes in the several ways which are meaningful to him. In developing his response he may take into consideration the shape, color, shading, or movement perceived in the blot. In addition, the focus on the whole, major parts, or details of the blot are taken into consideration, too. Intricate relationships have been worked out by psychologists concerning the personality attributes of testees who view the shading, color, form and movement in the blots. It should be emphasized, moreover, that although the original Rorschach test was used in psychiatric diagnoses, the form used in this study was standardized on a nonclinical population. Hence, psychiatric classifications and diagnoses of personality maladjustment were prohibitive. What the test reveals are the tendencies of normal people.

When the SORT personality attributes of Piedmont and Appalachian dropouts were examined, striking differences were noted between the two groups. But equally important was this: the most common personality rating dropouts received was *average*. Table VIII reveals the typical ratings of the dropouts in the two areas. For every attribute studied, moreover, the distributions ratings of Piedmont dropouts differed from those of the mountain sample. Not only are frequencies with which the low, below average, average, above average and high ratings received different for the two samples, for several traits the modes are different, too. The Piedmont sample was overly concerned with trivia. That is to say they were picayune and apt to focus on minute details. They were not, moreover, tuned into what the average person might be concerned with. In addition, they were less creative than the mountain sample. The mountain sample was more restrained, accepted roles in society less, was less stable, had a lower level of energy productivity, was more impulsive but was more adaptable to changing situations.

IN SUMMARY, the two dropout samples studied here seemed alike in some characteristics; were quite different in others. Moreover, although they resembled typical citizens in some respects, they differed from them in others. To delineate a single set of characteristics and to designate them as unique to the dropouts is not possible. Careful scrutiny of inter-regional and intraregional differences between school dropouts unequivocally demands programming of instruction to the assets and deficiencies of the *individual* trainee.

Chapter III

RESULTS

PRIOR to entry into the program, few trainees read a newspaper or a book. Most were unemployed and, therefore, had little contact with any demanding routine. Social contact was confined to a neighborhood friend or two who exchanged recently heard dirty jokes or gossip at the bowling alley or soda shop. The training program changed all of this. Each day was planned. Each day was to confront a trainee with new ideas, training tasks, and new social challenges.

INTELLIGENCE CHANGES

The stimulation from thinking about the new ideas, practicing new tasks and working with new friends, it had been hypothesized, would effect rises in intelligence quotients. Intelligence tests, it was assumed, measure a readiness to learn. The readiness is increased with learning experiences. In Table IX are the average gains of eleven OSC programs, two non-OSC training programs, and one nontrained group of dropouts. Only one of the OSC classes, sewing A-15, gained in verbal scale IQ. The untrained group, however, declined in IQ. Seven of the eleven classes made significant improvements in performance scale intelligence quotients. One class, masonry A, increased on the average more than ten points. The gains these classes made usually exceeded the amount of fluctuation one could reasonably expect from having taken the test once before. Five classes rose significantly in the full scale IQ. Special note should be made of the groups labeled *control.* They received no training and they did not change in IQ.

The evidence presented here supports the hypothesis that OSC training does change intelligence test scores. Such changes were observed for the full scale IQ, but more particularly for the intelligence tasks which involve manipulative skills, the perform-

TABLE IX

CHANGES IN INTELLIGENCE QUOTIENTS DURING OSC TRAINING

Class	*N*	*IQ Change*	*S. E.*	*t ratio*
Sewing—A				
Verbal Scale	15	+ 2.73	1.31	2.14*
Performance Scale	15	+ 4.93	1.87	2.63*
Full Scale	15	+ 4.13	.98	4.24†
Sewing—A				
Verbal Scale	11	+ 1.45	2.37	0.38
Performance Scale	11	+ 8.91	2.17	4.24†
Full Scale	11	+ 4.73	1.61	2.61*
Masonry—A				
Verbal Scale	7	+ 0.18	1.70	0.11
Performance Scale	7	+10.55	2.34	4.50†
Full Scale	7	+ 5.55	2.05	2.70*
Carpentry—A				
Verbal Scale	8	− 0.75	1.36	−0.55
Performance Scale	8	+ 7.25	3.68	3.84†
Full Scale	8	+ 3.50	2.37	1.47
Upholstery—A				
Verbal Scale	14	− 1.86	1.65	−1.27
Performance Scale	14	+ 7.64	1.87	4.08†
Full Scale	14	+ 4.36	2.08	2.10*
Upholstery—B				
Verbal Scale	21	− 2.75	3.00	−0.91
Performance Scale	21	+ 0.84	2.06	0.41
Full Scale	21	− 1.60	1.82	0.88
Welder—B				
Verbal Scale	17	− 1.20	2.10	−0.57
Performance Scale	17	+ 7.58	2.42	3.10†
Full Scale	17	0	2.59	0
Nurses' Aide—B				
Verbal Scale	13	− 3.23	2.12	−1.52
Performance Scale	18	+ 4.22	2.63	1.60
Full Scale	18	+ 1.22	2.04	0.60
Nurses' Aide—C				
Verbal Scale	13	− 3,23	2.12	−1.52
Performance Scale	13	− 1.62	1.11	−1.46
Full Scale	13	− 3.08	1.51	−2.04
Welder—C				
Verbal Scale	11	+ 0.36	1.73	0.21
Performance Scale	11	+ 6.64	2.44	2.72*
Full Scale	11	+ 6.73	1.31	3.93†
Auto Mechanics—C				
Verbal Scale	6	+ 0.33	3.31	0.10
Performance Scale	6	+ 4.67	4.71	0.99
Full Scale	6	+ 0.16	3.92	0.04

Class	*N*	*IQ Change*	*S. E.*	*t ratio*
Control—Masonry—B				
Verbal Scale	7	+ 1.29	2.52	0.51
Performance Scale	7	+ 4.42	3.71	1.19
Full Scale	7	+ 2.28	2.51	0.91
Control—Carpentry—B				
Verbal Scale	11	– 2.27	1.26	–1.80
Performance Scale	11	+ 4.91	2.41	2.03
Full Scale	11	+ 1.18	1.19	.99
Control—A				
Verbal Scale	19	– 3.57	1.34	2.66*
Performance Scale	19	+ 2.21	2.02	1.09
Full Scale	19	– 1.53	1.50	1.02

A—Piedmont.
B—Mountains.
C—Coast.
S. E.—Standard error of the mean, is the amount of fluctuation in the mean IQ change which could be attributed to chance.
t ratio is the IQ change relative to the S. E.
* This ratio could appear by chance fewer than five times in 100, N—1 degrees of freedom.
† This ratio could appear by chance fewer than one time in 100, N—1 degrees of freedom.

ance scale. No claim is made that *intelligence* improved. The fact that scores on intelligence tests increased in the trained group signifies, however, that either the underlying abilities or some factor associated with its measurement changed. The latter has been named by some *motivation*. Most trainees, then, refined the kinds of judgments and actions measured by intelligence tests. Without training, the control data indicate, such motivational or intellectual changes would not have been experienced.

ACHIEVEMENT CHANGES

Hypothesized also had been that the OSC training would effect improvement in academic achievement. The differences between the pretraining and post-training achievement scores are presented in Table X. Four classes improved significantly in reading; five in spelling; and three in arithmetic. On the average, the largest significant gain in reading was in the carpentry A class. This class improved almost one year within sixteen weeks. To be noted also is the fact that the only classes which made significant improvement in reading came from the Piedmont. Three of the five classes

TABLE X

CHANGES IN ACHIEVEMENT SCORES
DURING OSC TRAINING

Class	*N*	*Grade Change*	*S. E.*	*t ratio*
Sewing—A				
Reading	15	+ .47	.19	2.45*
Spelling	15	+ .33	.20	1.65
Arithmetic	15	+ .37	.32	1.16
Sewing—A				
Reading	11	+ .30	.17	1.76
Spelling	11	+ .72	.31	2.32*
Arithmetic	11	+ .10	.69	0.14
Masonry—A				
Reading	11	0.67	.27	2.50*
Spelling	11	0.03	.30	0.90
Arithmetic	11	0.70	.38	1.84
Carpentry—A				
Reading	8	0.88	0.30	2.95*
Spelling	8	0.41	0.17	2.42*
Arithmetic	8	0.90	0.36	2.51*
Upholstery—A				
Reading	14	0.60	.20	3.00†
Spelling	14	0.41	.18	2.26*
Arithmetic	14	0.49	.35	1.43
Upholstery—B				
Reading	21	+ .23	0.21	1.09
Spelling	21	+ .13	0.30	0.43
Arithmetic	21	+ .74	0.26	2.85†
Welder—B				
Reading	17	+ .42	.31	1.35
Spelling	17	+ .20	.60	0.33
Arithmetic	17	+ .65	.23	2.83*
Nurses' Aide—B				
Reading	18	+ .26	.60	.33
Spelling	18	+ .90	.64	1.12
Arithmetic	18	+ .35	.44	.79
Nurses' Aide—C				
Reading	13	+1.02	.50	2.04
Spelling	13	+0.50	.16	3.12†
Arithmetic	13	+0.23	.21	1.10
Welder—C				
Reading	11	+ .36	.23	1.57
Spelling	11	+ .23	.17	1.35
Arithmetic	11	+ .19	.13	1.46
Auto Mechanics—C				
Reading	6	+ .77	.63	1.22
Spelling	6	+ .25	.07	3.57*
Arithmetic	6	− .33	.30	−1.10

Class	*N*	*Grade Change*	*S. E.*	*t ratio*
Control—Masonry—B				
Reading	6	+ .99	.51	1.94
Spelling	6	+ .14	.20	0.70
Arithmetic	6	+ .74	.40	1.85
Control—Carpentry—B				
Reading	11	+1.09	0.57	1.91
Spelling	11	+0.27	0.16	1.68
Arithmetic	11	+0.48	0.17	2.82*
Control—A				
Reading	19	+0.26	0.16	1.62
Spelling	19	+0.14	0.15	0.94
Arithmetic	19	+0.25	0.23	1.08

A—Piedmont.
B—Mountains.
C—Coast.
S. E.—Standard error of the mean, is the amount of fluctuation in the grade change which could be attributed to chance.
t ratio is the grade change relative to the S. E.
* This ratio could appear by chance five times in 100.
† This ratio could appear by chance one time in 100.
* This ratio could appear by chance fewer than five times in 100, N—1 degrees of freedom.
† This ratio could appear by chance fewer than one time in 100, N—1 degrees of freedom.

which made significant improvement in spelling were also from the Piedmont. The largest gain in spelling was in the twelve week sewing A course. Two of the three classes making significant gains in arithmetic, however, were from the mountains.

One might speculate that there are regional differences in response to different types of instructional materials. Clearly, in the mountains, no measurable changes in language skills were effected by the OSC program. Might this be because they value verbal stimuli less than they do mathematical symbols? The hypothesis that changes in achievement would result from OSC training received some support. It needs revision, however, in light of the observed regional differences in intelligence, achievement, their interrelationships, personality attributes and response to the programmed instruction. These observations shed light on the gloomy path which ended only in blind alleys. Community factors, it is suggested here, shape the disposition and predispositions of its school dropouts. A more critical examination of institutions such as family, school, law, government, and business as well as of the community pursuits of work, leisure, and status may not only reveal what are the distinguishing characteristics of a dropout but what economical steps to take in rehabilitating him.

PREDICTABILITY OF OUTCOMES

Prediction of the behavior of trainees is an essential aspect of scientific studies of educational programs. Behaviors which we generally refer to as aptitude and achievement have been assumed to be associated with training. Changes in both aptitude and achievement were shown to be linked with OSC training. Links to the post-testing scores would reveal what are the essential pretraining characteristics associated with low and high post-training scores. Such correlations appear in Table XI. The high reliability coefficients suggest that the magnitude of change taking place during training is about the same for those who are high and low in ability and in skill. Note the stability coefficients for verbal IQ is .90; for performance IQ, .85; for full scale IQ, .92; for reading achievement, .97; for spelling achievement, .94; and for arithmetic achievement, .91. Clearly, those trainees who had been high in ability prior to training remained high; those who were low, remained low. The changes cited in the previous two sections affected the entire group in the same way.

These findings were anticipated as were those concerning the pretest intelligence test scores as valid predictors of post-test achievement test performance. Correlations between the intelligence predictors with reading achievement were on the order of .7; with spelling achievement, .6; and with arithmetic achievement, .7. The teacher is justified in having faith in intelligence test scores as reliable guides to academic behavior. What the present study revealed, moreover, was that teachers and counselors may pay increasingly more attention to the perceptual habits of the trainees. The SORT is a personality test which measures styles of perception. Ratings of personality attributes may be made by examining the relationships among the several perceptual tendencies. In the present study, the focus was on the perceptual tendencies themselves. Those trainees who had a capacity for

TABLE XI

PRE-TRAINING CORRELATES OF POST-TRAINING INTELLIGENCE AND ACHIEVEMENT SCORES

Pre-test	*Post-test* Verbal Scale IQ	Performance Scale IQ	Full Scale IQ	Reading Grade	Spelling Grade	Arithmetic Grade
WAIS						
Verbal IQ	(90)	71	88	78	65	74
Performance IQ	65	(85)	80	50	43	56
Full IQ	88	82	(92)	72	62	72
WRAT						
Reading Grade	87	65	82	(97)	93	59
Spelling Grade	80	55	72	92	(94)	55
Arithmetic Grade	70	58	68	59	55	(91)
SORT						
Whole blot (W)	36	21	30	40	33	43
Major Details (D)	–02	06	04	00	07	–14
Minor Details (Dd)	–32	–22	–30	–38	–34	–06
Form Resemblance (F)	–29	–33	–33	–22	–18	–16
Poor Form (F–)	–22	–01	–13	–22	–17	–28
Human Movement (M)	01	–04	–02	–12	–12	–23
Animal Movement (FM)	–05	–13	–07	–07	–05	00
Color and Form (FC)	42	36	42	45	36	49
Color and Poor Form (CF)	02	–13	–09	04	11	02
Shading (Fch)	21	26	25	24	14	37
Animals (A)	–12	07	–02	–10	–04	03
Human (H)	12	–11	03	18	19	–30
Modal Responses (P)	60	54	60	57	46	51
Rare Responses (O)	–63	–48	–59	–72	–64	–54
White Spaces (S)	–17	–10	–12	–13	–23	–14

Italicized pre-test scores correlated highly with post-test scores.
Correlations in parentheses are reliability coefficients.
Decimals omitted.

abstraction, that is, who tended to see wholes rather than fragments (SORT score W) made higher achievement scores than those lacking in this capacity. Good form and color perception (SORT score FC) is a perceptual tendency associated with those behaviors involved in social responsibility, tact, confidence, and flexibility. Correlations of FC with achievement variables ranged from .36 to .49. Perception of the test content which most people typically see is measured by the SORT score, *P*. *P* is linked to empathy and to conformity. The more a trainee perceives what other people typically see, the higher are his intelligence and achievement scores apt to be. *P* correlated with achievement almost as highly as did intelligence. More important, though, was the SORT score *O*. *O* measures a disposition to see the unusual, the unique and the uncommon. *O* is linked with eccentric, individualist, and nonconforming behavior. The high negative correlations of *O* with intelligence and achievement post-test scores suggest that the less atypical or the more conforming to social norms was a trainee, the more he appeared to profit from instruction.

The intelligence, achievement, good form and whole perceptions, high modal perceptions and low rare perceptions form the nucleus of the "attribute mix" which the writer hypothesizes distinguishes between high and low achievers in manpower training programs. This high achiever is successful, it is further hypothesized, because these attributes appeal to and are understood by his mentors and because they facilitate communication with the dominant society which shapes his behavior. Because of this attribute mix these trainees more easily cross the bridge into respectability, cultural advantage, and employment. Pictorially, the theory proposed looks like Figure 5.

In the case of Mary (Part II), the "attribute mix" of high intelligence, high achievement but low social receptivity is seen to produce someone who first enters training-unrelated work and

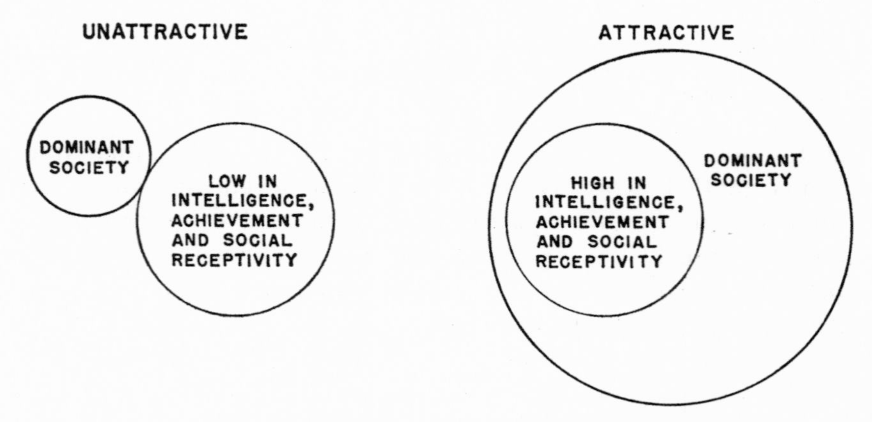

Figure 5. Theory of dropout achievement.

later, unemployment. Absent are the necessary social receptivity behaviors which permit communication with members of the dominant society. As a result, despite her ability, she misinterpreted the actions of her superiors and meandered nervously in and out of employment.

TABLE XII

PRE-TEST INTELLIGENCE, ACHIEVEMENT, AND PERSONALITY SCORES OF THE EMPLOYED AND UNEMPLOYED GRADUATES

	Means			*t ratios*		
	Training Related N=36	*Training Unrelated N=25*	*Unemployed N=78*	*TR vs. TUR*	*TR vs. UN*	*TUR vs. UN*
Intelligence:						
IQ						
Verbal	84.56	86.24	81.38	n.s.	n.s.	n.s.
Performance	84.75	80.70	80.50	n.s.	2.52*	n.s.
Full	83.52	83.72	79.25	n.s.	2.20*	n.s.
Achievement:						
Grade						
Reading	6.0	5.9	6.4	n.s.	5.71†	5.50†
Spelling	5.5	4.7	5.9	10.00†	5.00†	12.00†
Arithmetic	5.5	4.8	4.9	13.33†	12.00†	n.s.
Personality:						
Standard Scores						
W	40.6	36.24	37.71	n.s.	n.s.	n.s.
D	49.3	53.5	50.0	2.41*	n.s.	n.s.
Dd	64.3	61.5	66.5	n.s.	n.s.	n.s.
S	43.1	44.2	44.0	n.s.	n.s.	n.s.
F	49.6	52.4	57.9	n.s.	2.73*	n.s.
F–	57.54	57.92	57.89	n.s.	n.s.	n.s.
M	47.89	53.68	45.97	n.s.	n.s.	3.68†
FM	52.19	51.16	50.61	n.s.	n.s.	n.s.
FC	41.08	40.64	41.15	n.s.	n.s.	n.s.
CF	47.62	47.60	47.55	n.s.	n.s.	n.s.
Fch	51.62	44.12	46.73	3.14†	2.40*	n.s.
A	50.13	44.46	49.87	2.27*	n.s.	n.s.
H	52.38	53.84	48.73	n.s.	n.s.	2.46*
P	34.59	34.40	33.65	n.s.	n.s.	n.s.
O	53.59	56.24	55.56	n.s.	n.s.	n.s.

n.s. There are no statistically reliable differences between the means.

* The differences between the means are statistically reliable at the 5 per cent level of probability with $N_1 + N_2 - 2$ degrees of freedom.

† The differences between the means are statistically reliable at the 1 per cent level of probability with $N_1 + N_2 - 2$ degrees of freedom.

If we may add one more element to this theory, namely that the high ability, achievement, social receptivity attribute mix is attractive (+) and the low ability, achievement, social receptivity mix is repulsive (–), the subsequent employment experiences of the graduates become meaningful. Group statistics and individual case studies (Part II) will support this position.

This theory may explain how well a trainee learned from his courses. Another outcome with which this research was concerned was the employment of OSC graduates. In Table XII below are the average intelligence, achievement, and personality scores of the graduates who entered training-related employment (TR), training-unrelated employment (TUR), and those who entered no employment (UN). The pretest scores of the three groups were compared. It is obvious that the three groups of graduates were at the outset alike with respect to many characteristics, though different with regard to others. Attributes which distinguished between any two of the three employment criterion groups are presented graphically in Figure 6.

The TR group was significantly higher than the UN group

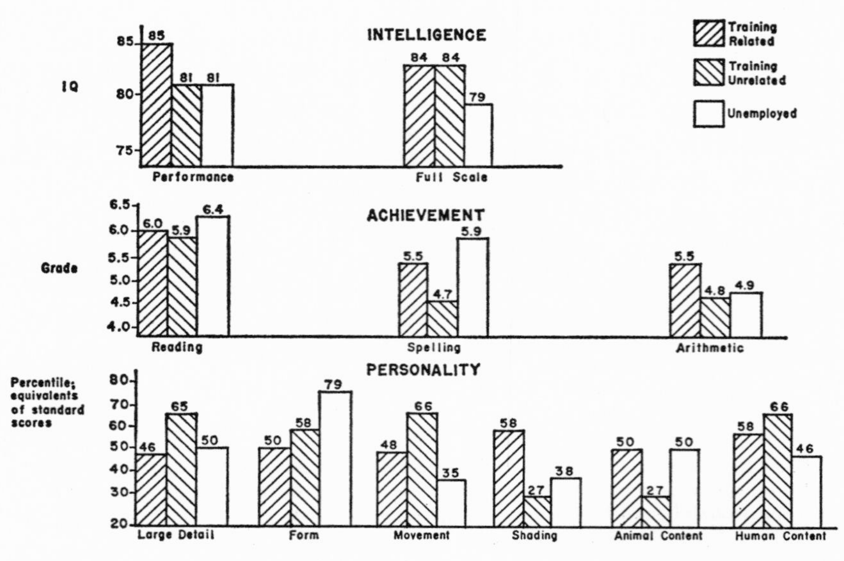

Figure 6. Pretest scores which distinguished between employed and unemployed graduates.

in Performance and in Full Scale IQ's. The reading and spelling skills of the UN group was greater than either the TR or the TUR groups. The TR group, however, excelled in arithmetic. The personality data also reveal distinct differences between the three groups. In the first place, the TUR group received high *D* scores. *D* measures the facility for dealing with concrete detail.

The TUR group may be viewed as very practical people. When faced with the possibility of leaving their home for twenty-five cents more per hour working at a training-related task or remaining at home and working at a training-unrelated task, they would choose the latter.

The unemployed group, the high *F* scores reveal, were very much aware of reality, more so than the other groups. Why then did they not take jobs? A partial answer is provided from the M scores. *M* is a measure of activity potential. The unemployed group had little drive or motivation for work. Further evidence of this low drive was noticed in the low *Fch* scores of the TUR and UN groups. *Fch* is a measure of anxiety. Anxiety is the tendency toward worry. True, all people worry somewhat. The graph reveals, however, that the TR trainees were concerned about themselves. This concern moved them to achieve success in the world of work. *A* is a measure of immaturity. Immaturity was not an attribute of the TR or UN groups. The TUR group appeared to be the most grown-up. Finally, *H*, the tendency to perceive human elements was found to be most characteristic of the TUR group and least characteristic of the UN group.

IN SUMMARY, those trainees destined to become employed had higher IQ's, higher arithmetic scores and greater drive than the subsequently unemployed. Those entering training-unrelated employment were more practical, less immature, and more sensitive to people than the training-related group. Regional differences in achievement suggested more intensive survey of community institutions and activities.

PRETRAINING HISTORIES

In addition to status immediately preceding entry into the program, the research team examined the previous school histories, family attributes, and age of entry into the OSC program. In Table XIII are the results of this survey.

TABLE XIII

PRE-TRAINING HISTORIES OF OSC GRADUATES: TYPICAL OBSERVATIONS

	Employment Status			
Characteristic	*Training Related N = 33*	*Training Unrelated N = 31*	*Unemployed N = 85*	*Chi Square*
Marks				
Reading: 1-3	B	B	B	n.s.
Reading: 4-6	C	C	B	6.93†
Reading: 7-9	C	C	C	n.s.
Language: 1-3	B	C	B	6.21†
Language: 4-6	C	C	B	4.95*
Language: 7-9	C	C	C	n.s.
Arithmetic: 1-3	B	C	B	n.s.
Arithmetic: 4-6	C	D	B	7.38†
Arithmetic: 7-9	C	D	C	n.s.
Decision to leave school	8	8	8	n.s.
Reason	Failure, disinterest, age	Age, failure, disinterest	Age, failure, disinterest	n.s.
Highest grade attained	9	9	9	n.s.
Age of entry into OSC	20	18	18	9.81*
Employment history	None	Worked one year	None	9.03†
Mother's empl. history	None	None	None	n.s.
Father's empl. history	Currently employed	Currently employed	Currently employed	n.s.
Level of present occupation	Skilled	Semiskilled	Semiskilled	9.14†

n.s. No significant differences existed between the groups.

* The differences in distributions of the three groups could be attributed to chance no more than ten times in 100 with 2 degrees of freedom.

† The differences in distributions of the three groups could be attributed to chance fewer than five times in 100 with 2 degrees of freedom.

Upon examining available school records, the following observations were made: in grades one through three, there had been no differences in reading or arithmetic between the trainees who subsequently got employment and those who did not; the unemployed group had significantly higher marks in language in grades one through three and in all subjects in grades four to six; and, in junior high school, there were no differences among the groups. All trainees left for the same reason; school failure and disinterest. The majority of the trainees left in grade nine. Those graduates who entered training-unrelated work had a longer employment history than those in either the TR or UN groups. Those trainees who were employed in TR work were older than the others and came from homes where the parents were engaged in skilled rather than semiskilled work.

The pretests and pretraining histories did provide clues to the employment outcomes. The three groups of graduates were different from the outset. The outstanding features of the attribute mixes which distinguish them from one another are presented in Figure 7.

IN SUMMARY, the theory which explains *learning* during the program, namely, social attractability, was not tenable in explaining *employability*. Motivation, pragmatism, interest in people and achievement in arithmetic were pretraining scores found to be most closely related to post-training employment. Age, employment history, and occupational level of the parents were historical attributes most closely linked to post-training employment. Hypothesized here is this: A parent inspires his children to model their work histories after him. The children of parents who have an occupational specialty tend to enter training-related work. Those trainees whose parents have no occupational specialty will enter training-unrelated work if they have high motivation, are practical minded and are interested in people; they will be unemployed if they have low motivation, have no high interest in people, and are not practical-minded. While test results did distinguish between the several groups, the challenge of manpower training is to remotivate the dropout who *seeks* unemployment and to engender high goals in all trainees.

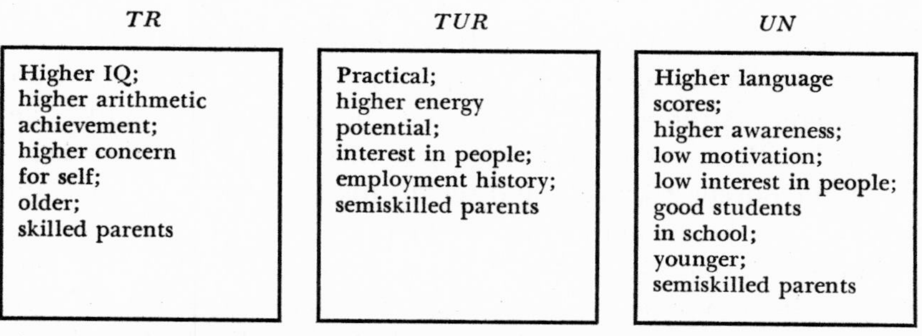

Figure 7. Attribute mixes of subsequently employed and unemployed trainees.

TRAINEE'S ESTIMATION OF OSC DURING TRAINING

At least three interviews were held with the trainees during the instructional period. The research staff gleaned from the interviews what each trainee was learning, the ways in which the program was meeting his expectations, what his future plans were, and how his family was responding to the training. It was hoped that from these interviews, suggestions to improve the program would ensue. Of great importance to future studies and programs was determining whether trainees who subsequently became employed differed during training from those who subsequently became unemployed.

Trainees, irrespective of whether or not they were later employed, agreed that the program was helping them but that the tools and equipment did not facilitate learning. One trainee said, "We need more metal, more acetyline torches and smaller books for those of us who can't read." Another emphasized the lack of opportunity to check his own progress. He did not like the idea of tearing down his wall after he so carefully lined up the bricks. Because of scarcity of materials, trainees had to take apart many of the products they finished in order to be supplied with materials upon which to practice further. One very verbal trainee put it this way, "I would like to sell the chair I make or put it in some room so I can compare the progress I make. This way, I have incentive to improve."

Most trainees did plan to enter the trade in which they were receiving instruction. There were several who consistently stated they had no plans to enter such a trade. Rather, they planned to do something else. One trainee stated, during the first interview, that he planned to open a cafe. He had no intention to become an upholsterer. Although he completed the upholstory course, he traveled with a carnival. To prevent this type of vagabondage, his father purchased a cafe and set up his son, now a trained upholsterer, in the restaurant business.

Trainees found OSC to be more satisfying than their previous public school experience. Most explained that OSC teachers were more sympathetic and that they cared about individual students. Others suggested that they could go at their own rate. The majority of the students were excited that they were improving in

TABLE XIV

TYPICAL TRAINING REPLIES DISTINGUISHING BETWEEN THE THREE GROUPS OF GRADUATES

Characteristic	*Employment Status*			*Chi Square*
	Training Related	*Training Unrelated*	*Unemployed*	
Geographical preference .	Local	None	Local	5.61*
Family reaction to program	Endorse all	Endorse all	Endorse vocational	13.50†
Willingness to move				
1. To get work	Anywhere	Anywhere	Up to 150 miles	6.60*
2. To do something important	Anywhere	Anywhere	Up to 150 miles	5.72*
3. To continue education	Anywhere	Anywhere	Up to 150 miles	7.47*
Plan to look for a job ...	Upon graduation	Upon graduation	Soon	8.14†

* Differences between the distributions significant at the 10 per cent level of probability.

† Differences between the distributions significant beyond the 5 per cent level of probability

reading, geometry, and history. Several, however, became bored with the vocational program because daily assignments were so repetitious.

Most trainees had no plans to continue their education. They did indicate that if it were possible to receive more training through OSC, they would continue in the program. Many would have liked to remain with OSC until they received a high school equivalency diploma. Although most trainees were willing to move, the majority preferred to remain in their home town for the remainder of their lives. When asked were they to have the opportunity to choose their own curriculum and train for forty weeks without pay or to be assigned a curriculum and train for sixteen weeks with pay, 82 per cent of the students selected a different occupation. The level of responsibility[1] of the chosen occupation was, however, the same as the one for which they trained. Fifty per cent of the trainees would have preferred being assigned to training but earning the $24 each week.

[1] Scoring system according to Roe, A.: *The Psychology of Occupations*. New York, Wiley, 1956.

TABLE XV

PERCENTAGES OF RATINGS RECEIVED BY TRAINEES

		Rating: 1—Low	*2*	*3*	*High—4*
		Primary interest in money; doesn't care what he does when the training is completed; finds no satisfaction in the course; doesn't tell anyone about the course; non-mobile.	Interested in trade; would like a job in the area trained; benefits somewhat from training; would accept other employment; doubts the value of the course but is willing to continue; would prefer not to move but would if absolutely necessary.	Interested in becoming tradesman; benefits from training offered; thinking about more schooling; tells friends of the benefits but does not get them into school; willing to move but not very far.	Interested in becoming tradesman; states he has benefitted from course work; tells friends about it and trys to convey value of training to them; deep involvement with training; would willingly move to work in area of new found skills in the trade.
TR	(36)	6	17	53	24
TUR	(26)	12	46	31	11
UN	(78)	6	35	51	8

When categories 1 + 2 and 3 + 4 are combined, the resulting chi square is 8.09. This is significant beyond the 5 per cent level with 2 degrees of freedom.

Most responses to training did not distinguish between those whose employment status differed later. There were several items, though, which did point to differences between them. These are presented in Table XIV. The training-unrelated group was most willing to relocate. It will be recalled from the personality study of the trainees that this group was the most practical minded. The unemployed group had throughout training most often cited restricted post-training mobility. The urgency in becoming employed was noted more often in the subsequently employed group rather than in the subsequently unemployed group. Typical of the responses of the subsequently unemployed to the question, "How soon will you look for a job?" was "In about two or three weeks."

The most significant factor distinguishing between the groups was the family reaction to the program. Those trainees who discussed both the academic and vocational aspects of the program were most apt to become employed. When asked of his family reaction to the program one unemployed graduate had said, "Vocational? Folks want me to get a job. Academic? We don't talk about it. They know I take it. (I) Say nothing to them about it."

The research staff developed a four point scale to rate each trainee. Ratings were based primarily on the knowledge gained about each trainee from the interviews. Seventy-seven per cent of the TR group, 59 per cent of the UN group, and 42 per cent of the TUR group received high ratings. In the judgment of the research team the TR group was ready for work. They predicted, however, that the unemployed group was also ready for work. The factors discussed in the last section were not known to them at the time.

Evaluations by teachers, however, did not prove to distinguish between groups. In Figure 8 is a sample of such an evaluation. In the table which follows is the rating scale and the frequency of observance of the several traits. What affects the low predictability of teacher ratings is their focus on academically oriented assignments. The unemployed group had good academic records. They may have been more highly motivated to receive a general education. The TR group was more highly motivated to go to work.

Name of student: Johnny

Directions: Please observe student after each week of the program, mark an X for statement which best summarizes his habits and attitudes. Make no mark if it does not apply.

	Week											
Behavior	*1*	*2*	*3*	*4*	*5*	*6*	*7*	*8*	*9*	*10*	*11*	*12*
1. Begins assignments promptly	X	X	X	X	X							
2. Selects additional assignments during free period		X										
3. Distracts others												
4. Records answers neatly	X	X	X	X	X	X	X	X	X	X		
5. Comes to class late		X										
6. Leaves class early												
7. Follows directions	X	X	X	X	X	X	X	X	X	X		
8. Requires more than usual individual attention, that is, more than one question per assignment												
9. Continues work after class												
10. Does not budget time						X	X	X	X	X		
11. Talks about his troubles in class												
12. Tries to exceed previous accomplishments	X	X	X	X	X							
13. Shows signs of boredom in the middle of assignments												
14. Talks about quitting program												
15. Reviews his work		X										
16. Skims over important ideas						X	X	X	X	X		
17. Tries to get general idea of assignment		X										
18. Discusses applications of what he studies		X										
19. Laziness	X	X	X	X	X	X	X	X	X	X		

Additional notes: Johnny seems to be a sly fox. He's a perfect angel to your face and very sneaky behind your back. 3/11/64. He admitted he had been drinking and was sent home. He returned to school, but has a habit of absenteeism.

Figure 8. Observations of work habits and attitudes.

TABLE XVI

TEACHER ESTIMATE OF WORK HABITS AND ATTITUDES

	1	*2*	*3*	*4*
	Interferes	Works occasionally	Works steadily most of the time	Works steadily all the time
	Does not work steadily	Interferes occasionally	Output consistent but low	Works independently —needs no supervision
		Output present but variable	Output high but does not work well without supervision	Output consistent and high
TR	3	17	31	49
TUR	10	42	24	24
UN	7	25	24	44

Merging 1 + 2 and 3 + 4 resulted in no significant differences between the groups.

IN SUMMARY, trainees did not differ much in response to questions put to them. Subsequently employed trainees, however, did impose fewer restrictions on their mobility, felt a greater urgency in obtaining employment, and were more deeply involved in the total program than were the subsequently unemployed graduates.

FOLLOW-UP

Four weeks after each training course ended, the research staff returned to the training site to assess the impact of OSC upon subsequent employment. Again the responses of the three groups were essentially the same. The majority of the graduates hoped to enter and to remain in the trade for which they were trained, imposed some restriction on their mobility, and expected to find friends at work or near home. Twenty-six per cent of the graduates were engaged in church activities, three per cent in community activities, 12 per cent in athletics, but 59 per cent in no organized activities. "A bunch of us get together at the bowling alley (pool hall, soda shop)," was the most common reply. Also, there were few differences between the groups with regard to how jobs were obtained. This may be seen most clearly in Table XVII. Most of the unemployed graduates did not look for jobs. On the other hand, most employed graduates found jobs on their own.

TABLE XVII

AGENCY FOR OBTAINING EMPLOYMENT: PERCENTAGE REPLY

	Did Not Look	*Self*	*Friends, Family*	*Employment Services*
TR	0	40	30	30
TUR	0	56	26	18
UN	79	5	0	16

The high percentage of unemployed graduates who did not look for a job requires some explanation. Thirteen per cent of the total unemployed group were girls about to become mothers. Several of these trainees, moreover, went to work shortly after their babies were delivered. Thirty-three per cent of the total unemployed group were from one nurses' aide class. No trainee in that class was placed. Rather, the girls were told that they were not ready to take on hospital responsibilities. It had been suggested to them, however, that by volunteering their services at the hospital they would become more competent and would get jobs. Many of them volunteered two to four days each week. Several months after graduation, the girls were still volunteering. There was no evidence, though, that any of them were hired as nurses' aides.

Unemployed trainees were always told by the research staff to check on employment opportunities with the local office of the Employment Security Commission. Several trainees in eastern North Carolina said they did not know how to locate the ESC office which was situated in an adjacent county. Others were frightened by this suggestion. They doubted, on the basis of previous experience, that they would receive "leads" to training-related employment. Several graduates rejected the recommendation to go to ESC. One stated, "I would not waste my time at an ESC office."

Material gathered at the follow-up interview showed that the TR graduates were earning more than TUR graduates; that TUR graduates imposed fewer restrictions on their mobility, that unemployed graduates had considered leaving school in high school, whereas employed graduates decided to leave earlier, and that

TABLE XVIII
TYPICAL FOLLOW-UP OBSERVATIONS

Characteristic	*TR*	*TUR*	*UN*	*Chi Square*
Earnings	$1.75	$1.25	—	9.72*
Mobility	Up to 150 miles	Anywhere	Up to 150 miles	8.35*
Recall of school leaving	Grade 8	Grade 8	Grade 8	7.68*
Reason	Legal age	Legal age	Failure	6.62*

* The distributions of responses are significantly different from one another beyond the 5 per cent level of probability with 2 degrees of freedom.

the reasons for leaving were *legal age* for the employed graduates but *failure* for unemployed graduates.

IN SUMMARY, the picture emerging of the trained dropout is that he still is quite alone, does not feel himself a part of any ongoing community activities, distrusts government agencies set up to assist him, and restricts his mobility even in the event employment were offered to him. Several trainees were hired to work in cities no more than fifty miles from their home town. Most returned in less than one week. One group of four boys returned home within two days. The bonds which tie the unemployed trainee to a region which offers few employment opportunities were not broken. The unemployed graduate returned to wander aimlessly in the community he was afraid to leave. He was observed to wallow in self-pity about his unemployed status, yet he did not go out to look for a job. In general, he had attended public school longer than the employed OSC graduate. Whereas the employed OSC graduate had found his public school experience irrelevant, the unemployed graduate did not. Rather, he saw himself a failure. One might speculate that the failure motivation was still strong. OSC had not taught him how to succeed in a competitive world.

One might well ask could not these failures be anticipated earlier in training and subsequently contained? Most of the failures were identified quite early. Program inflexibility and lack of instructor skill in penetrating student barriers to work spawned further failures. Ideally, a training program for disadvantaged youth must program success for all trainees despite their unconscious yearning for failure.

REGIONAL DIFFERENCES

As the writer reviewed his data he noted that in addition to differences between the subsequently unemployed and employed trainees, trainees from certain regions responded in certain characteristic ways. These are presented and discussed in Table XIX.

To insure reliability of response, the same question was asked in more than one way. When asked if they would be willing to move, vast differences were noted between trainees from the several regions. Piedmont trainees said they were unwilling to move, yet when asked how far they would move, these same Piedmont trainees were willing to move more than fifty miles. What this means is that the trainees from the Piedmont were unwilling to move beyond a "mobility radius" greater than fifty miles. In the mountains, on the other hand, the trainees were *willing to move* but within a "mobility radius" of fewer than fifty miles. Trainees in the Piedmont and the West did not consider a subsidy essential, yet they preferred to train but sixteen weeks. Trainees in the East did consider a subsidy essential but would have forgone the subsidy in order to train in a trade of their own choosing.

To some trainees, the subsidy was essential. One trainee had three children. Her husband had been sent to prison for nonsupport. The $24 subsidy permitted her to pay for her travel to school. Another trainee was in a similar position. Her husband had left her with two children, one of whom suffered intracranial trauma at birth. She was paying a $1,000 hospital bill from the money she saved from her subsidy. The subsidy was, however, a source of discomfort to other trainees. Trainees would accuse one another

TABLE XIX

REGIONAL DIFFERENCES IN RESPONSE TO INTERVIEWS

Item	*Piedmont*	*Mountains*	*East*	*Chi Square*
Mobility	Unwilling	Willing	Willing	40.4*
Mobility	More than 50 miles	Less than 50 miles	More than 50 miles	7.8*
Subsidy	No	No	Yes	13.6*
Training preference	16 weeks	16 weeks	40 weeks	n.s.

* Significant beyond the 5 per cent level of probability with 2 degrees of freedom.

of applying to OSC only because they received the training allowance.

One trainee said the allowances encourage poor working habits. "A kid," he began, "knows he don't have to do no work to get the money. So he don't. Now if he got money for what he done during the week, he wouldn't goof off so much." Another trainee pointed out that the allowances made him vulnerable. He felt guilty that he had to take the money. He did not want to feel indebted to anyone. Rather, he wanted to view himself as someone who could make it on his own. Although necessary in some cases, automatic disbursement of weekly allowances had a crippling effect on many trainees.

One further observation concerned the impoverished economic conditions that the trainees inherited. In talking with the trainees, the research staff discovered that being without money is not viewed in the same light in the several regions of North Carolina. In the East, being without money meant *poverty*. It was an unpleasant condition, one to avoid and to change. Male graduates took jobs and changed them less frequently than in the other areas. Many left the area and did not return. Several totally illiterate graduates took jobs as welders and were so dedicated and became so skilled that their employer who hired only high school graduates was willing to consider more OSC graduates. Among the western trainees, however, being without money was no sign of poverty. To them a minimum of money was always forthcoming, often from a governmental welfare agency. Fishing, hunting, and enjoying nature's gifts were more important satisfactions to pursue than accumulation of material wealth. Existing on a minimum of money was satisfying, other monies derived from undemanding tasks and efforts requiring little persistence were welcomed. During the follow-up interview, one trainee noted, "the dropout school was gravy."

Being trained, however, produced many inner conflicts for many graduates whether they were employed or not. Several felt they were not good enough to do the work expected of them. They often were on guard to spot their errors. "Making it," a term the graduates most often used to denote success involved overcoming their own high but unrealistic standards of performance. Sympathetic supervisors sensed the inner conflicts and paid no attention to the mistakes OSC graduates made. Rather they discussed only the excellent service each was performing for the company. There were graduates, moreover, who after becoming skilled in their trade returned to part-time work picking apples, mowing lawns, or baby-sitting. They earned enough money to take care of their basic needs. There were graduates, moreover, who did not develop any skill in the field for which they trained. After training they returned to farming, dishwashing, or no work at all. Finally, there were semiskilled trainees who desperately sought training-related jobs but could not find them. Frightened to leave their homes yet fighting themselves to emigrate, they were impotent to raise enough money that would have tipped the balance of their inner conflict. Thus starting life anew was for them a hopeless dream.

SUMMARY

Among the changes wrought by OSC were sharpened mental skill and improved achievement. Regional differences in these changes appeared. Subsequent employment status was also linked with the region in which the training took place. Certain personality characteristics like practicality, motivation, sensitivity to people, and concern for oneself were also related to employment status. Other correlates of job attainment were level of responsibility of parent, willingness to move, and family endorsement of the total OSC program.

Chapter IV

VIEWS OF THE TRAINING PROGRAM

THE broad spectrum of training activities were observed and evaluated critically by the coordinators, teachers, and students. The occasional visitors like the local advisory board could not help but pass judgment on the program. The phases of the program which each judge eyed were quite different. In general, the trainees spoke of their rebirth, the teachers, of their shortcomings, but the local advisory board focused on the financial and political implications of the program.

TRAINEES

Without any doubt, the OSC trainees endorsed the efforts of the government to teach them marketable skills. Convinced that their training was valuable, they recruited many bashful tyros for the program. With the sincerest of emotions, many trainees confessed that OSC made them search their souls. They discovered a new value in working together with people. A startling revelation befell several trainees. For the first time they felt a genuine fondness for others. They sought membership in the family of man.

Several OSC graduates returned to high school, others took high school equivalency examinations, still others took apprenticeship training. Although the trainees approved of OSC, they were not unaware of its drawbacks. More equipment and books, they agreed, as well as longer periods of training would have made them more competent workmen. Many resigned themselves to obsolete equipment and made every effort to use it to the fullest. There were other trainees who felt they were compromised by the program. Disgruntled at the late arriving and out-of-date tools and machines they fought every goal the program had endeavored to attain. By-and-large, these trainees did not get training-related jobs. Many were unemployed. They did not see the program as "helping" them at all. Their indifference to swimming with the tide, albeit in a forceable undertow, spelled the difference between success and failure in the program.

In summary, two distinct trainee views emerged. All trainees knew of the shortcomings of the program. Some sought the "good" in the program; others were so disappointed at the absence of modern equipment and facilities that they spent their time griping instead of learning.

FACULTY

Interviews with the teaching staff revealed certain striking similarities with the views held by the trainees. Had they been better prepared to teach, the trainees would have learned so much more. Several teachers expressed the opinion that they had failed the trainees. Most lamentable was their impotence in adjusting the academic and social climates to the individual trainee. The academic teachers had teaching experience but no orientation to the motivations and abilities of school dropouts. The vocational teachers had practical experience but did not know how to teach. Despite the sincere intentions of the teachers, their greatest weakness lay in not knowing how to shape student behavior.

To begin with, they were totally unaware of what a "dropout" was like. They had conceived of him as "dissolute" and "disadvantaged." These, they later admitted, were words which prejudiced them against the trainee. Obscure was the fact that each trainee had been endowed with life. But how much to expect him to learn was not known. Some teachers believed the dropout to be too dull to learn anything so they expected little of him. Others reasoned that if a trainee was to survive in the world of work, he had to be skilled. They made them "toe the line" at assembly line speed.

Another weakness was the scanty knowledge teachers had about instructional methods. One masonry teacher confided that he had not the foggiest notion how to get unskilled and unambitious trainees to lay brick to the line. A welding instructor did not know what to do with the trainee who was giving a "hotfoot" to the working students. All teachers felt they should be measuring the progress the trainees were making. They did not, however, know how to construct tests. Nor were they certain of which questions to ask.

The most serious handicap cited by the teachers was the late arrival of training materials. In two classes, materials were received *after* the course was over. "You can't teach sixteen welders if there are only materials for four," one instructor asserted. Teachers complained that many materials were defective or no longer used in the trade.

The dedication of most of the teachers connected with the program was extraordinary. Many purchased materials on their own. They felt the trainees needed the experience with tools and books if for no other reason than to sustain their interest in the program. The teachers recommended several plans which would facilitate their instructional tasks. These are presented here to emphasize the dedication of the teachers.

One carpentry teacher suggested that at the beginning of the program he be given money or materials. The trainees could build a five room house. With the profits from its sale, money would then be available to purchase additional materials. An upholstery teacher suggested that woodworking classes build a variety of upholstery frames. Those used by his class were so worn that they no longer could hold springs. Greater coordination of vocational and academic instruction was the unanimous opinion of all teachers. All teachers requested more materials to cater to the variety of student interests and abilities.

A great concern to all teachers was the slovenly work habits of the trainees as well as their unreliable attendance. Their dilemma was "overlook these and, perhaps, unwittingly reinforce the undesirable behavior or make them conform to high standards of workmanship, and, perhaps, scare the trainees away from the program."

In summary, although they endorsed the program, teachers felt they were inadequately prepared for their jobs. Materials were so scarce, late, or obsolete that their services were so much less effective.

COORDINATORS

Each project site had its own coordinator. In addition, coordinators were appointed in Avery, Mitchell and Yancey Counties. The overall coordinator of the educational phase of the program was the ARA supervisor in the Department of Community Colleges. The overall coordinator of the employment phase of the program was the ARA supervisor in the State Employment Security Commission office. Presented now are the results of the interviews held with each coordinator.

The OSC program had a favorable impact on the trainees, they observed. Not only did many illiterate students learn to read and to write, but several trainees became so highly skilled that they got jobs even before their formal training was completed. The social changes in the trainees were judged to be most significant. Dropouts adopted a new view of what it means to be a citizen. Many became mannerly. Certainly, all but a few became more tractable.

The coordinators, however, did not hesitate to point out shortcomings of the program, although they soft-pedaled them lest they be indicted for incompetency. All were concerned with the high absentee rates of the trainees. The lack of respect for the eight hour day concerned them, too. There were trainees who arrived as much as an hour and a half late and returned home early in the afternoon. Several trainees scheduled themselves for a five hour day. One coordinator cited a member of the community college system as saying that trainees had to attend but one day a week in order to qualify for allowances. Shortly thereafter the coordinator received an inordinate number of trainee excuses for absence due to death in the family and due to sickness.

One coordinator pointed out that most of his trainees were "welfare cases." They developed poor social habits because they did not have to exert themselves to make ends meet. Because of the scarcity of money, moreover, few trainees had telephones or automobiles. It was not always possible to "hunt down" an absent trainee. Not only did it take hours to locate the cove in which a trainee lived, but where in the heavily wooded mountains he might be hiding was anyone's guess. The roads connecting a trainee's home with the main artery were frequently unpaved. The main artery itself was in such poor repair as to be a challenge to even the most skilled driver. In several areas in which OSC programs operated, public transportation was unavailable. Inadequate communication and transportation facilities contributed to the high absenteeism and tardiness records of the trainees.

Delays in contract negotiations with ARA reviewers in Washington caused, in the eyes of the coordinators, the high rate of dropout from the OSC programs. Enrollees frequently called upon the coordinators to find out when they might begin training. Many enrollees had been preregistered for the program as much as six months before the training began. Several applicants became impatient with OSC and refused to affiliate with the program. The late arrival and inadequacy of the equipment explained further trainee losses. Recruitment efforts had been primarily through news media and letters. However, the frequent delays and program postponements retarded recruitment drives. The reason for this quite clearly was that key dropouts who understood the program had encouraged others to enroll. One adolescent would look to another for confirmation about the advisability of going into OSC training. Youth leaders, moreover, impatient with the progress of the training enterprise required few convincing arguments to get reluctant applicants to disaffiliate.

After training got underway, it was quite apparent that several trainees had been inappropriately assigned to trade classes. Offerings were too few and regulations too stiff to permit changes. Some trainees, then, were identified early as not benefitting from their courses, but nothing further could be done for them. To prevent this from recurring, it was recommended that more intensive testing, screening, and guidance of each trainee be undertaken. Each prospective trainee should be given an opportunity to visit the training site and talk with the staff. He would become oriented to the nature of the school. Both he and the staff would benefit from this first contact. The physical disabilities, one coordinator explained, were so abundant that it is a wonder the trainees learned as much as they did. One trainee was epileptic. It was not until his third seizure that his illness was recognized. It was a visiting graduate student who identified the illness. Other trainees had defective vision. Still others had chewed tobacco until they had no enamel remaining on their teeth.

Perhaps the most difficult task the coordinators faced was controlling the work habits and social behavior of the trainees. The only incentive they could manipulate was money. Unruly trainees would lose their week's allowance. This created a hardship for some trainees. And it rarely taught them to behave better. One coordinator recommended a full-time psychologist work with the program to "iron out" problems such as these. He felt, moreover, it was necessary to control trainees by prorating the weekly allowance in accordance with the number of trainee's misdeameanors. If a trainee gets money for his attendance only, he develops the notion that he does not have to put forth any effort to earn his money. This, he added, only teaches poor work habits. On the other hand, if allowances are accorded on the basis of student output, the trainee learns he has to work for his money. This, he felt, is the more realistic of the two approaches.

All coordinators agreed that the teachers were unprepared for their assignments. Many of them had neither experience nor qualifications for teaching. One coordinator remarked that he had no opportunity to talk with applicants for the teaching positions. The local office manager of the Employment Service had hired the teachers. This was confusing because he thought it was the coordinator's function to hire teaching personnel. Three teachers were replaced during the course of the training. This only contributed to the already shaky program.

The local advisory boards, moreover, the coordinators said, were too inactive during the program to give recognition and support to the trainee and staff efforts. The coordinators also stated that membership in the local advisory board was composed of key community figures. These people would be most knowledgable about employment openings. The coordinators lamented the fact that board members did not vigorously aid them in the placing of the OSC graduates.

Finally, the coordinators noted a lack of harmony with administrators in the state agencies. They were of the opinion that state coordinators of the program were unaware of the local problems. Clear definition of roles of coordinators had never been made. They, therefore, never knew when they exceeded their authority. One coordinator was chagrined by the reprimand he had received from an ESC representative. Through his own contacts and those of his teachers, he had recommended trainees for employment. In doing this he bypassed the local employment office. He could not quite understand why ESC would disapprove of his humane efforts.

Subsequent interviews with coordinators of the state agencies involved in OSC supported in part the lack of communication between state and local coordinators. Who was responsible for training, hiring, and placing had never been clearly specified. Multiple duties of the state coordinators made it virtually impossible for them to devote full time to the OSC project. Therefore, closure was never effected on many issues. Despite several attempts to improve understanding, the physical contact necessary to establish good rapport was not possible.

The view of the program held by the state educational coordinator was that OSC made each community aware that there is a problem with dropouts but it is not insurmountable. The successes of the program dispelled the prejudices that the dropout is a dissolute degenerate. The OSC program gave those dropouts who saw no need for education a new outlook on life. For the first time, many dropouts awoke to the possibility that they had talents. In many others, there was a noticeable increase in motivation. This was not merely augmented energy. Rather, the program spurred the trainee toward socially directed activities.

Better planning, he added, would improve the program. An essential feature of a program would be its flexibility. When an applicant comes to the OSC office, the coordinator could explain the testing and training phases of the program. After testing, a counselor would interpret an applicant's scores. At this session, the many training possibilities available at the OSC center would be explained. Every effort would be made to view the training needs from the applicant's point of view. Rather than fitting an applicant to a training program, the state coordinator suggested tailoring the program to befit the trainee. He stressed, moreover, that the program must be ready for the student as soon as he files an application. If a dropout applied, it signified that he was motivated *then*. "Strike while the iron is hot."

The interval between OSC registration and the beginning of instruction was so long that many deserted the program before it started.

Length of training was not carefully thought out. Many programs ran for sixteen weeks. Some trainees were skilled enough at twelve weeks to work; others would not have been ready for skilled work before twenty-four or thirty weeks of training. The hopes of the trainees were raised, but at the end of sixteen weeks many trainees discovered that no magic formula could make them carpenters, masons, welders, or upholsterers.

The state coordinator questioned the advisability of naming skilled craftsmen as teachers. Merely calling a person a teacher does not make him the person to whom trainees will turn to for support, direction and tuition. Several instructors were influential in shaping trainee behavior. Several others were, however, inferior models to emulate. A basic consideration should be the attitudes toward the trainee. The teachers should forget that his trainees are disadvantaged. Neither pity nor enmity promotes good work habits. The trainee, he advised, should be accepted for what he is: an eager learner who has known aptitudes, achievements, and interests.

The view of the ESC coordinator was not unlike that of the state coordinator. He emphasized improved program-planning, elimination of contract and purchasing delays, and trainee orientation to the world of work. Rarely, he added, did the program staff realize how unfamiliar the applicants were with such simple procedures as filling out an application blank. The feeling of trepidation OSC graduates experienced when applying for jobs is rarely sensed by personnel managers and employment servants. Somehow, the trust OSC trainees should have developed in the ESC did not materialize. The Employment Service provided the routine aid given any applicant. This was not sufficient for OSC trainees. An employment servant should help the graduates locate jobs, take them to the personnel manager, visit the plant, be assured that the trainee is employed, and then help him find a place to live if he needs one.[1]

Labor surveys in each area were not undertaken. Training courses were often determined on the basis of educated guesses. Fortunately, they were good guesses in most instances. The local advisory boards, he continued, could have been of greater help here. The members were insufficiently involved. A community project like OSC *demands* greater participation by all citizens. Some take a dim view of the dropouts' abilities to become great. One leading citizen pointed out that dropouts "come from strata of society that aren't worth a damn anyway." Training for economic self sufficiency for local and regional job opportunities is an integral part of community action.

IN SUMMARY, coordinators endorsed the program but opined that it could have been run more smoothly had the funding agency in Washington been more sensitive to the urgency of expediting processing of program approval. Manipulation of incentives might have taught the trainees to be more prompt in their arrival as well as more productive in their work. Finally, improved planning and consultation services would have permitted the program to operate more smoothly.

IMPRESSIONS OF EMPLOYERS

It was impossible to interview all employers of OSC graduates. Many of those who hired three or more trainees, however, were contacted. They were cordial, candid, and cooperative throughout the interview sessions.

Employers were in considerable agreement with one another concerning the OSC training program. Each supervisor or owner who was interviewed warned that one cannot generalize about the graduates the program "turned out." Some graduates were described as pushers; others, as drags; some were competent workers, others, too unskilled to perform tasks requiring manual dex-

[1] This was not idealistic talk. The state coordinator personally met five OSC graduates from the Eastern project at the bus stop at Raleigh, escorted them to a local plant, stayed with them until they were hired, and then helped them find a place to live.

terity; some were dependable workers; others, "goof-offs." These OSC graduates with favorable employer ratings were deemed better than the average non-OSC job entrant.

Most OSC graduates, however, were viewed as having inadequate training to qualify for pre-apprentice positions. The kinds of tools and equipment which had been used in the program were too inadequate to prepare youth for employment. Most supervisors added that they had to retrain the OSC graduates. One of the biggest disappointments the owners experienced was this. Many OSC graduates quit shortly after they had been retrained. The owners complained that they lost money on them. In one plant where seven boys were employed, all but one left within two weeks. In another, where five were employed, none remained after two months. In still another operation in which six boys were employed, only one remained nine months later.

The industrial leaders who were interviewed felt that they could have made suggestions for training which, if carried out, would place the trainee in a more competitive position in the labor market. They had never been consulted. The economy is ever-changing. Industrial managers know best what a worker has to learn in order to find a place for himself.

Several supervisors observed the trainees closely during the instructional period. This was especially true of the hospital administrators. They agreed that the girls in the nurses' aide classes were too inept to be hired at their hospital. Too many girls did not take their responsibilities seriously. Six weeks, they concurred, was too short a training period for most school dropouts. The supervisors had hoped to employ the trained girls. The Employment Service, they insisted, had promised them that the hospital staff would be involved in screening. Supplies would be forthcoming from the OSC project. Such was not the case. They were disappointed in the calibre of students. Too many girls were mentally retarded, illiterate, and slovenly in appearance to qualify for hospital positions. The supervisors remarked that the Employment Service had misled them.

In summary, most employers were pleased with the calibre of work put out by OSC graduates. They felt, however, that the training was not adjusted to industrial needs.

LOCAL ADVISORY BOARD

Serving on the Local Advisory Board (LAB) in each area were civic minded public servants and knowledgable representatives of private enterprise. The reason the LAB was organized was to provide guidance throughout the several phases of the project: recruitment, training, and placement.

When the OSC program came to an end, every effort was made to discuss its key features with them. Seventeen board members were interviewed. The interviews were structured around role definitions of the LAB, the achievements of OSC, and future community action plans.

Most of the members interviewed interpreted their assignment to the LAB as community service. Their lives were that much brighter because they were in positions to help others. Fully 25 per cent of the members were dissatisfied with their service to the project. Even among those who said they felt honored to be appointed to the board, there were several who had been too busy to be active in the project. Several board members complained that after the local coordinator was appointed they did not learn about the program's inception, completion or progress. They anticipated being called upon to render counsel. Instead, they were appointed only because they were well known in the area.

Few LAB members defined their roles in the program the same way. Some stated their sole function to be approval of the local project coordinator and his secretary. Others believed they were to locate dropouts or set up contacts with people who knew dropouts. Except for promoting the program, the LAB members were not consulted. OSC programs and policies, most agreed, were out of their fields. Several members opined that they had no idea what were their roles. One member said he received a letter appointing him to the Board and he "obeyed." Many doubted their counsel was ever needed because it was never sought. The local coordinators, they judged knew the right things to do. The coordinators, however, had expressed the wish that LAB members would be more active.

When asked the extent to which the LAB accomplished its purpose, more than a third said they were too uninformed to judge. The majority agreed that it had attained its goal but rarely could they specify the ways in which this was done. One or two board members did explain that trainees were offered alternative jobs from the sectors of the local economy which would be most apt to absorb them later. Apparently, these board members were misinformed as no such choices were given any applicants.

Next, their opinions of the training program were solicited. Several responded that they imagined it was useful but did not know enough about the program to judge. Others reported that the program built a self sustaining population, instilled ambition, and made the trainees more socially competent. Judging from the high employment rate, several board members stated, the program was a success. Apparently the board members were not informed here, either. The percentages of placements in all three areas were below fifty.

The recommendations for improvement of the program were few. They centered around the lengthening of the program, retaining a guidance counselor for the maladjusted trainees, and extending the program to young adults. One member suggested that the Employment Service function in the program be curtailed.

The writer believed that one indication of the impact of the program would be the community's continuation of it. Most board members agreed that the community would *not* take it over. Several felt it should do so but the county commissioners would have to be "sold" on the idea. It would cost too much money to run. If the state or federal governments wanted to finance the program for dropouts, the commissioner would not turn it down. One board member felt the OSC program should be incorporated into the public school system and supported by local taxation.

Finally, the LAB members were asked how they felt when they saw the program in operation. Two out of three members had not seen the program at all. Many of those who had observed were not there long enough to render a judgment. Only two board members visited frequently and were well aware of the advantages and limitations of the program.

IN SUMMARY, it is clear that the roles of the LAB were not defined, their activities were limited to passing on the qualifications on coordinators and to suggesting recruitment procedures, and their interest in the program waned before the program got underway. Unfortunately, too few members were informed enough to make evaluations of the program.

The warp and woof of the program wove an "irregular" fabric. It was tangled in too many places. That these coordinators, teachers, and trainees did not falter in vain, the shortcomings identified here should be removed and improved strategies to cope with the problems should be investigated. Some suggestions are presented in Chapter V. To comprehend them more fully, though, the reader should become aware of the impact on the community and the state of the training program which was the exciting life-focus of all participants.

OTHER EDUCATORS

One way to determine the impact of OSC was to learn how it influenced the views of educators in nearby communities. Eleven school superintendents from counties nearby to an OSC site were interviewed. Nine of the eleven had heard of the program. Few, however, realized that OSC operated in three areas of the State. None, moreover, had visited any of the training sites. At this point in the interview, the training program was described to them, after which they were asked if they had plans for a similar program in the foreseeable future. Most replied "No." A few stated that they probably had similar programs within the regular public school programs. One was seeking aid under the Economic Opportunities Act. All eleven agreed that the OSC programs had no influence on their decisions regarding retraining of dropouts.

IN SUMMARY, the idea of retraining dropouts had not been disseminated to adjacent areas in the state.

COMMUNITY

Another measure of the impact of an experimental demonstration program is how it is viewed by the community in which it takes place. Five counties participated in the OSC program. How did the man in the street view it? What did he think it accomplished? Would he like to have the program continued?

These were questions whose answers shed light on the community acceptance of OSC.

In each county, members of the OSC research team were stationed at the popular gathering places like supermarkets and department stores. Every tenth person was interviewed. In Table XX is a cross-section of citizen views of the program.

Briefly, this table reveals that the average citizen heard about the program, felt the dropouts benefitted, believed it should be

TABLE XX

CITIZEN VIEWS OF OSC

Items	*East*	*Region* *Piedmont*	*West*
Knowledge of OSC			
Yes	87	46	41
No	23	16	16
Value to trainee			
Yes	104	58	54
No	3	0	2
Value to community			
Yes	78	51	34
No	7	3	8
Continuation of OSC			
Yes	110	61	51
No	1	1	3
Administration			
Local	11	11	6
State	16	19	18
Federal	36	13	8
State and Federal	20	13	23
Don't know	17	3	1
Curriculum			
Like OSC	63	49	27
Farming	48	3	6
Other	12	0	5
Don't know	22	8	19
Effect of OSC			
Profit to community	24	18	5
Trained workers	16	16	10
Reduced crime	4	2	2
Brought in money	7	4	2
None	12	0	13
Too soon to judge	46	21	23
Solution to dropout problem			
Retain in school	42	32	21
Sent to OSC	47	19	21
Don't know	11	6	6

continued, suggested that state and/or federal government finance and control it, were not too sure how the community benefitted from it, but felt that future dropouts need to be educated either in school or in an OSC program. Few were excited about the program. Most resented the intrusion by local political stooges.

There were few regional differences. Those that existed reflected the mood of the people and strengthen the aforementioned hypothesis concerning views of the dropouts and their rehabilitation. Administration of the program, all regions agreed, should not be local. In eastern North Carolina with a high percentage of Negroes, 40 per cent of those interviewed preferred the federal government to administer the program. The combination of federal money but state control was favored in the West. In agrarian eastern North Carolina, a large percentage of the respondents recommended the trainees be taught farming. More than half of the respondents in all areas endorsed a program like OSC. While most respondents in the Piedmont and the West felt it was too soon to evaluate OSC, respondents in the East said OSC had no effect. Nevertheless, they favored OSC as a solution to the dropout problem. In the Piedmont, however, the respondents recommended returning the dropout to school.

Verbatim comments presented below will hopefully make the statistics more meaningful. Certain recurrent themes were noticed. The verbatim accounts which follow illustrate the tone of the citizen reaction.

To the question: "Do you know about the OSC retraining program?" One respondent said, "I think the idea of a dropout program is fine but the problem here is that there are no jobs. So people have to leave the area."

The views of the program ranged from "It's no damn good the way it is organized," to, "It's the best thing that hit our town." Most respondents pondered over the question and responded with utmost sincerity.

One person said of the program, "It could be a great value. However, those kids that drop out usually are content with being on welfare and hanging around. It is a habit like drinking and not easily broken. There is not much in this community so it cannot provide much because half of those boys attending welding (sic, OSC) got jobs, and if it can help just a few, it will be worthwhile."

Another respondent felt the training was useless because it prepared the dropouts for nonexistent jobs. Several said the program is valuable to the dropout "only if he is white."

Few respondents wanted the program discontinued. Of 227 respondents, 222 agreed the program should not stop. Most of the 222, however, qualified their positions.

One man did not want it continued "the way it has been run." Another wanted it continued but out of the hands of the county superintendent of schools. "He is one of the ten cent politicians who infests many small towns," he began. "He's a tool of the local half assed machine. So naturally when he was asked to pick local advisory board members he gave the job to the courthouse politicians." The people wanted the program to be continued but control of every phase of it should be changed. They disapproved of the Local Advisory Board, the coordinators, and the incompetent teachers.

Most respondents favored continuation of OSC, but they were divided upon how it should be administered. Few wanted the program in local hands. In the Piedmont and the West they preferred the program be controlled by the state government; in the East, by the federal government.

Some combination of federal funds and state control was suggested by many citizens. One put it succinctly, "Federal money—you could get more, but state control. Eliminate the rotten local local politics." Another said, "State or federal money—but state control—carefully screen local people to work."

Judging from the kinds of programs which the local citizens suggested be included in subsequent training programs, the OSC mission catered to local employment needs. Many respondents felt, however, that closer links with local industrialists would have narrowed training choices to those jobs which trainees could *certainly* enter. The local citizenry felt this was a better approach than "The probability of entry" one alleged to be that of OSC. One respondent felt that the training program itself was secondary to getting the trainees placed. He said, "Line up the needs. Then fill the needs. But, you must *get* jobs for them. They cannot get them alone because they don't have experience." Racial discrimination in employment was stressed by both Caucasian and Negro citizens. One respondent said that something must be done for the colored people. "A colored person," he began, "has no future here. Even if he does have education or skill. They need help in job placement. They cannot eat in the restaurants, go to pool halls, or get employment in the factories."

One aim of OSC was to help local communities help themselves. Most citizens felt it was too early to assess this effect of OSC. Some put it, "It helped, I reckon." Several assayed the increased level of occupational skill in the community as a decided asset. "The more educated the community citizens, the better is the community," replied one lady. Several respondents felt the program did not succeed. "The kids are not working their field of training," was one reply. "All capable (trainees) have moved away," said another.

"This community cannot really benefit," began another, "because just a few people own everything and have control. No industry or business can come in without their approval. And they don't want change. As it is there is not much opportunity for employment here."

Again, racial priorities were cited as a disappointing outcome of the program. "The white sector of the community has gotten jobs for its dropouts," one citizen stated, "but the dropouts from the Negro community are without jobs even after completing it."

One final test of the impact of a program is how it is perceived as solving the dropout problem. When asked what should be done about school dropouts, one respondent pondered for some time over the question. "OSC could help. I want people to have jobs and get ahead, but we need industry. Some of the older people won't sell any land to industry."

Another citizen weighed several alternatives and then commented,

> You can't give them something for nothing. Too many just do not want to work. They want to collect unemployment. Ninety per cent of the men and 50 per cent of the women collect unemployment will not work. The Appalachian program will not work either, because it is a handout. Make them build a road

> or something. You're getting an education so you can work. You don't want a handout. These people are basically good—different, but good. They have gotten used to handouts. They've been raised on handouts. . . . We don't have anything to offer young people here. If they have incentive, they must leave to do something worthwhile. If they have no incentive, they will stay here and live off handouts. It's not such a bad life if you don't know any better. And the kids get no encouragement from home. Their parents are so uneducated.

IN SUMMARY, the local citizenry endorsed the OSC program and to this extent the efforts to retrain the community dropouts met with their approval. Also the local community wanted the program to be continued. They intimated, however, that the staff and coordinators were not always competent, that the local board members did not represent community interests, and that there was little within the community to lure the more skilled graduates of OSC to remain there.

Chapter V

SUMMARY, CONCLUSIONS, RECOMMENDATIONS

OVERVIEW

INTEREST in OSC has been fervent. Journalists have sought newsworthy success stories; local legislators, accolades to credit community action; educators, solutions for the unmoored teenagers, and manpower officials, a breakthrough in massive unemployment of undereducated adolescents. OSC was an experimental and demonstration program aspiring to teach salable, vocational skills to unemployed school dropouts. Could OSC extrude skilled craftsmen? Would the local community take over the responsibility for the retraining of future dropouts? Would the idea be "legitimated" and be diffused to adjacent communities?

The observations recorded thus far were neither intended to be laudatory nor derogatory. Optimists may cull from them the remarkable accomplishments of OSC; pessimists may find its sham, waste, and hopelessness. The detached scientist, in perhaps the least exciting of reporting styles, must dispassionately view OSC in its entirety. He is bound by his devotion to truth to present to the reader all that transpired.

Many of the accomplishments of the program are now understandable. There are, however, observations about the program which are so tangled that they stubbornly resist theorizing. But this is typical of social science. View this report, then, as a description of idealogical links which connect questions about unemployed, undereducated school dropouts with proposed solutions.

Our probings revealed new loci, new terminals, new pathways. Most startling was the discovery that the world of each dropout was *round*. Our navigations to this point had been guided by *linear* equations. Straight-line equations, the writer suspects, only hint at the solution.

The home, the school, and the community form an arc which circumscribes the unique world of each dropout, and these sociological units are welded together.

No training program may be expected to place a dropout in a job without identifying *his world, the area of external reality in which it could best fit and the custom-made path to arrive there.*

Quite simply, one must present a program, and the degree of absorption will depend on the student's ability and the encompassing nature of the program.

Briefly, the program trained school dropouts for marketable vocational skills in three areas of North Carolina; the mountainous West; the Piedmont plains; and the forlorn farmlands near the coast. Trainees were taught both vocational and academic skills. Length of the training varied from the six weeks nurses' aide program to the twelve week sewing for upholstery program through the sixteen week carpentry, upholstery, welding, pre-apprentice bricklayer, and auto service station mechanic programs. In each area, trainees ingested the ideas fed them. Many anabolized them, improved in reading and arithmetic, and became gainfully employed. This was most indicative of the trainees in Lincolnton, the Piedmont training site.

Some trainees were disgruntled. Still others were unresponsive. They entered and left the program illiterate and unemployed. In the nurses' aide class in eastern North Carolina all fifteen trainees were unemployed as much as three months after the completion of their training. Although all three centers were located in areas recognized as areas flanked by poverty belts, motivation for learning varied. In the western project, trainees tended to view the conditions of squalor which surrounded them as the norm. They recognized that there were meager job opportunities in the area. Many fancied moving to greener fields. Most graduates could not, however, separate themselves from their homelands.

It was not a love of the region which was solely responsible for making them remain in Appalachia. Fear and, perhaps, even animosity toward strangers confined them to the mountains. Those trainees who did leave the mountains rarely ventured out. Rather they moved within an established network, the stations of which were inhabited by kin or close friends. Each network differed from trainee to trainee. One such network was Asheville-Charlotte-Spruce Pine; no cities in between. Another was Miami Beach; Columbus (Ohio), and Spruce Pine; no cities in between.

Observed also was that trainees in this center did not generally view themselves as poor, despite their low average family income and despite their being on welfare relief roles. The families of many a dropout were landowners. They survived on the fish, game, fruits and vegetables which are freely available to them. When the way became rough social welfare funds, they were sure, would rescue them. The mere scarcity of money does not make them poor. Nature and the Social Security System watch over them.

Rarely did one observe evidence of discontent with life. Admonishing them, moreover, about their not maintaining an eight-hour work day expected of all OSC trainees, brought about no new work habits in them. Several would maintain a six to seven hour work day or not return to the OSC classes for several days. This is not to say that trainees indigenous to Appalachia exist on an estivation-hibernation schedule. Rather, it does point out that their dormant talents are anelectric. Neither money nor promise of a better life moves them. Condemnation and disapproval do not change them.

The dilemma for manpower programs is the finding of incentives to which trainees will respond. The trainees are open to suggestions. Mere amenability, however, does not mean that they will follow the advice. The most effective strategies were neither negative (electrons) nor positive (protons). Rather they were the neutral agents (neutrons) which did not scathe their view of themselves as being independent, free agents.

The trainees in Lincolnton were also united with soil. They were willing to travel many miles to work but they wanted to live at home. One group of trainees made an eighty mile daily round trip to work so they could work but still live in Lincolnton. Even the Negro trainees who complained of racial discrimination wanted to remain in Lincolnton. Willingness to conform to routine was greater among these trainees than in other areas.

Excitement for the program never ceased. Here was a hope for a better life. The trainees aspired to improve their status. In contrast to the independence motives of the Appalachia trainees, Lincolnton trainees enshrined egalitarianism. They sought to prove they were as good as anyone else. The incentives they responded to were primarily positive. More money, more training, and a better life moved them to achieve greater heights.

In eastern North Carolina, trainees differed in several ways from those in the other two centers. In the first place, they viewed their abject poverty as an undesirable condition which they would like to alter. In the second place, most of them were accustomed to long hours and hard work. Several trainees spoke of working at gas stations and on farms twelve hours per day, seven days each week, averaging less than fifty cents per hour. Finally, they viewed themselves as marginal members of their communities. They saw no way to earn enfranchisement and so they aspired to leave the area for any promised land. Reminders of their poverty and generally desolate conditions hastened the decision to leave. Contrast this with the dropouts in Appalachia, who viewed themselves a part of the community and in the Piedmont on the community fringe.

In Figure 9 is a pictorial summary of these observations. Note that the dropout in the East finds himself psychologically outside of the community. Because of so many roadblocks to self improvement, he gives up. When his being is threatened—as well it is when he is hungry and out of work, he leaves the community

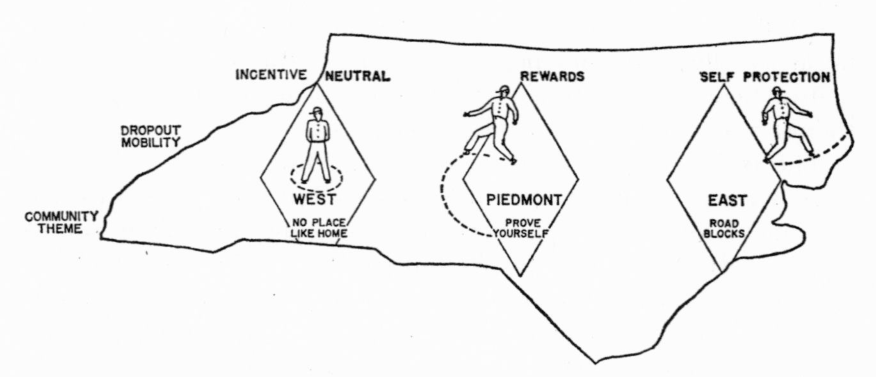

Figure 9. Incentives and view of community held by trainees in the three different centers.

to protect himself. In the Piedmont, on the other hand, the dropout is psychologically on the fringe. One foot is in the community, one foot is out. The community urges him to prove himself in order to gain their acceptance. He, therefore, moves toward those opportunities which will reward him with status.

In the Appalachian mountains of Western Carolina the prevailing theme is, "There is no place like home." The dropout is an integral part of the community. He is "in." There is little he can do to invite community wrath. Rarely will he have to excel or achieve in order to gain additional status. His self esteem is not in jeopardy. He moves about in circles. His movements, moreover, are highly circumscribed. Similarly, the mountain dropout is unaffected by reward or punishment. Neither vicissitudes nor pleasures move him. Rather, many a dropout from this area who does saunter toward work will do so when neutron-like events, often governed by whim, appear on the horizon.

The greatest improvement in general academic and mental abilities occurred in the Piedmont. Also, the largest number of trainees employed in training-related jobs was in the Piedmont. The largest number of trainees in training-nonrelated employment was in the West. Finally, the largest number of unemployed trainees was in the East.

What this means to community action workers is that the relationship which a dropout has to the rest of the community depends largely on the community itself. No recipe on how to manage a community's dropout problem can be written here. One ingredient to consider, though, is the community itself. There are

TABLE XXI

EMPLOYMENT STATUS OF OSC GRADUATES IN THE THREE REGIONS*

	Numbers			*Percentages*		
	Piedmont	*West*	*East*	*P*	*W*	*E*
TR	19	12	5	33	24	11
TUR	9	12	5	16	24	11
UN	30	31	17	51	52	78

* These figures are based solely on those OSC programs which were studied by the research staff.

certain communities which set up conventions and mores concerning social mobility. It is possible to step from low status to a higher one. Such is the case in the Piedmont. The dropout could earn respectability by his hard work. In the East, on the other hand, one's status was determined at birth. As long as the trained dropout remained in this type of community he was destined to work at those jobs permitted to his *caste*. In the West, though, the dropouts belonged to the same *class* with which most citizens were affiliated. Little effort had to be exerted to gain status.

Whether a dropout has to work for his recognition will have a determining influence on his behavior in the program. If a trainee sees his future as hopeless, he will attend classes and collect the government allowance. If he has no reason to doubt that his future will be as comfortable as his past, he has little incentive to improve. If a trainee has the slightest promise that he will better himself through training he will explore the possibility that learning a trade will earn him dignity. The characteristics of a community and the acceptance and rejection of it by the trainee cast the model which a training program will ultimately shape.

THE HELM

Despite the determining influences of the community, administrative planning might alter the outcome. In the following figure, the organization of the OSC project is presented. Briefly, the Governor of North Carolina appointed to a state planning committee representatives of such state agencies as Education, Labor, Welfare, and Employment services. Appointed to chair this committee was the State Coordinator. The State Planning Committee met frequently prior to receipt of the OMAT grant; infrequently, thereafter, with the advice of a member of the Governor's staff, the three areas in which OSC were selected. Contacts with local legislators and civic-minded citizens were arranged. The spade work for the project was completed and further decision making fell, perhaps by default on the State Coordinator. The State Coordinator together with a manpower consultant from the employment services met with Local Advisory Boards and with the local coordinator whom the State Coordinator approved. The Local

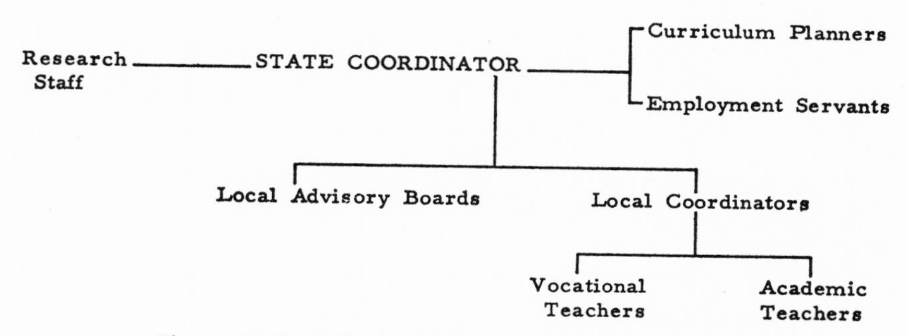

Figure 10. Organization of Operation Second Chance.

Advisory Board was active during the initial phases of recruitment; perhaps by default again, the local coordinator was given the responsibility for local decision making. Major decisions were approved by the State Coordinator. Delegated to the Department of Community Colleges (DCC) was the responsibility for drawing up approvable Area Redevelopment Act courses. Delegated to the Employment Security Commission (ESC) were the responsibilities of screening, counseling, and placing the youth enrolled in the program. The research staff assumed the role of investigating the outcomes associated with the OSC community projects. Clearly the pivotal point in this project was the State Coordinator. He interpreted the counsel of the State Planning Committee, participated in the formation of Local Advisory Boards, supervised the local project coordinator, and monitored the curriculum planning of the DCC and the interviewing and placement functions of ESC. He also performed liaison services to the Office of Manpower, Automation, and Training.

Were the detailed duties under each of the above headings to be enumerated, one might say that they were too many for one person to perform. Consider also the expanse of more than 400 miles of North Carolina which defined the geographical limits of the project. Visits extended from the spiralling highways cut through the State's rugged highlands to narrow, poorly paved, serpentine two lane county roads in the eastern end of the State.

Complaints of inconveniences, loss of trainees, program delays, ineffective personnel, and employment frustrations reached the coordinator's office. But the OSC coordinator was also manpower training coordinator for the Department of Community Colleges. Other manpower projects were beset by problems of their own. As a result, attentions divided among so many projects delayed OSC decisions, postponed supervision of local coordinators and in general weakened the vital role which the State Coordinator was endeavoring to shape.

In all fairness to the training staffs and the trainees, the State Coordinator cannot afford to be detached from the project for one moment. This is essential to the life of a project manned by subordinate local coordinators unschooled in manpower training and unauthorized to make major decisions. Trained coordinators are scarce, though. Too many of them are given additional responsibilities at the whim of their superiors. The lure of federal monies is so great and competent administrators so rare that the dowry obscures the waste.

Contributing to the crippling of the State Coordinators' authority were the long distances of each training center from one another and all centers from Raleigh. After conferences with local coordinators and teachers, each participant resumed his former duties apparently uninfluenced by the supervision of their superior. Implementing the State Coordinators suggestions was not always feasible in light of the conditions which existed in the communities. Many suggestions, moreover, were suitable for long-term, permanent projects and not for ephemeral, transitory projects.

Occasionally, representatives of employment services and the State Coordinator did not agree on policy or approach. While harmony was readily achieved, it involved compromise. With each compromise the authority of the State Coordinator became increasingly diluted. Interagency jealousy, moreover, was so intense that the needs of the trainee became secondary.

Were this project to be repeated, we would recommend that once again the State Coordinator be appointed to head it. His position should be full time with at least one full-time assistant responsible for training instructors in methods of teaching disadvantaged youth, for holding teachers meetings, and for drawing-up innovative instructional plans adjusted to provide preemployment experiences for trainees differing in attribute mixes in each community. To contribute to the maximum efficiency of a short-term project such as OSC, the respective roles of the several state agencies must be defined clearly. No individual or agency should be permitted to preempt the authority of, or to undermine the State Coordinator.

Once selected by the Governor, the State Coordinator should be empowered to make decisions demanded by the project needs. Not even the Governor himself should be allowed to intervene. If interagency cooperation fails and if compliance to the State Coordinator's plans are not immediate, then the training the dropouts receive is that much less effective. A full-time supervisor with complete authority over the project and with the foresight to appoint qualified instructors and the willingness to delegate roles and functions to them is necessary. Complete authority includes supervision of funds. Constantly emphasized in each interview with coordinators, state and local, was the long delays in procuring equipment for the trainees. These could have been averted had the State Coordinator complete jurisdiction over all funds granted for the project.

THE EMPLOYMENT SERVICE

The manpower staff of the Employment Security Commission was delegated the registering, counseling and placement of OSC trainees. This was accomplished through the staff available to the local employment office managers. In the Piedmont and mountain projects, the local offices were understaffed. Frequently, responsibilities like testing and counseling were delegated to experienced employment servants who lacked training in testing and counseling. This was immediately recognized as a blunder, but the urgency of the moment demanded expediency. Assigned to the eastern OSC project, the last to get started, were the best ESC counselors and examiners. The entire operation was overseen by its manpower coordinator. In addition, he counseled with trainees, visited them during training, and made contacts with employers for them. One might speculate that had a representative of ESC been so deeply interested in the trainees in the other areas, OSC graduates would not have been frightened to go to the local ESC office for counsel.

Few counselors truly understand the naiveté of underclassed dropouts. Few know that they fear rejection; few realize how limited is their scope of experience; few are aware of how unlearned they are in commonplace business procedures such as filling out applications or time sheets; and few sense how unsure they are of themselves. Should OSC be extended, it is recommended that the Employment Security Commission assign to it as a permanent member of the OSC staff, a vocational counseling psychologist. Such a staff member would be as thoroughly familiar with vocations, the local, regional, and national job markets, the psychology of the disadvantaged, as with the management of emotional reactions of trainees to schooling as well as of everyday frustrations on the job. In addition to preadmission testing, he would be responsible for giving occupational information as well as adjustment counseling to trainees with poor work habits and faulty work attitudes. As trainees become more skilled, he would take them on field trips to industrial plants. In fact, he would be the trainees' liaison with industry. If he places the best trainees in part-time employment, he would spur them as well as the others to improve.

When each trainee shows that he has mastered the skills which would permit him to perform at a beginning apprenticeship level, he will assist them to find jobs where they are available. This assistance should not be, "Go to Ajax Printing Company, corner L and Spring." Rather he should take the trainee there and introduce him to the personnel manager, take him on a tour of the plant, help fill out personnel forms and then return him home.

One Negro girl sent to a textile plant tried three times to see the personnel manager who had sent for her. His secretary would not permit her to enter his office. A vocational counseling psychologist would certainly have prevented this by accompanying her. There are countless unexpected frustrations on any job, moreover, mostly in relationship with co-workers and with supervisors. The ESC counselor would be available to continue his role as comforter and pilot of the OSC graduates.

The ESC counselor would become the bridge that connects the dropout with the prevailing society. He would ferry the dropout out of the wasteland of disenfranchisement across the desert of cultural desolation. He would be the one certain link between the trainee and the world at large before, during, and after training. This career of a vocational counseling psychologist should be filled by an experienced Ph.D. It deserves a high GS rating. The utter flexibility which this career demands, moreover, precludes its being entwined in the typical hierarchical jungle which only obstructs progress.

LOCAL ADVISORY BOARD

The Local Advisory Boards were composed of knowledgeable and influential citizens of a community. It was they who established the machinery by which dropouts would be contacted. Also, they were selected because they were aware of their community's economic resources and problems. Ultimately local board members, because of their special information, were to formulate the curricular action policies for their local training center. What was to be established was a local center under local control funded by the North Carolina Department of Administration under grants from the Departments of Labor and Health, Education and Welfare of the United States. Many members of the Local Advisory Boards were involved in more than one social action project. It should be pointed out, however, that in some instances, political stooges who had no special competence in training or in industry were appointed. One board member could neither read nor write. This could have been avoided had not the State Coordinating Committee felt the need to have the endorsement of local legislators.

In interviews with board members, the research staff discovered that they had confused OSC with programs sponsored under the Economic Opportunities Programs on whose advisory boards they also served. Also, it was quite clear that members of the board were busy people. Although the boards met infrequently, meetings were not always well attended. The mantle of responsibility for the local project fell on the shoulders of the local coordinator, who because of limited experience in manpower problems required the direction and counsel of the State Manpower Coordinator. Local citizenry, the research reveals, favored state supervision over local control. They viewed the Local Advisory Board as composed of power figures who were insensitive to the employment problems of every John Doe in the town. In one community, the respondents viewed the local coordinator as the same inept person who had in the first place contributed to the children dropping out of school.

If a community is to solve its own problems concerning unemployed, disadvantaged school dropouts, the Local Advisory Board must be a strong educational-policy-making body. To be sure, it did set into motion recruiting procedures. By and large, however, OSC recruitment had not been influenced by impersonal media like TV, radio, or newspapers, but rather by the personal letters and visits of the local coordinator and more especially by word of mouth spread by the dropouts themselves. The Board moreover, should not only be composed of citizens representing education, welfare, and civic organizations, but should also include a member of the Employment Security Commission because of his knowledge and understanding of the local, state and national employment trends and because of his familiarity with manpower legislation. Most boards were over-represented by government servants. Industry, most aware of its own expansion plans and current manpower needs, was almost completely neglected. But industry is the climax of a job training program. Its counsel concerning educational policy is needed together with that of the public servants.

Frequently, OSC trainees practiced on obsolete machinery which in no way was like modern processing equipment. Industry's advice is needed here, too. Reciprocal benefits await both the trainee and industry when cooperative agreements are arranged between the training program and representatives of business. Studies cited earlier indicated that industries cooperating with job training programs tend to hire their trainees.

One further recommendation concerning the composition of the Local Advisory Board is in order. Despite the sincerest of intentions, the Board did not understand their dropouts. Some board members alleged the dropout was a misguided stray, was destitute, or a ne'er do well. Their lack of contact with dropouts veiled their attempts to comprehend and, consequently, to help them. Coleman's research,[1] however, indicated that adolescents understand one another's language, feelings, and hopes. An adult, on the other hand, does not. Hence, he may have less influence on an adolescent than does a teenager. Why not appoint to the Local Advisory Board model adolescents and dropouts who command the esteem of their little bands of followers? They would not only explain the behavior of early school-leavers to the sages on the Local Advisory Board but, as community ambassadors, would interpret the planned training programs to the community's dropouts.

Fluid communication within the several subgroups within a community results in improved social action. Mutual understanding ensues from an interchange of ideas, beliefs, hopes, and facts. But lines of communication not only have to be open within the community but between the local policy making body and training staff, state supervisors, and Local Advisory Boards in other communities. Certain local board members testified that not only did they not know when OSC training began in their community, but they were never notified what courses were offered, what problems were met, what successes were achieved, and when the program was completed. Had there been a newsletter containing summaries of local and state OSC activities, the data necessary for board members to reach intelligent school policy decisions would have been readily available.

PROGRAM STAFF

More frequent communication between teachers and coordinators and teachers and trainees would have facilitated solution of mutual problems. Communication is not merely a student replying to a teacher's question, it is a *sharing* process. In Lincolnton this was accomplished in two ways. The coordinator held weekly meetings with his teachers. Insights into managing certain center problems were shared. Similar sessions were held with students. Problems were not denied; rather they were exposed, defined,

[1] Coleman, J. S.: *The Adolescent Society*. Glencoe, Free Press, 1962.

faced, and solved in an atmosphere of faculty-student give and take. Student morale and loyalty to OSC was, moreover, highest at this center.

Communication with and understanding of trainees by staff can be facilitated by preservice and in-service teacher training. The reason for this is plainly that teachers and trainees come from different social classes. Language, customs, traditions, values, and general conduct of the two classes are unlike. Social conflict is inevitable because both teacher and trainees organize their lives from different points of view. Prescience of the motivational patterns and reaction systems of economically disadvantaged, community economics, occupational information, and methods of teaching nonverbal learners would have removed many barriers in the teacher-trainee relationship. Many trained teachers come equipped with such knowledges, skills and insights. A short-term project with no definite starting date and with no assurance of tenure rarely attracts teachers with such qualifications. Rather, the faculty and coordinators who were hired were themselves out of work. A few had never been in the labor force; others had been retired from it. Temporary jobs with no foreseeable tenure do not elicit the highest of motivations. Certainly OSC had dedicated instructors who took their jobs seriously and were masterful teachers. Faculty meetings which the research staff conducted at Lincolnton frequently lasted until 2:00 AM. This is evidence of the staff dedication.

The argument presented here is that the *mere availability* of a person is an insufficient criterion for assigning one to a teaching or to a supervisory position. Neither should acquaintance with a local legislator be an employment criterion. Rather, the teacher to be hired should demonstrate that he understands disadvantaged youth, does establish contact with them, and is expert in his chosen field. This does not mean that all teachers must have earned a degree in professional education. In the writer's view, the most successful teacher held no degree; she knew how to sew and was poised in demonstrating how to stitch. She wanted her girls to imitate and to learn. Above all she was a model of what was proper and reasonable.

In addition to understanding the economically disadvantaged

school dropout, the local coordinator should be schooled in educational and/or industrial administration, personnel management, and vocational education. Records which contain the fundamental information which describe the activities of any enterprise were occasionally too inaccurately kept to be of value to anyone concerned with OSC. Employment statistics gathered from independent sources rarely agreed with the local OSC center records.

To maximize the value of a program to retrain dropouts, responsible staff must themselves demonstrate accurate work habits, professional competence, and willingness to meet the trainee half way. This was not always the case. Many teachers took more "breaks" than the trainees and allowed their classes to go unsupervised. It was presumptious of them, moreover, to berate the trainees for sloppy work habits.

MIDWIFE TO THE DROPOUT'S REBIRTH

What special knowledges do program planners and staff need to develop disadvantaged dropouts into better citizens? The exegesis which follows is intended to be a composite view of dropouts.

The dropout views himself a disenfranchised, second class citizen. He is not a part of the mainstream of the local social groupings. He craves social acceptance. Moreover, he wants to "amount to something" so that he will be treated like any other human being. Frequently, he lacks the connections which would plant him in the mainstream of the community. Had he the connections, his lack of social courtesies would prevent him from entering into the mainstream. He feels, he hopes, he accepts rejection stoically, he despairs, he hopes again, he aspires to improve himself in the face of many social barriers. Sometimes he gives up; most often he drives onward anticipating social rejection. Often he has difficulty expressing his feelings in articulate English. One trainee expressed with every muscle in his body how much he wanted to become a welder. His words were vague, but his emotions were vivid. Many a dropout had confined his circle of friends to a radius of less than five miles. The world known to them was an area frequently less than eighty miles. The roads, houses, people, activities, flora and fauna which they knew very well extended over an area fewer than twenty-five miles. Many trainees in Spruce

Pine heard of Charlotte but had never been there; many, moreover, had never visited Asheville. In eastern North Carolina, there were trainees who had no idea how far it was to Williamston, a nearby town, let alone Raleigh. The narrow and limited experience of the dropouts prevented their developing ideational maps of towns. How then could they plan activities in a location other than near home. Rarely, did the dropout want to leave home. If someone was available to teach him landmarks in another area, he was willing to risk it. This often meant being alone in a strange town; but when two or more friends or acquaintances lived in another town, the trainees would not hesitate to emigrate.

Lack of understanding of the narrowly defined world of the dropout cost one trainee his job. One qualified carpentry graduate applied for a job in Charlotte. He was accepted but was told to go across town where the work gang was. The streets of Charlotte were unfamiliar and appeared like a complex of mazes which led nowhere. The boy got in his car and returned home. One could easily misconstrue this event as indicative of indifference to work. Such was not the case. The boy was paralyzed by the fear that he would get lost. Contrast this, though, with the representative of the Employment Services who personally met OSC graduates at a bus terminal, escorted them to a personnel manager's office, helped them fill out applications, helped them find a place to live, and made certain that they had transportation to and from work.

Those who have worked with OSC dropouts have learned that nothing may be taken for granted. This was poignantly demonstrated to a research staff member while testing an applicant.

> "When were you born," the psychometrist asked. "I don't know," was the reply. "Well how old are you?" "Seventeen and a half," was the quick retort. Yet a quick glance at the records on file at the OSC office indicated that he was nineteen years and four months. The psychometrist showed him the birthdate he wrote on the registration card. The applicant broke into laughter. "I can't read." He explained, "I copied what the boy sitting next to me wrote." A quick check of the birth certificate on file at the county courthouse revealed the applicant to be seventeen and a half.

A major starting point in any retraining program for dropouts, I must insist, is starting each trainee with a clean slate. The data presented in this report refute every conceivable prejudice about dropouts, their ability to learn, their wanton moral character, their personality, their economic conditions, and their motivations. Preaching, lecturing, forgiveness, and oversolicitousness they neither need nor seek. They do deserve compassion. Above all, most of the dropouts registered in OSC programs wished renascence, they wanted to be reborn to carve out a new life for themselves. The writer is of the opinion that this rebirth may take place through an informed training faculty as well as through the curricular experiences a program offers.

CURRICULUM THEORY

The curriculum which produces the best results has as its underpinning a functional philosophy of education. A fundamental principle should permeate all instructional activities. A training program does not merely consist of appending one course to another. Student aptitude is one theme around which a program may be focused. If so, abilities must be measured and instructional activities adjusted to the capabilities of the trainees. Vocational interest is another theme around which a program may be organized. Often, however, the expressed interests of a trainee belie his true interests. Both ability and interests permit a wide latitude of vocational offerings, so wide that it would be impractical in short-term, transitory projects to fashion a training program at all. Job openings in the local labor market is still another theme around which to build a training program, though student ability and interests might be ignored. More important, such a program would not recognize mobility patterns in the South.

ABILITY

Ability, the OSC results revealed, was only somewhat related to accomplishments in the program and post-training employment. Not only that but significant changes in IQ were observed in several groups. Attempts to assess interests, moreover, were futile. After standardized tests of vocational interest failed, the

Employment Service counselors began to ask program applicants what are the jobs which interest them the most. At one training center, the majority said "truck driver," other trainees expressed interests in careers for which there were not available programs, e.g., electronics repairman, secretary, and beautician. All applicants were assigned to programs which corresponded closely to their interests and for which courses were available. The girl whose first choice was "beautician" was assigned to the nurses' aide course. At the end of three weeks, she said she liked hospital work so much that she cannot understand why she chose "beautician." On the other hand, a trainee who aspired to become a secretary became a most successful sewing machine operator. In her evenings she was studying office practice. A trainee who selected "electrician" became such an exceptional brickmason that he began apprenticeship training in brick masonry.

PERSONALITY

Ability, motivation and interest in people, this study revealed were trainee characteristics linked with post-training employment. Total student involvement in training often determined whether or not a trainee would later become employed. Unrestricted mobility was also a factor in subsequent employment. Local openings are vital considerations in developing a training program for economically disadvantaged dropouts. What if local job openings call for abilities which a trainee does not currently possess? Can these abilities be trained? What if the local job openings are not within the vocational interests of a trainee. Can his attitudes change? What if there are few jobs available locally. Can he be trained for regional or even national job openings? OSC programs took place in high unemployment areas. Competition for the few available jobs was keen. Often the OSC graduate was squeezed out of personnel offices by older applicants. In short-term and transitory training, though ability, interests and local job openings are worthy orientations to a curriculum, they are not practical.

What the current research indicated is that abilities do change, interests are modified, and job opening orientations may be broadened to include a radius of some 500 miles. One belief which must be dispelled is that an individual is predestined to enter a specific career. In this research, the level and field of interest which a trainee would have preferred entering was the one and the same for which he was trained, namely, semiskilled. Instead of catering to a trainee's idealized image of some career, general work values and response styles should be the starting program. Emphasized earlier was that each trainee is motivated to maintain and enhance his self-esteem. A program which is not designed to heal wounded egos and to rebuild self-respect closes the dropout out of the labor force. Much attention of late has been focused on the delinquent breakers of civil order who have been denied access to ego-building opportunities. In addition to despoiling social institutions, human talent is thwarted.

Through a training period, the dropout has to define where he is, where he is going, and what skills he will need to get there. Briefly, *a program should begin with a plan for the individual trainee.*

OCCUPATIONAL INFORMATION

What does the trainee have to know? In essence he must realize that whatever goods he processes and whatever services he performs are creditable and indispensable. In return for his labors, he is able to purchase the goods and services of others. Each individual has gifts and talents. Some, however, go untapped, as in the case of many an OSC dropout. When the trainee does utilize his talents, however, not only are his labors rewarded, but jobs are created for distributors of the product, and money is earned for the company owners. These owners retain a part of the profit since they risked investment. Also, part of the profit is returned to the company to improve its equipment.

Each worker is vital to the nation's economy. Contrast this with the advice one instructor gave his class. "You are going to be on the assembly line. You gotta be fast. And don't rub the boss man the wrong way." Those principles may be important to survive in a job, but it reduces the worker to a pair of hands, a pair of eyes, and a pair of legs. It violates the one personal goal the dropout has namely, acceptance as a total human being. The same adaptive behavior which the instructor seeks to instil may be fashioned by having the trainee develop the notion that what he does for his boss benefits him, too. It, moreover, insures the dropout that he is a part of an enterprise, what he desperately seeks, rather than apart from it.

Other occupational information which trainees need are the interrelationships between raw materials distributors and processers; between processers and distributors of finished products, and between consumers and producers. Needed today also is a sketch of the careers which have short lives and which are rapidly becoming obsolescent. Today's trainee cannot think that the education he is currently receiving is either final or lasting. Periodic retraining should be stressed. Dress and language during personnel interviews, practice in filling out job applications, and the importance of favorable recommendations round out the basic occupational information each trainee should receive.

The content of training is inextricably bound to its length. The coordinators, teachers, trainees, Local Advisory Board members, and community citizens unanimously agree that there was an insufficient amount of time to equip an inept, unskilled dropout for employment. We must turn our backs on such cliches as the "trainee with a weak mind has strong hands." There is no substance to this belief. Specialized training such as brick masonry, carpentry and welding demand proper coordination of eyes and hands, learning to make refined movements, and then learning the many tasks requiring variations in these movements. These all involve mental judgments. The ideas trainees learn about these movements transfer to the performing of other related skilled actions. Without developed thought processes, the craftsmen cannot become skilled.

CURRICULUM PLANNING

The OSC curriculum was highly specialized. A trainee spent sixteen weeks learning the unique functions of the tradesmen in his field of interest. Some trainees needed from eight to sixteen weeks just to learn to comply with school rules and to set high standards of workmanship.

In the writer's opinion, the first sixteen weeks of training school dropouts should not be specialized at all. Rather it should consist of a core program which prepares generalists. Specialization may take place after generalist skills have already been developed.

GENERALIST TRAINING

Today's labor market calls for generalists who, as semiskilled workers, may obtain jobs as helpers to plumbers, electricians, carpenters, and masons. Such training is practical for another reason. Whether they are functioning as carpenters, masons or plumbers, generalists often use the same tools, e.g., chisels, pliers, saws, wrenches, screwdrivers, awls, and hammers. They also have to know the uses and limitations of common materials such as metals, stones, woods, and plasterboard. Wiring, motors and generators cannot be foreign to any tradesman. Interpreting a blueprint is a must in each trade. There are, moreover, educational advantages to generalist training. Careful teacher and counselor observations of trainees performing generalist tasks would yield the kinds of information which may serve as guides to subsequent career specialization counseling. The trainee should have a chance to explore woods, metals, and stone; to use large and small tools; to build and rebuild; to visualize large and small operations; to translate and to create designs; to arrange work elements in logical and time orders; and to work for speed as well as for accuracy. At the close of the generalist training, a judicious decision could be reached concerning remaining a generalist and training further as a specialist. Not only that but that specialty which a trainee is most gifted in will have already been discovered.

Any frequent visitor to OSC training sites would see many reliable, industrious trainees. They would also see "goof-offs" and equipment destroyers. In one OSC class, a trainee was sent to the doctor because another trainee had fastened his finger with an upholsterer's power stapler. In another class, a trainee gave a "hot-foot" to a boy lapwelding thick steel. One trainee was "sleeping off a drunk" in the back of a car he was supposed to be repairing. Are these nonadjustive trainee behaviors inevitable? The writer thinks not. More carefully organized curricular experiences and incentive manipulation would virtually eliminate these problems.

EQUIPMENT

Materials, tools, and books make a short-term vocational retraining program. If any or all arrive late, the trainee is denied much learning opportunity. Several courses suffered from welding, masonry, nurses' aide, and auto mechanics equipment which arrived when the course was half over. In one course, the materials arrived on the last day of class. This means that available materials were rationed. When equipment was in use, moreover, some trainees were idle.

Ordering procedures for large equipment are regulated by state law. Sealed bids must be made. Delay in ordering equipment may be between four and eight weeks. The ordering of small equipment and books was assigned to personnel in the closest state area school. Because of other faculty responsibilities, OSC orders were not given the highest of priorities. Delivery of materials, moreover, was retarded by low inventories maintained by distributors as well as the poor highways connecting the training centers to the distributors. It was not at all uncommon for the machinery delivered to be obsolete and in need of constant repair.

Projects like OSC pressed for time and anxious to hold the motivation of volatile trainees can ill-afford to be dilatory. In light of OSC experiences, we recommend that high quality equipment be ordered from the office of the State Coordinator. No training program should be allowed to start until all tools, books, and materials have arrived. Strong program organization eliminates behavior problems.

RECRUITMENT

There were other sources of chaos, though. Applicants who were recruited were most eager to be trained. Training plans were submitted to ARA, however, only after a nose count of applicants justified the existence of a course. Sometimes several months elapsed between the registration of an applicant and the submission of training plans to ARA. In one center, several months intervened between submission of training plans and ARA approval of the courses. Applicants became demoralized. Only 40 per cent of the registered and tested applicants were available for training in the Spruce Pine area. When the OSC program was about to get underway there, the training slots exceeded the available enrollees. An intensive, hurried search for applicants followed. More dropouts enrolled, but with the absence of training equipment OSC became a false promise, and many of the recent recruits left the program.

Some trainees viewed the delays with anxiety but stoic resignation. Others expected to be trained immediately. After all was there not a rush to sign them up and to get them tested? With each succeeding week of delay, excitement for training faded. Some hopefuls became despaired. "Another dirty deal the good white trash pulled on us," was the view of one trainee. The most propitious moment for training had passed. Despite their forbearance, trainees who waited several months for the program to begin were disappointed. The loose organization of the curriculum and the tardy training equipment caused motivation to ebb to a low. Students arrived late, left early, and extended to a half hour their coffee breaks. The staff did not bear down on them because they knew how bored the trainees were.

INCENTIVES TO LEARNING

Another factor which contributes to the smooth operation of a program is the kinds of incentives for learning which are dispensed. Training allowances, merits, points, time off, longer coffee breaks are what many program planners point out increase a trainee's productivity. On the basis of more than a thousand interviews with OSC trainees, however, the writer protests this view. Trainees construed these as bribes. Instead of the program controlling trainee productivity through disbursement of training allowances and the like, the trainees controlled the behavior of teachers and coordinators. At one center, the trainees overheard one of the program administrators say that a trainee had to be present but one day each week to qualify for allowances. Shortly thereafter, there was a rise in trainee absences. Further evidence that the training allowances were not viewed as incentives comes from the effect of withdrawing them from the intractable and the frequently absent trainees. After denying trainees their weekly allowances, they might withdraw from the program, give it less than "their all," but this action did not change the unacceptable habits in any discernible way. Rarely did the denial of allowances have the effect anticipated.

There was one instance when a trainee was refused his allowance because he returned from lunch with beer on his breath. He later became one of the most capable carpenters in the class. Cause and effect cannot be imputed here, though, because his father also "tanned his hide."

PROGRAM

The purpose of the external incentive is to move a trainee to establish good habits of workmanship. One upholstery instructor approached his light-hearted trainees in this way. He promised to award a pennant to the best worker of the week. This pennant would hang over that trainee's work bench. In addition, he was given a reward of a dollar bill. To qualify, a trainee not only had to work assiduously but would have to keep tools and work bench clean, neat, and tidy. If no one qualified for recognition at the end of the week, there was no award. According to all indications, this incentive mobilized better work habits. An important question to raise is whether this incentive sustains good habits. Soon trainees realized that the likelihood the reward would be received by certain trainees is greater than it is for others. Habits began to slacken off. The advantage of this incentive is as a captivator. It mobilizes good habits, but it does not sustain them.

SELF

In the writer's view, the internal incentive was the most powerful of all. First, to be an incentive, the sign, symbol or act of reward must be *personally meaningful to an individual trainee,* must be something which increases effort after it is received. "Personally meaningful to an individual trainee" is emphasized because a sign or event which mobilizes good habits of workmanship in one trainee may not do so in another. The origin of the internal incentive is the *trainee's view of himself as a worker.* Whatever it is a trainee produces in a program, it must make him feel he has personally accomplished something and that this new learning experience has brought him one step closer to the kind of worker he would like to become. More than anything else, a trainee actively seeks esteem-building classroom experiences. If this is so, one coordinator asked, why do the trainees fool around so much? The reason is plain that it is easier to achieve recognition by joking and fooling than it is by hard work. Whenever two paths to a goal are available and one is easier to traverse, the easier path will be chosen. By planning a program around individual trainees instead of groups, such incidents would be averted completely. More than half of the OSC trainees testified that without further allowances they would continue their training until they became more skilled craftsmen. They asked, however, for better equipment. There were several OSC graduates who applied for further training to established educational institutions.

How potent a source of energy is the trainee's self-view has perhaps not been recognized. This self-view is the frame of reference with which a trainee faces, interprets and responds to training. One's self-view is an internal automatic self regulating operation. When a trainee perceives that the service he performed is below his own expectations, his self-view is impaired. On his next try, he will endeavor to organize his habits to do a better job. If the service he performed is perceived at or above the trainees expectations, he will be self-reinforced. But not only that, he will increase his level of aspiration. He will strive for new heights. If, on the other hand, the trainee views objectively poor workmanship as a self-fulfilling, adequate performance, the self-view will also be reinforced but the subsequent trainee endeavors would remain as examples of poor workmanship.

FEELING OF ACCOMPLISHMENT

The self-view also processes the data received by the sense organs. Take the trainee who always wanted to "make something of himself." He was assigned to a brick masonry class. He was quick to lay bricks on the line; he was accurate; he found no task objectionable; he sensed the admiration of his instructor, and discovered that he influenced other trainees to develop better work habits. The feedback from his labors, his instructors, and his fellow students enhanced his self-view as a trainee. After graduation he aspired to be an apprentice mason. The feedback from his labors, his boss, and his co-workers enhanced his self-view further. Now he aspires to be a supervisor. Might he some day control his own company? This trainee who aspired to be a mason accomplished more than the mason trainee who aspired to be an electrician. Why? Because the data fed into his self-view as an electrician was always interpreted negatively. Laying brick, mixing mortar did not bring him one iota closer to his persistent goal of becoming an electrical worker.

THE FAMILIAR

Working with the familiar is another incentive to some trainees. They do not fumble with tools they know; they do not make mistakes. Their self-view is not injured. There are some trainees who respond to the familiar in the opposite way, though. They apply themselves better to tasks which are new and out of the ordinary. Likewise, it is ego enhancing for some trainees to work with that which is simple. The simple task is no incentive to the trainee who likes to tinker with intricately complex machinery. Some trainees are averse to repetition of the same task each hour, day, and week of the year; but to others it is ego enhancing. They do not see the repetitiousness as monotonous. Rather, they seek the opportunity to perform the same task all of the time. They are proud of their accomplishments. Should the task be varied, a decrease in productivity would ensue. Large tools are incentives to some; small ones, to others. Working indoors is an incentive to some; outdoors to others. What makes a sign, symbol or act an incentive is that by experiencing it, the trainee looks upon himself as being important. This good feeling is one he would like to reexperience, so he tries even harder the next time and produces even more.

CHOOSING INCENTIVES

How do you find out which incentives work for which student? A psychometrist could give the trainee a checklist to fill out or ask him point blank in an interview. This procedure is neither valid nor reliable. Students check items on lists even if they don't understand the questions. Also trainees who never have worked with large tools are in no position to judge whether such tools are attractive to them. Should the generalist training idea be adopted, however, the signs, symbols, and practices which are incentives for a trainee would readily be discerned. In the beginning phase of generalist training, a wide variety of tasks should be presented to all trainees. Among these tasks would be included simple and complex ones; repetitive and varied ones; and familiar and novel ones. Also those tasks requiring large muscle manipulations and, those which require small muscle manipulations. Tasks using woods, metals, stones, and fabrics would reveal inclinations for certain media. Several opportunities to practice with these tasks would show how quickly the trainee learns it. Rapid learning, it may be assumed, breeds the wish to continue such tasks. Another test to apply is this: Interrupt several tasks. Proclivity for one task rather than another may be inferred from those which the trainee resumes. Also, after experience with many and varied tasks, provide the trainees with an opportunity to select whatever tasks he would like to work with. Those he selects again are most apt to reveal which tasks will serve as incentives.

Are these the only source of incentives? No, these are incentives readily observable from working with elements inherent in a trade. There are other incentives, though. One trainee idealized his instructor. He wanted to be just like him. When he did the things the instructor did, he felt important. He had an ideal view of his self, with each act he came closer to his model. Wanting to fashion one's behavior to resemble that of the ego model is also self enhancing. The desire to work hard and aspire to greater heights is an incentive when it brings a trainee closer to the person he idealizes. These incentives are no less powerful than those inherent in the act of work. This is, moreover, something that most people can spot. It is not the sole province of the psychologist. It is easy to identify because all people have at one time or another imitated the behavior of people they admire.

THE SELF IN CAREER

A different type of incentive for training is the perception of evidence that the trainee is a carpenter, plumber, welder, or upholsterer. During the training, he views himself as a trainee in carpentry or some other trade. What is proposed here is that qualified trainees be released to work in industry a few days per week. These students would need no more supervision than regular workers. The students who qualify will be known as "carpenters" or whatever is the career name for the duties they will perform. It is recommended that they be paid the starting rate for beginners. They will be distinguished from other trainees. There is a difference between viewing oneself as a trainee in carpentry and viewing oneself as a "carpenter." The student who is elevated to the status of "carpenter" has the incentive to maintain his reputation. Also, when he returns to class he will influence the students in two ways: one, he becomes a model they will seek to imitate, and second, he can explain to the others what are the real demands of industry.

RECOMMENDATIONS FROM TRAINEE VIEWS OF PROGRAM

Contrary to what was popularly believed, the dropouts in OSC did not unanimously reject academic training. Instead, they developed respect for it and tried to learn to read better. There were trainees, moreover, who sought more academic training on their own. Some returned to the academic class at the end of the school day to pick up where they left off, some went to the library to take books out on carpentry and welding, and others went to night school. The academic program had to be basic for the many trainees who functioned below the grade five level. Such students lacked the tools to learn on their own. They did not know how to analyze words. They did not know the sounds which certain letters made. They did not know what to do with the tens in addition and subtraction problems like:

$$46 + 55 = \qquad 33 - 17 =$$

Converting per cents into fractions was also bothersome. One 21-year-old boy insisted he did not know how to measure with a ruler until he attended the OSC classes.

Trainees lacking basic reading and arithmetic tools require more intensive and individualized training than was given them. Two hours each day is insufficient for them. Also, programmed instruction which presupposes that a student knows how to learn may not be the most satisfactory method of learning. Those trainees not functioning on the minimal adult literacy level also tended to experience difficulty in the vocational and technical courses. So that such trainees could profit from instruction, complete physical and psychological examinations should be given to determine any medical causes of the slow learning. This would include eye, ear, and teeth; muscles and glands, and neurological functioning. Acetylcholine-cholinesterase imbalance has been observed to be related to poor flicker fusion and hence to inefficient reading habits. Nutritional deprivations are certainly linked with motivation. Modern knowledge of learning disabilities is expanding at such a rapid rate that programs which cater to poor learners could easily avail themselves of this knowledge.

In addition to medical information, intensive diagnosis of the reading problem should be made. What are the symptoms of the disability? In OSC, there were trainees who did not know all of the letters of the alphabet, others did not know all of the sounds made by the letters, others could read words but not put them together to make sense. Particularly impairing rapid development were long-standing but incorrect pronounciations which distorted the meaning of the sentence. In another area, local pronounciation for "t" was "k." Trainees would speak of their "kraning." In addition to individualized instruction in reading, speech therapy for the widespread articulation errors would catalyze reading improvement.

When discussing the academic program with the interviewers, the trainees would emphasize what they were learning which helped them in the vocational class. They frankly admitted that if they could not see the link, they would not exert effort. How can a trainee know what are the links? Some links are less obvious than others. For instance, few beginners may see any value in learning the word "scheme," yet it appears in instructions for electrical wiring in expressions like "schematic circuits," in carpentry as "schematic drawings," in plumbing as the architect's scheme for pipe-laying the kitchen sink and dishwasher. Writing and reading stenciled words may not seem to have value to the beginning slow learner, yet in electricity, plumbing, and auto service repair training, the name of much equipment is stenciled. *Fragile* is but one such word.

Suffice it to say that most trainees do not have the judgment to decide what is and what is not necessary for them to know. Appeal of a task to a trainee is no criterion for its inclusion in a program. The only suitable criterion is "Will he be expected to perform this task on the job?"

Through individualized instruction, the teacher could make obvious the more subtle connections between verbal and metric language and the knowledge necessary to become a competent tradesman. In addition, the teacher can select high incentive content to teach the trainee. Even basic phonic principles like short and long vowels can be taught by using vocabulary spoken by tradespeople. Budding carpenters can learn the phoneme "in" by viewing the words "in," "pin," "tin"; "ine" in "fine," "pine," "line"; the long "a" when followed by "i" as in "nail," "pail," "stain" and "paint." Also, arithmetic could be taught meaningfully. Have trainees order materials for some real project, say the building of a fireplace. "How many bricks would be needed? How much cement?" After practice with one to one dimension problems, scaled models and diagrams may be used. Hence, one inch on a diagram may be equal to eight, ten, or twelve-and-a-half bricks.

True, the slow learners assigned to trade classes are at a greater disadvantage than the better achievers. By means of remedial instruction with high incentive tasks adjusted to the particular strengths and weaknesses of trainees, many obstacles which impaired the learning of our trainees would have been removed. Length of training of the slower learners should not be the same as for faster learners. They have missed prerequisites, are slow to grasp, and slow to apply what they learn. In flexible programs such as is being advocated here, there is no set date when the course terminates. The training for a future craftsman should be over when he passes the tests which qualify him for membership in the next level of craft, usually the apprenticeship level.

Thus far, the peculiar needs of the slow learners have been

discussed. What about the faster learners? They benefitted from the variety of programmed materials given them. Many did not need two hours of it per day. Several learned as much in one hour as others did in two. Had they spent the wasted hour practicing their trade they not only would have become more skilled, but they would not have been disruptive influences on the students who were slow learners. Literate students are able to learn on their own. Teacher domination of them, moreover, is crippling. Such students are independent and they resent teacher interference in their activities, and rightly so. While they improved in reading and in arithmetic, this was frequently a function of how relevant the materials appeared to them. High incentive programmed materials are generally unavailable for the trades. It is recommended here that programmed instruction materials for carpenters, electricians, upholsterers, and brickmasons be developed. In this way, the most important verbal and metric prerequisite, knowledges, skills and understandings could be taught in the academic class. Doubtlessly because of the high incentive content, students would complete it in fewer than sixteen weeks.

One further advantage accrues from such flexible programming. As each OSC program got underway, interested dropouts would appear at an OSC office to register for the program. In many instances they had to be turned away. Occasionally, they were told that they would have to wait several months before another training program would begin. With generalist individualized training, such disappointments and delays could have been averted because an applicant could be assigned to training immediately. Not only that, but the level of trade competence of a larger percentage of economically disadvantaged dropouts would be increased.

IN SUMMARY, what is advocated here are more intensive diagnoses of trainee strengths and weaknesses, greater correspondence between academic and vocational training, greater individualization of instruction, regulation of course length to meet the criterion of "beginning apprentice," and greater awareness of the trainee's view of himself as a worker.

In spite of delays and inadequate equipment, the trainees approved of the OSC program. They were grateful to have had the opportunity to be given a second chance. One trainee said, "This was the best thing the government ever did for Lincoln County."

Teachers and coordinators endorsed the OSC program. Although delays hampered OSC, they agreed that the school dropouts enrolled in the program added a new dimension called "self respect" to their personalities. Many teachers asserted that as the program drew to a close, it was only then that they truly began to understand the trainees.

Mere endorsement of OSC by trainees and staff does not insure the continuation of a retraining program in a community. The evidence is quite clear that no community in which OSC operated took the program over when federal funds ran out. Inquiries of the key community figures on the Local Advisory Board indicated that while they, too, approved of OSC training and their community desperately needs programs like it, financing it out of local funds, though possible, was not likely. One reason for this was the meager local funds available; another, the success of the program had not been demonstrated. While local board members praised the program and registered few complaints, their views should be interpreted with caution since very few board members ever saw an OSC class in action. To prevent this from recurring, board members should be given periodic tours of their training center.

Knowledge of a demonstration like OSC, it would be reasonable to expect, would filter down into the community. Results of surveys in each of the three communities in which OSC operated did indeed prove this to be true.

The vast majority of local citizens interviewed exhibited considerable knowledge about the program. The primary source of their information was "word of mouth." Objection to the program was absent. The local citizens interviewed felt very strongly that the OSC program should be continued. Opinion was divided, however, with regard to how the training program would be financed. A few respondents held no opinion. A sizable percentage of local citizens felt the federal government should finance the program. Several citizens added that complete federal control of the program would mean that local, incompetent politicians and leaders would not have a chance "to ruin it for us common folk." Frequently cited in interviews was the lack of industry in the area which would allow dropouts or anyone else for that matter to use what he knows. The majority of the respondents felt that OSC helped the community by keeping trainees off the welfare roles, provided people with skills which they could use, brought money into the community, and raised the general cultural level of the community. The solutions offered to the community dropout problem, though expressed in different ways, indicated that citizens were optimistic that programs which offered vocational training would restore dignity to each youth. Several citizens, moreover, recommended that a dropout be counseled before entering the OSC program.

Citizens of the community legitimated the need for the training programs and suggested a variety of training courses which if offered dropouts would improve the community welfare. Yet another concern of any social action program is the extent to which it was diffused to adjacent communities. County school superintendents whose districts were contiguous to counties in which OSC operated were contacted. Most of them had heard about OSC, although they did not know the programs in detail. None visited a training center. The majority had no plan to initiate a retraining program for dropouts. Several had vocational training programs which they felt could easily substitute for OSC. Counties with programs, however, had not been influenced by OSC at all.

Closing words are not easy to find. Beyond any doubt the destinies of the trainees who participated in the program were changed. All trainees began life anew. At the last interview some graduates were still zygotes; others, embryos; others, fetuses; others, children; but many of them were adults. The dignity which they rightly deserve as people could not have been earned without OSC. The slow growth of some trainees and the relatively low employment rates cannot be solely attributed to inadequacies of the trainees. Social attitudes are often so rigidly fixed and economic opportunities within a community so limited that the environment does not promote growth. Yet leaving the environment that nurtured them is precarious. In conclusion, it may be said that OSC awakened dormant human talent. And we saw it and we say it was good.

> *And the Lord said, if I find in Sodom fifty righteous men within the city then I will forgive all the place for their sake.*
>
> *Genesis 18:26*

PART II

CASE STUDIES

Norman M. Chansky and James B. Jones

INTRODUCTION

IN July, 1963 The Office of Manpower, Automation and Training entered into a contract with the State of North Carolina to develop and assess vocational training programs for high school dropouts. Such programs were established in several areas of the state known to have high dropout rates. A center was established in each of the three major geographical areas of the state; the mountains, the Piedmont, and the coast. The following criteria were used in selecting a center: high dropout rate, designation as an Area Redevelopment Act (ARA) county, propinquity to an Employment Security Office as well as to a community college, and agreement of the local advisory board to comply with the terms of the contract.

Governor Terry Sanford appointed James Ellerbe to coordinate the program called Operation Second Chance (OSC). After consulting with the local Steering Committee in a designated area, Mr. Ellerbe approved the appointment of a local coordinator. The local coordinator surveyed the school records for all dropouts between the ages of sixteen and one half and twenty-two. He contacted them by mail. Later, there was a follow-up home visit. In the meantime, news media gave the program some coverage.

Applicants to the program were registered by Employment Security as well as by the local OSC office. The Employment Service tested the applicants and recommended training programs which in their best judgment the applicants would benefit. The Division of Community Colleges drew up instructional programs for the students. These programs were approved of and funded by the ARA agency. Training allowances were $23 per week at first, later it became $24. After the students were trained, it was the responsibility of the Employment Security Commission to place them.

The writer was invited to evaluate the OSC program. Evaluation presupposes the existence of criteria or standards which were to be met. As those were not clearly defined in any of the transactions of the State Advisory Committee responsible for instituting the program, the writer took it upon himself to narrow the program objectives to (1) remotivating the dropouts by the training program and (2) placing the graduate in training-related employment. To be sure, the students who were trained changed in many ways unknown even to themselves. Scientific studies of vocational rehabilitation in order to have any value, however, must limit themselves to predicted outcomes. Monday morning quarterbacking, while providing abundant hypotheses about what might have happened, does not explain what did happen. Therefore, this report will be in keeping with scientific method. Any evaluative statements will be made in terms of the two main objectives. Because the research staff made other observations about the program and the trainees, these will be included. They are not to be construed as evaluations but rather as a verbal commentary written only to guide future community action planners in the country.

What was the program like? Approved applicants were given training in brick masonry, carpentry, upholstery, welding, auto mechanics, sewing for upholstery, and nurse's aide. Each day for six hours, the students received vocational training. Another two hours each day was devoted to teach them the verbal and number skills necessary to adjust to the world of work. All instruction was of the programmed variety. Instructional materials were so adapted as to utilize language and mathematics skills with which each student entered the program. The wide range of achievement of the students made this mandatory. Students varied in achievement from the nonreader to the one who was proficient enough to compete with college freshmen.

How was the program evaluated? Prior to training, a battery of tests was administered to each applicant. These consisted of (1) the Wechsler Adult Intelligence Scale, (2) the Benton Visual Retention Test, (3) Wide Range Achievement Test, and (4) the Structured Objective Rorschach Test. All tests were administered individually except for the Rorschach. The Rorschach, moreover, was administered individually to all functional illiterates. At the close of the training programs, these tests were readministered. The nurse's aide program was completed in six weeks, the sewing in twelve weeks, and the others in sixteen weeks. During the course of the program, the research staff interviewed the students on three separate occasions. One month after the completion of the program, each graduate was interviewed for the last time. Some graduates continued contact with the writers and with the teachers at the school. As a result, somewhat more is known about them than the others.

Student response to the program varied. Not only that, but realization of the program goals differed from graduate to graduate. Some students were remotivated. The program stimulated many to become more dependable workers and more responsible citizens. Not all students, however, benefitted from the program. Many graduates looked for jobs but could not find any; others did not care to look; still others did find employment in training-related areas. Those who could not find such jobs took any job that came along. Because their quests and achievements were so unique, the writers endeavored through the case study method to report the hopes, joys, disappointments, attainments and failures of the Operation Second Chance alumni.

The present part is dedicated to the idea that no two dropouts are alike in background, traits and achievements. If we can learn nothing else, it is that a retraining program will fail when the dropouts are sterotyped and the differences between them go unrecognized. To succeed, training must be adjusted to the proclivities of the trainees. In addition, it should be well known in advance that there are job openings for trained individuals with these talents. Even in this individualized approach the reader will note that trainees had many characteristics in common. What these case studies show is that the individual ways each trainee wears his talents vary widely.

In Part One of this report are the findings made on all groups on every test administered and on every question asked them during the interviews. Also in this volume are assessments made by the local coordinators and teachers, as well as conclusions about OSC and recommendations for future programs.

Thirty trainee files were selected *at random* to *represent* three training outcomes: training-related employment, training-unrelated employment and unemployment. Although the study officially ended one month after graduation, contacts were made periodically with these treasured thirty up to eighteen months after graduation. All relevant historical data are included in each case. This was done with scientific detachment to ensure a just evaluation of the training.

Share with us the joys of the trainee who is reborn; understand the striver who fails; know the indifference of the recruit who values neither money nor a good name. The writers endeavored to describe the trainee as he from objective evidence appeared to them. Therefore the reader should neither try to look for flattery nor disparagement of the program. What follows are representational paintings of thirty personalities.

Many case studies in this section were developed by James B. Jones, Research Instructor in Education. He endeavored to establish rapport with the trainees and then to maintain contact with them. His ardent devotion to the project is gratefully acknowledged. His contribution as co-author of Part II is appreciated.

NORMAN M. CHANSKY

CASE STUDIES*

UNEMPLOYED AT THE TIME OF FOLLOW-UP INTERVIEW

Greg

Greg is an eighteen-year-old who was one of the very first applicants to the program. He was assigned to the brick masonry class. His father is a farmer and his brother is a store keeper. His mother died before Greg entered the first grade. A review of his school records indicated Greg received D's and F's in grades one and two. No marks appeared on his record thereafter; nor were there any further comments. He left school as a total nonreader in grade eight. His reason for leaving was that he could not do the work. He has never been gainfully employed.

Pretraining Tests

Several intelligence test scores revealed that he is severely retarded mentally. Although his Wechsler Adult Intelligence Verbal Scale IQ would place him in an educable classification, his ability to perform tasks requiring manual dexterity, eye hand coordination, and organization were so low as to result in an overall classification as "trainable." Specifically, his Intelligence Quotient was 45. When he was tested, he was found to be very cooperative, but at no time did he look at the examiner. Was he shy or was he ashamed of his ineptitude? Achievement testing revealed him to be a total nonreader. He was achieving as well as the average child entering first grade. He could not, however, spell his name.

Some observations made about his personality were that he would become lost in detail, he was unable to think in terms of categories, or to discover underlying principles of common elements. Once having discovered a solution, albeit an incorrect one,

* The names in all case studies are fictitious in order to protect the rights and dignity of each student.

he would stick to it. He would, moreover, pay strict attention to his task. He was not in tune with everyday happenings but rather made unusual observations about reality. He was very persistent. He did not feel socially responsible or receptive to the group standards of conduct. Although not at all confident about his abilities, he was nevertheless a cooperative trainee.

Training Observations

In general, his response to training was favorable. He liked laying brick to the line without making a mistake. A nonreader, though, he was unable to read blueprints or the bricklayer's manuals. His teacher was convinced that Greg wanted to learn to read very much. At one point he held the opinion that Greg had "come up." He added that he would never become a bricklayer. Although he laid the bricks straight, he was too slow. He could, at most, lay 100 bricks a day. In addition, he needed close supervision. After laying a line of bricks Greg would sit down and light up a cigarette until the teacher told him to return to his work. Greg would then lay another line, sit down, and not resume the work until spoken to again. He had not grasped the principle of the continuity of work. In addition, he was unable to generalize from one class day to another. Each day began with the teacher repeating the lessons previously given and already acquired by the other students, but not comprehended by Greg.

His academic teacher observed Greg to be self conscious about not knowing how to read and to write. During the instructional period he made slow but continuous progress. Some of his achievements were learning to write his own name and to spell words like "cat" and "go."

Greg was a conscientious student who absorbed little. His work habits were satisfactory. He was neat; he followed directions, and he tried to exceed his previous accomplishments. He did need considerable individual attention. At the close of training, Greg was learning how to count, how to tell time, and how to add and subtract. He could not do these without supervision.

Although being trained as a bricklayer, when asked about his work plans, he said he wanted to work in a chair factory. He, moreover, did not want to leave home for any reason, whether it was to improve himself or to get a job. He sensed he could not set out in the world on his own.

Post-training Tests

A noticeable change in Greg was observed during the retesting session. Throughout the testing his eyes met the examiner's. He was proud of his achievements. There was no change in intelligence test scores, but there were noteworthy changes in academic achievement. He gained .4 of a year in reading to grade 1.1, 1.6 in arithmetic to grade 2.5 and .6 in spelling to grade 1.6. Despite these sizable changes, qualitatively he was still a nonreader. There were, moreover, very few qualitative changes in personality. The personality vignette observed on the pretests was observed once again. Certain measured changes should be cited, however. He became more tactful, more confident, and less nervous. These changes determined from standardized testing parallel those observed by the teachers, by the research staff, and by Greg himself.

In general, Greg is a slow learner who was not able to profit from the vocational program, as it was presented. Brick masonry is undoubtedly a calling requiring more ability than Greg could demonstrate. Yet he was motivated to learn. Not only that, he did learn. He was not able to put ideas into categories and so his learning consisted of making simple verbal or manual gestures to selected sounds he heard or sights he had seen. At the close of the training he had not grasped the principle that "an," "pan," "can," "tan," had common sound and sight elements. When asked about training, he said he would rather train for forty weeks without pay than sixteen weeks with pay. He was aware of his limitations. He sensed, however, that only through extensive training could he become sufficiently skilled to become a workman.

Follow-up

Greg went to work with a construction crew. His job was mixing cement and carrying it to the workers. He was fired, however, after one week. He could not work continuously without supervision. On his own he did not know that after each delivery of mortar to the masons he had to mix new batches and tote these, too. Rather, he repeated the same pattern of behavior noted during training, namely, after he completed one task he would sit down and smoke until the supervisor told him to bring a second batch. The ire of the brickmasons was so intense that Greg was asked not to return to work.

When interviewed, Greg was unemployed. He was still looking for a job, but added, "I might as well give up." In retrospect, he felt kindly toward the training because he had developed some friendships. Most of the people he had known prior to OSC had ridiculed him; his fellow trainees, on the other hand, were kind.

During this interview, a change in motivation was noted. He neither wanted to be an upholsterer or a mason. Rather he wanted to study welding for sixteen weeks with pay rather than any other course for forty weeks without pay. He still would like to become someone. He wants to show others he can do better but he does not know how he can prove himself worthy. He does not plan to get additional training unless supported by the government. He was confused about what direction to go. Money has become his main incentive.

In conclusion, Greg was registered in a program which from intelligence test scores it would have been predicted that he would fail. In addition, evidence from training confirmed this prediction. He, therefore, was ill-equipped to cope with assignments on the job. Although motivation for work and self confidence about his abilities were high at the end of training, his hopes were false. His work habits were decidedly unsuitable to adapt to the world of work. The result was further despair. His buoyancy waned. His bubble burst. The training staff had, indeed, supported him as an individual. He had confused this with approval of him as a worker.

A contact made with him six months later revealed him to be unemployed. A final contact made fourteen months after graduation showed Greg to have been working for two weeks as a delivery boy for a soft drink company. This was the only job he had ever held.

Key features of the case. Trainable mental retardation; inability to read; motivation to learn; improvement of reading and number skills; improvement of self confidence; inadequacy of response to vocational training; failure in first job, and despair.

Jill

Jill was sixteen and one half when she entered the sewing for upholstery program. She had never held a job. She had only recently left school. Her father was earning $85 per week as an upholsterer; her mother worked part time in a rug plant. In elementary school, Jill was a model student. She received A's and B's. Her teachers found her especially talented in music and art. In junior high school, her average improved. She received A's. Throughout her school career her marks in arithmetic centered around B. She had no C averages at all. She was an A student in art, music and social studies. Upon withdrawing from school in grade ten, her marks were 95, 93, 88, 80 and 79. She left because she was dissatisfied with her "79" in biology. She felt she was a failure.

Pretraining Tests

Upon entering the program, her Wechsler Intelligence Scale scores were: Verbal Scale IQ—96; Performance Scale, IQ—92; and Full Scale IQ—94. Her reading grade was 8.5; arithmetic grade 9.9; and spelling grade 9.6. Some noticeable personality characteristics were talents for inductive reasoning, high interest in people, high motivation, and high conformity. She paid strict attention to detail. At the same time, she was found to be impractical, lacking in originality, lacking in persistence, and apprehensive.

Training Observations

Jill made steady progress in the first six weeks of training. Her excitement tapered off, though, after the sixth week. During the first interview she reported that she had always wanted to learn to sew. She valued arithmetic and spelling above the reading parts of the course. Her academic teacher had been more helpful than any she ever had. In public school, she asserted, "they tell you once and that's it. At Operation Second Chance, the teacher will explain several times if you don't get the point." During the second interview she felt that she had not learned anything new in sewing. Concerning the academic program, she stated, "I like it very much, but I don't like the teacher." At the third interview, she expressed considerably more hostility toward the academic teacher and said she did not learn anything in the academic course. She added that she learned very little more in sewing. Sewing, however, was so important to her that she would have been willing to go to class for forty weeks without pay.

Despite the feelings which Jill expressed, her teachers showed no awareness of her hostility. The academic teacher judged her a good worker, one who began assignments promptly, selected additional assignments during her free period, followed directions, tried to exceed previous accomplishments, reviewed her work and tried to get the general idea of her assignments.

The vocational teacher described her as someone very interested in people. In addition, she found Jill to be a neat, clean, dependable and trustworthy worker. She summed her up as "a good sewer."

Throughout training Jill said she hoped to get a job near home, earn at least $1.25 per hour, and get married. Her life plans were short-term and involved a balance between home, work and marriage.

Post-training Tests

The retest data revealed that Jill changed in some highly significant ways. First with regard to intelligence, her performance on nonverbal IQ rose sixteen points to 108. In addition, her Full Scale IQ rose eleven points to 105. Her lowest subtest score was vocabulary. In fact, this score was in the mentally retarded range. Despite a meager vocabulary, Jill exploited her knowledge of words to the fullest in solving other mental problems and extended the frontiers of her mind. One could only speculate how much more she would contribute to her community if her vocabulary were larger. Despite her distaste for reading, she improved 1.5 grades. At the end of training she was reading on the tenth grade level. Her spelling achievement declined slightly to grade 9.1. A significant decline in arithmetic of 1.8 grades to grade 8.1 was examined. Skill in the fundamental operations in arithmetic were demonstrated on both tests. The errors were primarily in converting fractions to percentages, e.g., .45 was expressed as 66⅔ per cent. It appeared that Jill was so anxious to demonstrate her knowledge that she became confused.

With regard to her personality attributes, Jill deemphasized certain observational tendencies and adopted different ones. She became less theoretical but more perfectionistic and more practical. This meant she paid closer attention to detail in preference to broad categorizing. Inductive and deductive reasoning remained high as did interest in people. She became less in tune with everyday events than formerly. This was accompanied by greater self confidence. Declines in cooperation and in conformity were especially noteworthy. As she became more aware of and more confident in herself, she became less receptive to the social demands of the environment.

Follow-up

She was holding no job when she was interviewed after training. She said her parents were helping her find a job. She did try to get a job, but the factories she approached (all close to home) were not hiring. She was not at all disappointed. She summarized her experience in the sewing program as helping "to know what a job is. Sometimes we really worked." If the opportunity presented itself, she added, she would like to receive more training as a sewer and did not care if she did not receive any training allowance.

When asked if she would accept a job out of town, she said she does not expect to move even to get a well-paying job. Her plans call for her to live in the same town next year.

Attracting her to work were her wishes to do something useful, to make use of time, and become someone, that is, achieve status. She feared becoming lazy. Her hope is to become a sewer and to earn as much as her father. She said she would not quit a job for any reason other than its monotony.

At the last interview, Jill left the impression that she is just beginning to find herself. She is trying to throw off the parental yoke but has not done so entirely. She is motivated to work but still has unrealistic notions about the demands of a full-time job. The boredom of home drives her to the labor market. She feels she has to have some talents to cash in on. Sewing, to her, was as good as any. Although she developed skill, she did not develop speed. Jill was never reconciled to her failure in high school. The sewing course was an outlet available to make her feel useful. She was unable to accept herself as a sewer. The internal discord was most apparent halfway through the course. She was unable to find a smooth road to maturity.

Two months after graduation she got a job as a sewer but was laid off within the month because of her inadequate output. Eight months later she got a job in a glove factory. She is currently employed and earning $1.40 an hour. Her recent marriage has undoubtedly given her a purpose in life.

KEY FEATURES OF THE CASE. A good student in school; could not face failure; a good sewer; a good reader; increased mental capacity; friendly; self centered; ambitious but lacks persistence. Strong protestations to become a sewer and with such success in the training program, the subsequent unemployment may be a curiosity. Jill was in conflict, however, about her becoming a sewer. The low persistence observed on personality tests, the uneven progress in the academic training and her aversion for repetitive tasks are offered to explain her unemployment.

Herb

Herb was twenty years old when he entered the upholstery program. He had held jobs as a presser in a garment factory and a cook in a restaurant. Although he had several years of gainful employment he had been out of work for one year before the training program began. His father was a laborer and his mother a domestic. He had three siblings, one of whom was a college professor; another of whom was a laboratory technician. In his first three years in public school he received B's in language and in arithmetic. He received C's thereafter. Some unusual statistics, however, appeared on his school record. He had been retained in grade two. At the time of his retention he had received eight B's and three C's. The next year in grade two, he had received one A, seven B's, two C's and one D. In grade five he was retained again. His marks in this grade were eight B's and four C's. In the second year he was in grade five he received one B, three C's, two C–'s, and three D's. In at least two grades, then, he received passing marks but was not promoted. His achievement the second year in a repeated grade was always lower than in the first year. The only comments appearing on his record was that he is "a very lazy boy." He left school because he had fallen behind in his work. In addition, he had been ill. Herb said he withdrew from school to go to work. "I ran up a hospital bill of $1,300," he explained.

Pretraining Tests

At the beginning of the upholstery program, Herb's IQ on the Wechsler was about 80. This is borderline retarded. His scores on the Benton were essentially the same. His reading level was grade 3.9, spelling 3.1, and arithmetic 4.1.

On the personality test, Herb was observed to be deficient in developing main ideas, overly concerned with detail, mentally aware but with narrow interests, especially in people. He was also found to be lacking in persistence and in social responsibility. He did not adapt flexibly to situations.

Training Observations

At first, Herb responded favorably to the training program. As the program drew to a close he admitted that he dreaded going into the academic class. He spoke confidently about his becoming an upholsterer. His interest was so deep that he said he would have been willing to take forty weeks of training without pay. He added, "A trade means more than $23 per week." (Reference to the training stipend.)

His original vocational choice had been to become a barber. Now he had his heart set on becoming an upholsterer. If he could not get work as an upholsterer, he said he would take any job that comes along. He added, moreover, that he does not think he could get a job without having received the upholstery training given him. He planned to save enough money to start an upholstery enterprise in his own home.

His academic teacher observed him to begin work promptly, to be neat, to follow directions, to exceed previous accomplishments but to lack self-confidence. In addition, she rated him a consistent and hard worker.

His vocational teacher felt that Herb was a good upholsterer. Despite his tendency to "goof off," he was a skilled worker. The teacher added, however, that it will not be easy to find a job for Herb because he is a Negro. Had he been "white," he added, "there would be no trouble." He worked well with other students. The harmonious racial relationships in the class, the teacher attributed to Herb's easy-going manner.

Post-training Tests

At the end of the training program, intelligence retests revealed intelligence quotients in disagreement with each other. On the Wechsler he had a borderline IQ but on the Benton, in which perceptual acuity is measured, he attained "superior" mental ability ratings. This is a significant change over his "borderline" designation on the same test administered prior to training. Reading scores improved 1.3 grades. His reading level was now 5.2. Arithmetic and spelling improved slightly to grades 3.2 and 4.5 respectively.

There were few major changes in personality. Those characteristics which did change, however, deserve comment. Herb showed improvement in concentration, and in interest in people. One of the most significant shifts was toward greater persistence. Social responsibility, tact, confidence, motivation, and flexibility scores improved. There were several attributes uncovered which may continue to interfere with his mental functioning. These were "low generalization skill," "perfectionism," and "compulsivity." In other words, he fails to see a principle behind an action. Rather, he is aware of the details only, and these he doggedly pursues.

Follow-up

At the time of the follow-up interview, Herb reaffirmed his wish to become an upholsterer. The major attractions of any job would be its proximity to his home as well as the salary. He added he would be willing to commute up to forty miles per day, but did not want to leave the area. He was grateful to the program for teaching him a trade. Now he felt he could hold his head high alongside his brothers. Prior to this interview, Herb had been working as a delivery boy for a soft drink company. One week after this interview, he got a job in the shipping department of an upholstery firm. He worked for six months, received one raise, and had good ratings from his supervisor. His supervisor did reprimand him for staying out of work without notifying the company. He had been warned should he repeat this, even if he were very ill, he would be fired. Herb was fired two months later. Six weeks later he went to work as a short-order cook in a luncheonette.

KEY FEATURES OF THE CASE. Unusual scholastic history of satisfactory marks followed by nonpromotion. Left school and worked to pay his hospital bills. High ratings of work habits by academic teacher. Fair ratings of work habits by vocational teacher. Considered a good upholsterer by teacher but not likely to get a job in a training related field because of his race. Aversion to mobility. Good progress academically. Inconsistent measures of intelligence quotients. A willing worker, but inconsistent work habits.

Chip

Chip is a 21-year-old who was registered in the carpentry program. Prior to entry into the program he had been a helper with a construction crew. He had been gainfully employed for three years. There was no record of his parents' work history. An aging grandmother had been his guardian as long as he could remember.

His school record revealed marks for grades nine and ten only. His marks in language and in mathematics were D. He repeated both grades. Chip received no higher grades each year he repeated the grades. In grades nine, the ratings of such personal and social assets as cooperation, courtesy, dependability, initiative, and maturity were "average." In grade ten, these ratings were below average. Teachers recognized that Chip was an able student who would not study. Other teachers noted he was lazy and refused to learn. One teacher indicated that Chip had "an inferiority complex." This same teacher concluded, "he hangs out with the wrong boys. Could be a very nice person if environment was changed." A third teacher noted, "there is absolutely nothing school can do for this boy . . . stays out of school to caddy. No interest at home." Chip left school in grade ten. He felt his teachers persecuted him. He explained he had been "pegged" as dumb and placed in the lowest track.

Pretraining Tests

The results of the intelligence testing revealed him to be of low average ability (IQ 92) on the Wechsler, but mentally defective on the Benton. The latter emphasizes visual memory. His achievement in reading was grade 5.3. In both arithmetic and spelling he was functioning on the grade four level. Several attributes measured by the personality test suggested personal instability. He was found unable to think in terms of topics or categories, rather he focused on details; he was deficient in inductive and deductive reasoning; he was unresponsive to those events which the average person regards as relevant to all people, and was unable to concentrate. With regard to traits of temperament, Chip was found to lack persistence and drive, to have little feeling of social responsibility, to be uncooperative, to be lacking in tact, to have little confidence in himself, to be very apprehensive and moody, and to be very impulsive.

Training Observations

During the training, Chip made slow but steady progress in reading. His attitude toward the program was decidedly favorable. Despite his preference for the carpentry program in contrast to the basic education program, he did learn to read and to solve arithmetic problems better and faster. He enjoyed carpentry, especially outdoor work. House frames and borders were his specialties. He found arithmetic to be a difficult subject, but as long as he could work alone without teacher pressure (as he indeed did through programmed instruction) he enjoyed it.

From the very beginning of training he felt very strongly that he would succeed as a carpenter. He knew there were openings for trained carpenters. He expected to earn from $1.50 to $1.75 an hour. When asked how he would feel if he did not get a job as a carpenter, he replied it would probably be due to his race. Luck, to him, is essential to the getting of a job. If he were not lucky enough to get a job as a carpenter, he would return to "rolling bricks" on construction jobs. He was optimistic, though, that his talents would be recognized and that he would be advanced to a supervisory position.

Chip's motivation for work appeared to be quite genuine. He would like to have additional training. Had he the opportunity he would like to go to school for forty weeks without pay to learn to be a TV repairman. Despite this preference for a vocation for which no training was offered, he felt he had become a skilled workman. He tried to recruit friends for the training program but they doubted anyone could become a skilled craftsman in sixteen weeks. Chip felt that his own accomplishments would change their opinion.

In retrospect he believed both the academic and vocational programs were helpful to him. Although sixteen weeks is insufficient time allowance to become skilled, he felt he began to learn. In addition, he saw himself as more mature. He feels a greater self responsibility.

His academic teacher assessed Chip's work habits as those necessary to succeed in the world of work. She stated he begins his assignments promptly, he selects additional assignments during free period, he records answers neatly, he tries to exceed previous accomplishments, he reviews his work, tries to get the general idea of his assignment, and discusses applications of what he studies. She summarized her view as follows: "Although colored, Chip has a very fine attitude. He does not like for any of the other students to bother him at all while he is working. Chip is well mannered and puts in a good day's work."

His vocational teacher summed up his views as follows: "He's good. He works. He gets along well with others. He has imagination. He will not copy the work of others. He is good in class. Given a chance, he'll make good. He has been recommended to Savoy Construction Company. If anything holds him back, it will be his color. What he does is right. A dependable worker."

Post-training Tests

Retests at the end of the course indicated no overall change in intelligence on the Wechsler. A loss of eight points was observed for the Verbal Scale; a gain of nine points for the Performance Scale. There was a significant increase in perceptual acuity and visual memory IQ's on the Benton. He went from "defective" on the pretest to "average" on the retest. Significant gains were observed in academic achievement. He improved two full grades in reading, and one grade in arithmetic and in spelling. His reading level was now grade 7.4; arithmetic grade 5.4; and spelling grade 5.4.

Several changes in personality were noted on the retest. Although still a perfectionistic thinker with low generalization ability, he nevertheless began to examine the relationship between rules or principles and examples more carefully. He became more mentally aware and began to concentrate more intently. Changes in temperament were noted, too. He became more persistent, more socially responsible, more cooperative, more tactful, more self confident, less anxious, less moody, more goal directed, more flexible and more conforming.

Follow-up

At the follow-up interview Chip was very bitter. He had gotten a job in the carpentry trade. He was not, however, allowed to do any carpentry work. On the job he was allowed only to be a carpenter's helper. He said, "My boss did not think a colored man could be a carpenter." Chip quit after one week of work. Throughout his training, he increasingly viewed himself as a carpenter. His future plans revolved around becoming a successful carpenter. His self image fell apart when he was not allowed to use his talents.

Because he is the only person taking care of his grandmother, he added, he would be reluctant to leave home to take a job in another part of the country. He would move, though, if he knew he could become a carpenter. He was motivated to work in order to better himself. He added that he might quit if his salary and relationships with his supervisor were inadequate.

Despite his disappointment at not finding work, he continued to speak favorably about his training. He said the program "has given me hope and something to look forward to. It has helped build confidence in myself. I know I can do the work if given the opportunity."

In conclusion, Chip, a highly rated worker and skilled carpenter, found he could not work at his trade because Negroes were not hired to do skilled work.

Months later, Chip did get a job working as a carpenter with his former instructor. He was earning $1.25 per hour. After two weeks he had to quit because the carpentry gang moved on to another city. Chip had no transportation to the new site. For several months Chip was again unemployed. His next job was as a laborer on a brick masonry project. He wanted to save his money to buy a car. With a car he said he would become mobile enough to accept a job as a carpenter. He quit this job to work part time as a carpenter. For four months he worked two to three days per week. Finally, he went to work full time in a dry cleaning establishment. He did not care for this kind of work. Currently, he is seeking training in the Job Corps. His ultimate goal is to do "clean" work.

Key features of the case. Poor scholastic record in public school; lives with and takes care of grandmother; wanted to be a TV repairman. Made great strides in program; improving in reading, spelling, arithmetic, and intelligence. Better personality adjustment was noted, too. Considered a good worker and an able carpenter. Employed as a carpenter's helper and quit in disgust. Racial prejudice a factor, but not the sole contributor to his unemployment. Resistance to mobility and lack of persistence prevent him from establishing himself on the job.

George

George was nineteen years old when he entered the program to train as a carpenter. Although he had two years of gainful employment as a farm hand, he had been unemployed for several months prior to the Operation Second Chance program. When George was fourteen years old his father died. Since then the Welfare Department has supported George and his family.

A review of his school record revealed that he received all D's except for an A in citizenship in grade six. He first thought about leaving school when he was fourteen years old. He left at the age of seventeen because he could neither read nor write. He had quit school several times before. One Monday he got a job on a farm and never returned to school.

Pretraining Tests

Upon entering the carpentry program, he was given the battery of intelligence, achievement, and personality tests. Both Wechsler and Benton IQ scores were in the educable mental retardation categories. His reading achievement was at the grade 3.4 level; whereas his spelling and arithmetic were at the grade 2.8 and 2.7 levels respectively. Scores on the personality test indicated several deficits. Among these were the absence of developing guiding principles to thinking, especially in inductive reasoning, disinterest in people, lack of anxiety, and absence of conformity. He was found to be highly persistent, highly consistent, very perfectionistic, and inflexible in his thinking.

George was interviewed several times during the program. He felt that the program in general was good for the county. "It gives us a chance to learn to do a job." He was quite serious about this. When asked how he was progressing in his training, George would always joke. He recommended, moreover, that the school needed more equipment. In subsequent interviews he continued to praise the program but avoided relating the program to himself.

Training Observations

At the first interview he bluntly indicated that he would not become a carpenter. When asked what he planned to do when he completed the carpentry course, he said, "take another course—sometimes I think I'd kinda like to go back to school. People need a lot of education now-a-days." In his earliest vocational plans, then, carpentry had no place. By the second interview, he said he would probably become a carpenter but he did not think very highly of his abilities. While he thought he was better than a helper, he sized himself up as "half as good as a carpenter." At the end of training, he indicated that he did not know what kind of job he would be looking for. When asked to discuss his plans for the coming year, he asserted that he expects to be working on a farm.

His overall evaluations of the program were that it gave him a good reputation and work experience. In addition, he learned how to get along with people. He felt the carpentry program benefitted him the least, and the upholstery program, in which he took no formal instruction, helped him the most. He was asked to elaborate on his comment about "good reputation." To this he related that he lives on the edge of town and if anything goes wrong in town, the police subject him to questioning. Since he has been going to "dropout school" the police leave him alone. They feel George is trying to make something out of himself.

Although George began his assignments promptly in the academic class, his teacher observed him to have poor work habits. He distracted others, came to class late, did not budget his time, and skimmed over important ideas. His teacher summed him up as follows: "The only problem with George is his laziness and he likes attention. Talks out a lot in class." She added a phrase which will be of utmost significance later, namely, "he is tight with his money—puts it all in the bank. He says it is for his old age."

The carpentry teacher said that George worked only when supervised. He would wander away from class with his hammer swaying in his belt. Often he would barge into other classes and pull out his hammer, a symbol of power, character, and attention. This would "break up" the other vocational classes. Although George was seen as a good boy, unafraid of work, and cooperative, he would rarely stick to a task long enough to learn it. In summing him up, the carpentry teacher judged, "George doesn't have skill. He'll never be a carpenter."

George planned to quit after he was in the program only three days. Since he was not present at school to sign up for his allowance, he received none for the first two weeks. The coordinator spoke to him and convinced him to return to the program. After this, the teachers noted an improvement in work habits. About halfway through the program, the following incident took place.

George went out to lunch but did not return to school until the next day. He received a note from the coordinator explaining why he was found ineligible for allowances. The note read, "According to the training faculty you told no one that you were leaving and could offer no legitimate excuse as to why you left. This isn't in line with the conduct expected from trainees and you have therefore been determined ineligible." Interviews before and after the disallowance reveal that George had a deepening interest in the program. He was not going to quit. Shortly after this last disallowance, George began to seek the attention of his classmates and teachers through various gambits. It was not until they were thoroughly exasperated that he would stop.

The disallowance was a disciplinary action to maintain order in the school. To George, however, it was of greater significance. His mother lived on a pension and the modest sums brought home to her by George and his brother, also a trainee. The loss of the money used to maintain himself was an especially stinging blow. Although he never again left school at noontime, he also made little further progress in school. At no time, moreover, did he speak disparagingly about the program. Rather he encouraged other dropouts to register for the program. George moralized a great deal. He knew what was right and proper. However, he could not demonstrate the virtues he espoused. By the last interview he had given up becoming a carpenter. He wanted to become a mill worker.

Post-training Tests

At the end of training, retests of intelligence revealed that George was still mentally retarded. In fact, his Performance IQ declined thirteen points, and his Full Scale IQ declined six points. While he improved one half year in reading, he made no progress in either arithmetic or spelling. With respect to changes in personality traits, few changes were noted. The changes which took place were generally toward greater maladjustment. His organization of reality became increasingly blurred. In addition, he was unable to concentrate. He became less persistent, more moody, and more impulsive. In general, the events in training interfered with his growth. His low abilities, immediate unresponsiveness to carpentry training, and distracting work habits predestined him to failure.

Follow-up

One month after the completion of training George was unemployed. He had held two jobs in the interim. One as a construction helper, the other as a farm laborer. He left the first job for two reasons: he did not work all day and he resented his Negro co-workers. On the farm he found solace. Because farm work is seasonal, he could only work part time.

George wanted to work near home. His reasons for this is that he does not want to have to depend on other people (for transportation). He added, if anyone got sick in the family, he could be contacted and his help would be forthcoming. "If you get hurt, they could call home," he added. He does not want to move any more than two miles in order to get a job. His plan to become a spinner in a cotton mill leads him to expect to be gainfully employed at this calling.

In retrospect, he felt the program made him understand more. It was comforting for him to know that someone wants to help him. He felt someone cared about him. With regard to his failure as a carpenter, he said, "It was my own fault. I didn't get much out of the program, I feel I just don't know enough about carpentry to do a good job." The strength of his motivation to learn may be seen from his wish to continue his education. He said he would like to take a course in mechanics for forty weeks without allowances. "If the training is good enough, you do not need to be paid."

For six months after his graduation from OSC, George held jobs primarily as a farm laborer. He was helping his brother who occasionally paid him fifty cents per hour. He had been to Employment Security regularly but could find no job leads. He held part time jobs mowing lawns and milking cows. In retrospect, he felt the OSC program was good but he could not put any of his knowledge to use. He is in a quandary. He would like to make better use of his time, but seems to do everything wrong. He wanted to join the Job Corps but would not affiliate if it meant he had to leave home.

In conclusion, George did not benefit from the carpentry program. Lack of mental ability, poor work habits, and resentment toward his teachers played prominent roles. He does not have any clearcut vision of what kind of work he would like to do. His motivation for learning is high but he could not find within the program those occupational tasks which he could pursue successfully.

KEY FEATURES OF THE CASE. Low mental ability. Devoted to family. Living in abject poverty. Saved his training allowances. Improved in reading, but declined in psychometric mental ability. Maladjusted personally. Maladjusted vocationally. Motivated to learn. Feels personally responsible for failure.

Ronnie

Ronnie was a 17-year-old who was registered for the upholstery class. He had never held a job. His father, the principal wage earner, is a handy man with a construction company.

He left school in the ninth grade "to help out at home." There is no evidence from available work history records that this, indeed, was true. Rather it seems more likely that he dropped out of school because of a long history of academic failure. He was retained in grade one. His marks in language and in arithmetic for the eight grades he attended were all D's. He, however, consistently received A's in citizenship. Although rated average in social and personal assets for the first six grades, in the seventh and eighth grades he received below average and low ratings, especially in industriousness, leadership, and personal appearance.

Pretraining Tests

Ronnie was examined prior to training. The five IQ's obtained on him placed him in the educable mentally retarded category.

In addition, he was found to be a total nonreader. With regard to arithmetic and spelling skills he was observed to be functioning on the first grade level. The results of the personality tests revealed that he had low generalization ability and was overly concerned with detail. His range of interests were narrow. Such temperament traits as social responsibility, cooperation, anxiety, and conformity were found to be below average for adults.

Training Observations

His response to the training was nonspecific. He said that he likes everything. Rarely did he communicate spontaneously. Rather he would find single word answers to close the interviews as quickly as possible. He did seem to enjoy the work and when asked to elaborate he specified that he liked springing the seats, backs, and arms of chairs.

During the second interview, he said he planned to get a job in an upholstery firm. But at the third interview, he did not cite upholstery at all as a trade he would take up. Rather he said he would look for any kind of job. His plan for the following year was equally uncertain. While he was unwilling to move out of the area, he said if he were sure he could get a job he "might" move to the nearest large city.

His academic teacher viewed him as a willing worker who began his assignments promptly, recorded his answers neatly, and followed directions. Due to his meager sight and speaking vocabularies, however, he required more than usual individual attention.

His vocational teacher viewed him as a willing worker who was too slow to keep up with a production line. He felt he could not work without supervision.

Ronnie said that if he were given another chance, he would like to study auto mechanics. Acceptance of the program would be contingent upon the granting of training allowance.

Post-training Tests

Upon retest, gains of one year were registered in reading, arithmetic, and language. Since he was reading on the grade two level, he was still considered a nonreader. Losses in intelligence test scores, on the other hand, were considerable. His Verbal IQ dropped seven points; his Performance IQ eight points; and his

Full Scale IQ dropped eleven points. This may very well have been due to the lack of communication skill necessary to demonstrate one's abilities. Previously his IQ's placed him in the educable mental retardation category. Now he was in the trainable category. Changes in personality were slight. A shift toward wider interests, greater social responsibility, and greater cooperation were noted.

Follow-up

One month after completion of the program Ronnie was unemployed. He said he did not look for a job because a representative of the Employment Security Commission told him he was too young to get a job anywhere. When asked how he felt about not working, he said he was not disappointed. He added he would wait until his eighteenth birthday before looking for a job. Should a course in housepainting be offered and should he be given training allowances, he would probably take it.

In conclusion, Ronnie's mental ability was insufficient to profit from the upholstery program. He did make strides in the academic program. Toward the end of the program, he sensed he could not get a job in the field for which he received training, and he gave up. A contact made with him one year later revealed him to be unemployed .

KEY FEATURES OF THE CASE. Nonreader; mentally retarded; intelligence scores declined during training; willing, cooperative worker, requiring supervision.

Ed

Ed was a 17-year-old who was assigned to the welding class. His mother was a housewife; his father died of tuberculosis the year before OSC was initiated. He had been a mica miner. The family subsists on social security payments.

In the first three grades in public school, Ed received A's in language and in arithmetic. In grades four through six, his language marks averaged B, but his arithmetic marks averaged A. In junior high school, a reverse trend was noted. His language marks were B but his marks in arithmetic fell to C. Throughout elementary school his teachers evaluated his personal and social assets such as industriousness, maturity and leadership as either average or above average. In grades nine and ten, Ed's overall ratings were average, but initiative and industriousness were rated below average. During these two years, his teachers commented that he was sweet, nice and cooperative. In the beginning of the tenth grade, Ed said his marks began to fail. His teachers were "very hard." He did not like them. On several occasions he asked his father to allow him to quit. Reluctantly he consented.

Pretraining Tests

The tests administered at the beginning of the program revealed him to be of low normal mental ability. His Verbal IQ was 95; his Performance IQ 90, and Full Scale, 93. His reading on the grade 9.5 level; spelling 6.9; and arithmetic 5.6. Arithmetic errors were primarily those of carelessness (e.g., $4 \times 240 = 680$). The results of the personality tests indicated that Ed's reasoning abilities were adequate. He was particularly facile in inductive and deductive reasoning. Although lacking in mental awareness, he had a wide variety of interests. With respect to attributes of temperament, he could be considered persistent, cooperative, tactful, confident, flexible and conforming. The impression made was that of an adequate personality.

Training Observations

During the training he was interviewed several times. He spoke favorably about the program. He enjoyed learning to run better "beads" and to write his name with the welding equipment. Working with others was a new experience. He liked it. In addition, he found the programmed instruction exciting because he was able to detect when he was improving.

Ed was planning to become an electric welder. He anticipated earnings of $2.00 per hour. His immediate goal was to move to a larger city where he could work and at the same time continue to learn more about welding. Ed made considerable progress in the welding class. His teacher considered him one of the most skilled and dependable trainees.

His academic teacher observed him to be a good worker but not consistently so. He would begin his assignments immediately most of the time. He would always follow directions, but did not always review his work, budget his time, or select additional assignments. For the most part, he took his work seriously. He was never absent without a good reason.

Post-training Tests

At the end of the training, retests of intelligence revealed a slight improvement. On the Wechsler his Verbal Scale IQ was 101; his Performance Scale, 96; and his Full Scale, 99. The most sizable improvement in achievement was in arithmetic. He improved four grades in sixteen weeks. This was primarily due to his working more rapidly. His arithmetic score was grade eleven. Improvement in reading comprehension was noted, but spelling ability did not change at all. Few personality changes were observed. Mental efficiency was reduced by his poor emotional control.

Follow-up

At the time of the follow-up interview, Ed stated he could not get a job because he was too young. He had made no applications. After his eighteenth birthday, he added, he would look. Welding was what he wanted to do. But he was convinced he was a good learner and wanted to further his education. This was demonstrated by his willingness to take additional courses in electronics without training allowances. If he could earn a high school diploma through Operation Second Chance or the U. S. Army courses, he would. In retrospect, he felt the program helped him to learn to work with others. Learning the rules of the "bossman" was very helpful.

In conclusion, Ed is a skilled welder who made considerable progress throughout his training, but who perceived himself as too young to get a job. Ed was unemployed for eight months. He finally got a job painting steeples, earning $70 per week.

KEY FEATURES OF THE CASE. Made considerable progress in training program. Judged a skilled welder. Motivated to learn. Unemployed because of age.

Deke

Deke is a 17-year-old boy enrolled in the upholstery class. Prior to entry in OSC, he had never been gainfully employed. His father, who earns $65 per week, is currently employed as a maintenance man in a thread factory. He had worked in a mica mine until government subsidization of mica mining was terminated.

In his first three years in school, Deke earned B's in arithmetic and in language. His average marks in language in grades four through six was C; his marks in arithmetic remained at B. Junior high school averages in these and most other subjects were C. In the first three grades, teachers rated him about average in cooperation, in courtesy, in maturity and in self control. Thereafter, he was rated "average" in these traits. Beginning in grade six and continuing through grade nine, "below average" ratings were given him for dependability, industriousness, and initiative. The only teacher comment on the record appeared in grade nine. The teacher wrote "slow and lazy." Deke first thought about dropping out in grade six. He found junior high school enjoyable so he did not again consider quitting until he was in the tenth grade. It may be of only parenthetical interest but the enjoyable years in junior high school were the years in which he received his lowest marks and ratings of personal qualities. In tenth grade, he said, "the teacher rode me." His parents and friends urged him to stay in school. By the Christmas vacation he decided he had enough of teachers and principals and never returned to school.

Pretraining Tests

Upon entering the program, he was given several intelligence tests. His overall ability was classified "dull normal." His IQ was 83. He was reading at the grade 5.7 level; his arithmetic achievement, grade 3.9; and his spelling, grade 5.1. The results of the personality tests suggested that he had very low ability to generalize. Rather he seemed to approach life fragment by fragment. Inductive and deductive reasoning were both low. He had narrow interests. Nor was he in tune with everyday happenings. With respect to his temperament, he was tactful, confident and cooperative, but not concerned with his social responsibilities. He was observed to be moody and not too ambitious.

Training Observations

The vocational program had great appeal for him. He learned how to "spring" frames. When his task was completed, he was proud of the chair he had assembled. Occasionally, it would "aggravate" him to start a chair and then someone else come along to finish it. Benefits from the academic program were sizable. He noticed especially that his reading had improved.

From the very beginning of his training he planned to become an upholsterer. He expected to get a job in an upholstery factory and earn $65 per week. Although he would prefer not to leave home, he said he would move if he had to. His long-range plan was to be an upholsterer and to be working in one of the upholstery manufacturing centers in North Carolina. What attracted him most about a job was the opportunity to become someone. It was important to him to have "skill to do something." He was determined to be an upholsterer. If a job were not available, he said he would look until there was an opening.

The academic teacher thought Deke to be a good student, one who was serious and interested. She said he began his assignments promptly, recorded his answers neatly, followed directions, and tried to exceed his earlier accomplishments. In addition, she found him quick and alert. Deke, she concluded, "enjoyed working in all subjects and eagerly."

His vocational instructor gave him the highest ratings in knowledge about upholstery. Deke, he said, "could be expected to work quickly and independently."

Post-training Tests

At the conclusion of the course, intelligence tests were readministered to him. A loss of twelve points was observed in the Wechsler Performance Scale IQ. The Full Scale IQ decline was five points to seventy-eight. The greatest change was not in reading, but in arithmetic. He improved 1.5 grades in the four months of training. Spelling, moreover, improved 1.3 grades. Slight changes were noted on the personality test. Although his range of interests increased slightly, he was still quite perfectionistic. In addition, he had less control of his impulses.

Follow-up

Four weeks later, he was found to be unemployed. He had sought advice from the Employment Security Commission. Otherwise, he did nothing else to look for a job. He had mixed feelings about going to work. He wanted to return to high school to earn a high school diploma, but he also wanted to receive further subsidized training. In retrospect, he felt the program helped him learn how to work with others.

Fifteen months after graduation he got steady work as a mason's helper. His father explained that Deke did not talk much about his job except that he was "pushing a wheelbarrow of wet cement."

In conclusion, Deke wants very much to be a skilled upholsterer. He made considerable progress in the academic program. His personality profile reveals him to be unambitious and lacking in good emotional control.

KEY FEATURES OF THE CASE. Works hard. Young. Made progress in academic courses. Is in conflict about working. Wants to return to school.

Georgia

Georgia is a 20-year-old girl who entered the nurses' aide program. She had never held a job. Neither parent was employed. The family was subsisting on her father's pension. He had been a mechanic with the highway department.

In grades one through six, Georgia had received A's in language and B's in arithmetic. Thereafter her marks steadily declined. In grades nine through twelve, her marks averaged D. Several failures were recorded. Ratings of social and personal assets were generally average or above. In her senior year in high school, however, she was rated below average in industriousness, initiative, and leadership. Her fifth grade teacher noted that she tried hard to be popular with the other students. In twelfth grade, her teacher noted that she lost interest in school work. Her record states, moreover, that she got married during her senior year. Despite failing marks and waning interest, she graduated from high school.

Pretraining Tests

Upon entering the program, the battery of tests was administered to her. Her Full Scale IQ on the Wechsler was 82, placing her in a dull normal category. On the Benton, her IQ's were in the average and low average categories. Her achievement in reading was on the grade 9.8 level; in arithmetic, grade 5.2 level; and in spelling, grade 8.2 level. The results of the personality tests revealed her to be unable to visualize the whole picture. She was perfectionistic. Inductive and deductive reasoning received low ratings as did her interest in and empathy for people. She did not seem to be ambitious or persistent. Below average ratings were recorded for both social responsibility and conformity. Mental awareness and concentration ratings on the other hand were quite high.

Training Observations

From interviewing her, it was learned that she liked training as a nurses' aide very much, but she did not think very much of the academic program. Her parents approved of the vocational program because now Georgia "could always get a job." The academic program, on the other hand, was never discussed at home.

She planned to enter a hospital where she could work as a nurses' aide. She expected to be paid $24 per week. This, incidentally, was the same amount as her training allowance. If she could not get such a job, she would consider moving to Greenville, South Carolina. Her long range plans called for her moving out of the mountains. She was not sure, though, if she would be working in a factory or in a hospital. On one occasion she said that when she gets enough money saved she would get some training as a practical nurse.

Her academic teacher found her to be an inconsistent student. Georgia worked for short periods and then gossiped. She distracted others, came to class late, budgeted her time unwisely, and was often bored. She did neat work when she put her mind to it.

Her vocational instructor rated her fair in both responding to a patient's bedpan signal and in giving him extra nourishment. She was rated poor in perineal care. All other ratings were "fairly good." These included discharging patients, emptying bedpans, giving fresh water, and feeding patients, taking pulse, sterilizing water, and picking up forceps. Georgia received no ratings of "good," the highest possible one.

Post-training Tests

At the end of the course, she was retested. Gains of ten points in Wechsler Verbal and Full Scale IQ were observed. In addition, IQ ratings on the Benton were "superior" and "high average." No change was observed in reading or in arithmetic. A gain of .9 of a year in spelling placed her in the grade 9.1 level. Changes on the personality test were slight. After training, her interest in people ratings increased as did her ratings on social responsibility, flexibility, and ambition. She was observed, however, to be less tactful. Despite less than favorable teacher evaluations, Georgia had benefitted from the training program.

Follow-up

During the follow-up interview, she said she was unemployed but would take any kind of work. She had been looking for a job on her own since the end of training. She wanted to do something useful. Just sitting around was deplorable. There was a note of indecision in her long-term planning. While she did not want to leave the area, she wanted to move to Greenville, South Carolina. In addition, she was not sure if she would be working in a factory or as a nurses' aide. Had she the opportunity to become a beautician, moreover, she said she would go to school for forty weeks without training allowances.

In conclusion, Georgia was stimulated by the vocational program but responded unfavorably to the academic. She felt she could cope with most tasks expected of a nurses' aide. Yet she was not sure that she was truly suited to hospital work. Ten months after graduation she got a job as a waitress in a resturant, earning $18 a per week plus tips.

KEY FEATURES OF THE CASE. Poor work habits in academic course. Fairly good ratings in vocational program. Increase in intelligence quotients. Low generalization ability. Perfectionism. Increased awareness of her responsibility to people. Inconsistency.

Cindy

Cindy is a 19-year-old girl registered in the upholstery class. She had never been gainfully employed. Her father bagged mica for a living.

Reviewing her school records, it was observed that she received B's in language and arithmetic during her first six years in school. In junior high school, her language average was D and her arithmetic average C. Thereafter, there was a continual decline in school performance. In tenth grade she received four D's and an F. Through grade eight, teachers evaluated her average and above in dependability, maturity, and personal appearance. In grade nine, her teacher wrote "not a very smart student, but tries hard to make good grades." The steady decline in achievement was not discussed in her record. It is worthy of note that ratings of personal and social assets remained average while she was failing scholastically. In grade ten, Cindy left school, but then returned. She began the eleventh grade and quit after two days. She gave two reasons for leaving: dissatisfaction with her schedule and her mother's illness. Had she received the right schedule, she added, she would have returned.

Pretraining Tests

Intelligence tests were administered to her prior to entry into the training program. Her scores on the Wechsler were in the dull average range, namely between eighty-two and eighty-four. Her scores on the achievement tests were as follows: reading grade 7.1, arithmetic grade 4.5 and spelling grade 6.2. The arithmetic score was lowered by her not paying attention to the sign. Results of the personality tests revealed her to be very low in generalization ability but very high in perfectionism. Range of interests, especially interest in people were low. She was also rated low in persistence, in confidence and in drive.

Training Observations

Cindy was interviewed several times during the program. She was very excited about the upholstery class. Despite a lack of sufficient equipment, she utilized what was available. Throughout the several interviews, she spoke positively about upholstery, yet she had no plans to become an upholsterer. After training was completed she said she was planning to look for a job "in an overall or shirt factory close to home." She was sure a neighbor could get her a job. Getting along with other people had been a problem for her. As a result of the training program, she thought she would have no difficulty getting along with coworkers.

Her academic teacher rated her work habits very high. Cindy began assignments promptly, selected additional assignments during free period, recorded answers neatly, followed directions, exceeded previous achievements, and reviewed her work. The teacher summed her up as "quiet and studious, but has a definite enthusiasm. She works full time and enjoys selecting extra subjects when she finishes one. She takes pride in her work."

The vocational instructor rated her as one of the best sewers in the class. Good eye-hand coordination combined with knowledge of when to tuck set her apart from the other trainees. Despite being *registered in an upholstery class,* Cindy did not at any time learn how to upholster.

Post-training Tests

On the retest of intelligence, Cindy was found to improve six points in Verbal and Full Scale IQ's. Her Wechsler Full Scale IQ was 88. Benton IQ's were also in the low normal range. Her reading was on the grade 8.3, a gain of 1.2 grades; her spelling, 6.4; a gain of .2 grades; and her arithmetic, 6.2, a gain of 1.7 grades. Retest on the personality tests show significant changes in some attributes. There was improvement in generalization ability, inductive reasoning, confidence, social responsibility, and ambition.

Follow-up

On the follow-up interview, Cindy stated that she had been looking for work, but she would not consider any job requiring her to leave her home in the mountains. Transportation was difficult to arrange. Her long-range plans called for her remaining in her home town. She acknowledged the fact that there were very few openings close to home. To her, being near home was more important than working.

In conclusion, Cindy made considerable progress during the training program. She was rated very highly by both academic and vocational teachers. Yet she is insecure about her abilities. She was reluctant to leave home. Ten months after graduation she was contacted by the OSC staff. She was still unemployed. She had tried to get a job in the textile industry but her applications were never favorably reviewed. In retrospect, she felt the OSC program did her no good. Yet she was glad she took it. Had she the opportunity she would take more. She felt that the OSC program built up false hopes for employment. "They promised," she said, "to get you a job." Two months later she got a job turning collars in a shirt factory. She proudly stated that she is working steadily. Her wages were $1.25 per hour. This she viewed as a reward for her diligence. She had started at $1.10 per hour.

KEY FEATURES OF THE CASE. Modest ability; a conscientious, skilled sewer; sincere interest in learning; high motivation to work; high motivation to remain at home.

SUMMARY

Vignettes of ten unemployed dropouts demonstrate unequivocally what vast differences there were between them. Not only do they have no common public school history, but withdrawal from school was for vastly different reasons. Progress in the Operation Second Chance program varied, too. Some of the unemployed were poor risks as trainees because their mental abilities were inadequate for the tasks they had to perform. Most, however, were generally highly rated as skilled workers by their vocational teachers. In addition, their vocational teachers evaluated their work habits and attitudes quite favorably. The improvement in intelligence quotients and in basic literacy and numerical skills were of such magnitude that they could not be considered due to chance. Rather there is strong evidence that the trainees studied were highly motivated to succeed. So much was this in evidence that they were willing to forego training allowances to receive forty additional weeks of further instruction. Since most students lived in abject poverty, placing the training above the allowances is a dramatic demonstration of their sincerity.

No simple single thread runs through any of these cases. There are, to be sure, certain personality attributes which the several unemployed trainees had in common. Those were low generalization ability, high perfectionism, and low persistence. They did differ in all other personality attributes. In addition, they differed with respect to all the other measures, that is, intelligence and scholastic achievement.

The diversity among the unemployed dropouts, their abilities, their achievements, their personalities, their employment histories, and their progress in the rehabilitation program make it difficult to give any single explanation for their not working. Recasting all observation in terms of the *attractability* of an employee and the *attractability* of an employer, it might then become possible to understand the employment status of the trainees discussed thus far.

The cases presented suggest certain features which make a job applicant unattractive. In the first place, he must meet the minimum age requirements of those generally accepted for employment. It is not only impractical but it is also inhumane to train youth for jobs which they will not be able to hold for at least a year. The program builds up the hopes in the trainee that he will achieve a good name by going to work. The constant failure in securing a position for which he was trained and in which he invested so much energy merely chips away at an already fragile self esteem. Next, the race of the applicant was observed to be related to attractability of an applicant. In all fairness to the readers, there were qualified Negroes who did get jobs in the trades for which they were trained. Those cases discussed here were selected at random and irrespective of race. Employment traditions in some trades have systematically discriminated against the Negro. The loss of talent to the economy and the degradation experiences is in violation of the basic tenets of our democracy.

Next, mental achievements and ability to cope with the tasks to be performed is linked to employment potential. Finally, willingness to work is a trait which the employer is certain to investigate.

The question of how to organize a training program so as to maximize employment and minimize failure may be answered in part. Assigning trainees to programs which will make him most attractive to future employers calls for more incisive scrutiny of the age requirements for placement, the mental achievements for the skillful carrying out of the tasks on the job, and the work habits expected of a candidate. With respect to racial discrimination in employment, there is little that a training program can do directly to improve this situation. Representatives of the several agencies concerning itself with labor and commerce have a mandate to open all sectors of the labor market to all skilled and willing workers. To change in the employer the racial criterion in judging applicants is a necessary step in establishing equitable employment practices. Such practices are consonant with an ever-changing democratic America which relies on the maximum use of the talents of all of its citizens.

The employer, however, must be attractive to the applicant. In the majority of the cases presented, the attractability of an employer hinged on his geographical distance from the applicants home town. Most of the graduates did not want to leave home. A second factor, in determining the attractability of an employer, is the fairness of the "boss man." Comments about the partiality shown by a supervisor were observed in some of the follow-up interviews. A third factor was how the applicant could learn to feel important in a job. A final factor was salary.

Many of these OSC graduates unemployed at the four week follow-up interview remained jobless for more than a year. All graduates had at least one job within the eighteen month period in which the writer remained in contact with them. Not one of these graduates worked at training related jobs. Several boys delivered beverages for a soft drink company, one welding graduate was painting steeples, an upholstery graduate was working as a construction laborer and one girl was working as a waitress.

In understanding the employment history of the dropouts discussed thus far, their attractability to an employer and the employer's attractability to them must be known. Unattractive employees were young, Negro, unskilled, and undependable. Unattractive employers were physically distant from the applicant's home town, were perceived by the trainees as not being fair to all employees, provided no outlet for an applicant to feel important, and paid him low wages. What is seen here is that the unemployed trainee who made no attempt to secure employment had premonitions that employers would not hire them. Therefore they did not look for a job.

If students are unwilling to move out of an area, then the training program must equip them with those skills necessary for immediately successful employment. On the other hand, if there will be no job opportunities in the local labor market, guidance must be given the students in selecting and migrating to more promising geographical locations.

This guidance, it is clear, should not be limited to occupational information. It is also quite clear that this group of trainees were afraid of worker-supervisor relationships. Work itself was not feared. What they were apprehensive about was their acceptability to their employer. It is toward mitigating the feelings of personal inadequacy in the trainees that guidance and counselling procedures should be dedicated.

EMPLOYED: TRAINING UNRELATED

Jay

Jay is an 18-year-old boy who entered the welding class. For two years prior to training he had been employed at a nursery. His father is a retired fish warden. The family lives on social security. In the summer Jay's father supplements his income by looking after a neighbor's yard.

In his first five years in public school, Jay received C's in language and in arithmetic. The last year for which there were any marks was grade five. In that year, he earned eleven D's and one A. The A was in citizenship. Teacher ratings of social and personal assets was below average and low from the very beginning of his school career. He consistently received low ratings in cooperation, personal appearance and in self control. His first grade teacher wrote "too old for grade . . . parents failure to cooperate."

A second grade teacher wrote, "Is capable of fair work if he would attend regularly." Another teacher wrote, "Shy . . . quiet . . . will not participate in class activities." His last teacher wrote, "He needs to be in special class." Jay withdrew from school at age fifteen. He stayed away from school. No one tried to get him to return. Jay told the Operation Second Chance interviewer that he could not learn anything and did not get along with the teachers.

Pretraining Scores

Upon entry into the program, several intelligence tests were administered. All scores placed him in the educable mental retardation category. His reading test score was grade 1.7; his spelling grade 1.9; his arithmetic grade 4.0. Results of the personality tests suggest that Jay's inadequate emotional control might interfere with his mental functioning. In addition, it was noted that he lacked persistence. He was also rated low in conformity. For all the other personality attributes he resembled the average adult. Some of these attributes were interests, social responsibility, tact, confidence, and cooperation.

Training Observations

During the first interview he expressed the belief that he could learn welding but that he could not read the manuals. In subsequent interviews, he was still uncertain of his capability as a welder, but he was sure "he was catching on." By the second interview he had made so much progress that he expressed pride in his learning how to spell, how to read, and how to add and subtract.

Jay hoped he could become better educated but he did not specify how he would accomplish it. He wanted to remain near his home and get a job as a welder. How much income he might expect never crossed his mind. He was formulating his goals, moreover. He asserted, "the day is going to come when a man can't get a job without a trade and some education." His main attraction to a job was that he "could become someone." Jay's long-range plans call for him staying at home and working as a welder. He expects to work hard and not fool around.

The academic teacher noted that Jay began his assignments promptly and recorded answers neatly. Toward the end of training, he had improved in "following directions." The impression he left with her was of a slow, quiet worker. He never embarked on any assignment with enthusiasm. Also noted was that he did not associate with any of the other students. Failure, he feels, is always before him. When he first came to the training program, he hid behind a tree. An instructor had to bring him to class.

The vocational instructor noted that for the few days after each new lesson, Jay would be absent from school. A representative of the program went to his home and encouraged him to return. His ratings as a welder, however, were among the highest. The instructor anticipated Jay would succeed at any welding job.

Post-training Tests

At the end of the program, retests were administered to him. He had lost ten points in Verbal Scale IQ, three points in Performance Scale IQ, and nine points in Full Scale IQ on the Wechsler. Jay's IQ's on the Benton were in agreement with the educable mental retardation classification already ascertained. He made his greatest gain in the academic program. He improved .6 of a year in reading, one year in arithmetic, and a year and a half in spelling. He was observed to manifest poor motor coordination on the Wechsler. Reluctant to attempt tasks which he doubted he could succeed in, he often refused to try the task. The changes noted on the Rorschach were in the direction of greater maladjustment. On the retest, he received very low ratings on generalization ability. He was perfectionistic to the point that it would interfere with his mental functioning. While he did become more aware of his environment, he was not at all in tune with people. Ratings on persistence and aggression increased. Several interferences with mental functioning were observed. These were: low generalization ability, perfectionism, compulsivity, and poor emotional control.

Follow-up

One month after completing the program, Jay was interviewed again. He was employed at his old job digging shrubbery at a nursery. He was earning $1.00 per hour. Although he liked welding better, he did not know who to contact for a job as a welder. His primary attraction to work is that it is "interesting." He did not elaborate upon what interested him. He feels he can do a good job digging white pine. He knows this work well and succeeds easily. He does not like burlaping the plants, though. He finds it too monotonous. His long range plans still call for his becoming a welder. He would be willing to move if he were sure he could be a success.

In retrospect, he felt the program helped him learn to read and to spell. He asserted that the program did not help him get a job. He did not have a feeling of success because he was trained as a welder and was not employed as one. Yet he is reasonably certain he could hold a job as a welder. Motivation for training was seen to change also. He concluded that if more welding instruction were given, he would take it without receiving training allowances.

In conclusion, Jay is a mentally retarded boy who made great strides in both the academic and vocational classes. He did not know to whom to turn to get a job as a welder so he returned to the tranquility of his former job. His reticence and low self esteem make him hesitate to ask anyone for a job. One year after graduation he was still working at the nursery.

KEY FEATURES OF THE CASE. Reticence, fear of people, fear of anything new. Improvement in reading and arithmetic. Non-training-related employment.

Al

Al is a 17-year-old boy who entered the welding class. He had never been gainfully employed, but at the first interview he expressed the hope to become a truck driver. His father, a farmer and miner, had been killed in a mine accident. The family subsists on social security and allotment checks received from Al's brother who is in the U. S. Navy.

In his first three years in school, Al received B's in language, in his next three years, he received C's, thereafter he received D's. In arithmetic, on the other hand, he received B's in the first three years but thereafter received D's. At first, his teachers found him to be average in self control, dependability, and industriousness.

In grade six, they began to rate him below average in dependability, industriousness, and initiative. His teachers commented that Al was slow in his work and timid. His fourth grade teacher wrote, "Al made a noise with a toy one day and we all felt like applauding because he is usually so quiet." He first began thinking about dropping out in grade eight. The change from elementary to high school was too much for him. There were too many people there and the books were harder. He had been in ninth grade about three weeks when he withdrew. No one tried to persuade him to stay.

Pretraining Tests

Several intelligence tests were administered to him prior to entry into the welding class. All scores place him in the educable mentally retarded classification. His reading and arithmetic achievements were at the grade 4.9 level; and his spelling was at the grade 4.4 level. The personality test scores indicated the following: perfectionism, lack of awareness of the environment, restricted range of interests, lack of empathy, lack of persistence, lack of tact, lack of confidence, lack of conformity. Signs of ambition, flexibility, and cooperation were also noted.

Training Observations

Interviews with Al revealed that he had accepted the training program. He was telling his friends what he had learned about welding. In addition, he stated boldly that he wanted to become a welder in his home town.

His academic teacher observed him to have good work habits. He began his assignments promptly, recorded his answers neatly, followed directions, did not budget his time, and showed signs of boredom. She found him to be "quiet and neat." She added, "does not seem very interested but has progressed." He did not give the teacher any sign that he was enthusiastic or displeased with his progress. This indifference was of great concern to the teacher. She wanted very much to get through to Al, but he gave her no response. He would do what was required, no more, no less. The vocational teacher observed him to be a good welder, one who could be trusted with any job given him.

Post-training Tests

At the close of the program, readministration of the Wechsler intelligence test revealed an overall loss of ten points, hence reaffirming the educable mental retardation diagnosis. Scores on the Benton, however, indicated that he was functioning on the low average level of intelligence. This test requires no verbalization by the testee; whereas the Wechsler does. Al avoids talking as much as possible. He prefers quiet. Scholastic improvement was considerable. In reading, he improved 1.5 grades and was now reading on the grade 6.4 level; in arithmetic, he improved 1.7 grades and was now at the grade 6.6 level; and in spelling, he improved one grade and was now at the 5.4 level. Some changes on the personality test were noted. He became less perfectionistic, more interested in people, more cooperative, less anxious, and more conforming. He still was rated low in tact, persistence and self confidence. The greatest impact of the program was on Al's social behavior. The boys in the program took him under their wing. He felt very comfortable with them. When a teacher or interviewer tried to talk with him, though, he became frightened.

Follow-up

One month later he was interviewed again. At the time he was picking apples in a local orchard. Local employers, he asserted, would not consider him for welding jobs because he was too young. When asked to whom he applied, he answered he had not applied anywhere. Nor had he checked at the Employment Security Office to determine if there were openings in his specialty. Yet he did not hesitate to criticize the program for not getting him a job as a welder.

In conclusion, Al is a very shy youngster. He is unsure of his abilities, but hopes to become a welder.

He had taken no steps, however, to apply for a welding job. He made some scholastic and social gains during the program although his IQ declined. One might speculate whether the oral test used to measure his intelligence may have suppressed the true IQ. Al rarely talks. It appeared that he feared opening his mouth lest some danger befall him. With regard to employment, Al took the first job that came along. In his estimation, however, the program did him no good because he did not become employed as a welder. He could not understand that he was to show some initiative in looking for a job. One further contact was made eighteen months after graduation. He was not working at the time. Previous to this he was working but a day or two each week and then only to earn enough money for dating.

KEY FEATURES OF THE CASE. Reticence, low self confidence, low persistence. Flat affect, sizable increases in basic literary and number skills. Decline in intelligence. No verbalized vocational plans. Employed as an apple picker.

Mary

Mary is an 18-year-old who aspired to be a beautician. As there was no available ARA class, she was placed in the nurses' aide program. There was no record of her ever being gainfully employed. Both of her parents work in textile factories. Their combined income was $600 per month.

Her school records reveal that in grades one through six her average marks were B in reading and in arithmetic. In grades seven through nine, her averages in both subjects were A. A dramatic shift in her marks was noted in grade ten. She received all F's. Upon repeating grade ten, she received B's and C's. She received average ratings and above for cooperation, dependability and self-control. Her teachers found her to be a good student but absent too much. Her last teacher wrote "too good to lose to the dropout world. An excellent student who just couldn't get up in time to get to school regularly—finally gave it up and quit." Upon further investigation by the writer this was found to be an accurate observation. What was not known by the teachers was that Mary was responsible for cleaning house, preparing breakfast and dinner, and cleaning up after dinner. She could not keep up with her assignments because she had no time. Mary's version of her withdrawal was, moreover, different. She said she did not get along with her geography teacher. When she received failing grades in geography, she withdrew. Her parents did not interfere, nor did any representative of the school talk to her about returning.

Pretraining Tests

At the beginning of the program, intelligence test scores on the Wechsler were: Verbal Scale, 118, Performance Scale, 96, Full Scale, 109. On the achievement tests she scores grade 12.4 in reading; 11.2 in arithmetic and grade 11.3 in spelling. The results of the personality tests indicated that Mary was perfectionistic, lacking in persistence, but highly motivated. In addition, she had a wide range of interests and was facile in inductive reasoning.

Training Observations

Interviews with Mary during the training revealed that she was sincerely enthusiastic about becoming a nurses' aide. She felt it was helping her develop her personality. Hospital work thrilled her. Exciting her almost as much was the academic program. She felt she needed the training because she was getting "rusty."

When she completed training, she planned to become a nurses' aide. She expected to earn $120 a month and to live at home. She wanted to work in order to be useful. Her explanation for this was that she "wanted somebody to need me. I feel like a nobody sitting around doing nothing." She feared, however, that she would not be good enough for the job. Her long-range plans called for her working in the hospital in town. She felt the Operation Second Chance program did much for her. Her personality developed, she became a happier person, and she was easier to get along with.

During her free periods Mary began her assignments. Her academic teacher found her to have good work habits, follow directions, and try to exceed previous accomplishments. "She has a good mind," the teacher concluded, "and has been serious about her work. She has a good attitude."

Her vocational teacher considered her the most competent trainee in the class. The director of the hospital placed Mary immediately upon completion of the training. He assigned her to the laboratory technician staff, however, Mary did not work as a nurses' aide.

Post-training Tests

At the conclusion of the program, retests were administered. On the Wechsler, her Verbal Scale IQ became 117, her Performance Scale IQ became 123, an increase of twenty-seven points, and her Full Scale IQ became 125, an increase of twenty-one points. On the achievement tests, gains were noted, too. She increased 1.8 grades in reading and 1.1 grades in both arithmetic and spelling. Her final achievements were grades 14.2, 12.3, and 12.4 in reading, arithmetic and spelling, respectively. Changes on the personality test were toward greater maladjustment, however. There were losses in inductive and deductive reasoning. Interests became narrow. Lower ratings were received for social responsibility, tact, confidence, drive and flexibility.

Follow-up

The follow-up interview was suffused with excitement. Mary was bubbling over with joy. She said on the day she graduated, she was offered a job as a laboratory technician. The hospital provided her with training in laboratory technique and in x-ray methods. In addition to certain fringe benefits, the hospital paid her $25 per week. Mary was satisfied with this arrangement even though she earned but one dollar more per week than she had received during training. One of the reasons she enjoyed work so much was that she had never done anything useful before. She felt she was helping others by testing them so the doctors could prescribe treatment. Also she was amazed to discover things she had never known before.

Her long range plans called for her remaining in her home town and working as a laboratory technician. She did not want to leave home. In addition she wanted to advance in her chosen field, but regretted that she could not without a high school diploma.

In retrospect, she felt the program helped her in understanding sick people. She learned how to become more patient and enduring. If she could receive more training, she said she would like to take additional training for forty weeks without training allowances. She added that she would pay her own way.

In conclusion, Mary is a bright girl who made great progress in the nurses' aide and academic programs. She was placed immediately as a laboratory technician. She lacked persistence, was perfectionistic, and was unsure of herself. Two weeks later Mary became dissatisfied with the quality of her work, and resigned. She took a high school equivalency exam and passed it. Later she took a job in a nearby town as a nurses' aide. She wrote that she feels better about herself. It was difficult to reestablish contact with Mary. No one had heard from her. She had no telephone. Several letters were written; she replied to none. Five months after the last resignation she phoned one of the writers. She had been out of work and, furthermore, was afraid to look for a job. At the last hospital she worked she was given assignments in obstetrics. Never having been trained to assist delivery of babies, she was afraid she would make a mistake. Feelings of personal inadequacy welled up within her. She could not sleep at night. Her dreams terrorized her. Agitated and weary worn, she quit. Once again she knew she was a complete failure. For the next six months she was jobless. She refused to leave her home. Her parents did not know what to do for her. She spent her time reading and wallowing in self pity. She had occasion to be hospitalized for appendicitis. After she saw how understaffed the hospital was, she applied for work.

Key features of the case. High intelligence. Enthusiasm. Progress in course. Lacking in persistence. Low self esteem. Employment in training-unrelated field.

Len

Len is a 17-year-old boy who has never been gainfully employed. His father, deceased for many years, had worked in a saw mill and farmed his own land. The family is on relief.

An examination of school records reveals that Len was a capable student through grade seven. For years his marks in language averaged A and in arithmetic, B. In grade eight, his marks in these subjects declined to C+. In grade nine he failed all the subjects he took. For the first six years his teachers rated his social and personal assets "above average" and "superior." In grade eight, he received ratings of "low" in industriousness, initiative, leadership, maturity, and personal appearance. Through grade seven his teachers consistently remarked, "is a good student —very capable." In grade nine, Len started to stay out of school. He gave as his reason for staying out of school, "I didn't like to go to school with colored boys." "After I got into a fight with a colored boy," he concluded, "the principal said he would expel me or give me a whipping—so I left."

Pretraining Tests

Upon entering the program, the Wechsler Verbal Scale IQ was measured to be 113, the Performance Scale IQ, 89, and the Full Scale IQ, 109. This places him in the high average IQ category. His IQ classifications on the Benton were "superior" and "average." On the achievement tests, his reading grade was found to be 7.7, his arithmetic grade, 7.8, and his spelling grade, 7.8. Personality test data revealed average mental functioning scores. He received low ratings in mental awareness and concentration. He was found to be impulsive as well as nonconforming. All other traits of temperament were rated "average." His mental efficiency was reduced by poor emotional control.

Training Observations

Interviews with Len revealed that he liked the program and that he was receiving adequate training in order to obtain a job. He felt he learned a trade. Also viewed favorably by him was the academic program. He felt the arithmetic helped him most in his trade.

He hoped to become a welder. His cousin in Newsport News could help him get a job as a welder in the shipyards. Anticipated earnings were $2.50 an hour. His long-range plans called for his working as a welder. At the last interview, he said, moreover, he was leaving for Virginia in two weeks. High salaries drew him to this area.

His academic teacher found him to be quite inconsistent. Some weeks he would begin assignments promptly, other weeks he did not. The same was noted for selecting additional assignments during free periods, following directions, and exceeding previous accomplishments. "Len," his teacher wrote, "has periods of real concentration and study and again periods of disinterest, but I believe his home life is upset and he has no roots. . . . He is a good boy but he needs guidance and someone to encourage him."

The vocational teacher judged him to be a highly skilled welder. Occasionally, he needed supervision. Most of the time, however, he would work conscientiously.

Post-training Tests

At the conclusion of the program, Len was retested. A decline of seventeen points in Verbal Scale IQ, an increase of nine points in Performance Scale IQ, and a decline of thirteen points in Full Scale IQ were noted. His IQ was now 96 and in agreement with the IQ classification of "low average" on the Benton. There were, however, gains in scholastic achievement. His reading vocabulary improved 2.8 grades to grade 10.5 on one test, but declined 1.5 grades on another reading test; his arithmetic achievement was now at grade 8.6, a gain of .8 of a grade; and his achievement in spelling declined .3 of a grade to 7.5. Personality changes were slight. He was observed to receive higher ratings in persistence, cooperation, concentration, and mental awareness.

Follow-up

One month after the completion of the program, he was interviewed again. He was now picking apples. He was earning $1.00 an hour. He had looked for a welding job in two different towns, but he was told they were not hiring welders. He still maintained that he would like to become a welder. In retrospect, he felt that the program helped him become successful. It especially made him aware that a job is important.

In conclusion, Len was a skilled welder who made uneven progress in the training program. He had planned to move to another area to get a job but he did not follow through with it. One year after graduation he was working part time only. Some weeks he worked two days; others, none. He explained, "I'm not really interested in finding a steady job now 'cause the army's gonna get me soon anyway, I guess." Upon further inquiry, it was learned that he had not registered for the draft.

KEY FEATURES OF THE CASE. Personality inconsistency. Scholastic gains, intelligence test score losses. Training-unrelated employment.

Emmet

Emmet is an 18-year-old boy who was registered in the welding program. He had been employed as a farm hand prior to entry in the program. The family lives on the $40 per month Social Security allowance, the father being deceased.

In grades one through three, Emmet's marks in language were B and in arithmetic they were C. In grades four through six, an improvement was noted. His average language mark was A, his average arithmetic mark B. In grades seven through nine, his marks declined to C. In his last year in school all of his marks were F. The teachers' ratings of his personal and social assets were "average" through grade six, thereafter, he was given below average ratings in cooperation, courtesy, dependability, industriousness, and initiative. His last teacher wrote "he is a good student but will not apply himself." Emmet left school in grade nine, when he began to "mess around with the fellers." He started again one year later, completed the ninth grade, but went no further because he was so far behind. His father opposed Emmet's decision to quit school. It was at the time that Emmet was considering leaving for the last time that his father died. Now he felt he had a good reason to leave, namely to help support his family. He did not, however, go to work.

Pretraining Tests

Intelligence tests were administered at the beginning of the training program. On the Wechsler, his Verbal Scale IQ was 96, Performance Scale IQ 89, and Full Scale IQ 93. Scholastic achievement was as follows: reading—grade 9.2; spelling—grade 6.5; and arithmetic—grade 4.8. Personality ratings obtained on the Rorschach were low for generalization ability, for interest in people, for social responsibility, for drive, for flexibility, and for conformity.

Training Observations

Interviews with Emmet indicated that he was enjoying the welding course. He said, "I believe I could work right smart on heavy steel." He planned to move to Cleveland to get a welding job in a fuse box factory. While he was enthusiastic about the welding program, he disliked the academic part of the program.

His academic teacher found him to be inconsistent in his habits. Although he followed directions carefully and continued to work after class, he would also distract others. His teacher noted, "He is intelligent and can do excellent work, tries harder at times than others, but likes to talk (i.e., disturb)."

His vocational teacher found him to be a skilled worker, but he felt that Emmet needed considerable supervision. Left alone, Emmet would interfere with his co-workers by telling jokes.

Post-training Tests

Retests at the end of training revealed on the Wechsler that though Emmet lost six IQ points on the Verbal Scale, he gained twelve IQ points on the Performance Scale. This resulted in an overall gain of three points on the Full Scale IQ. Slight changes in academic achievement were noted. His reading score went down .4 of a grade, but his arithmetic score rose .8 of a grade to 5.6, and his spelling score rose .6 to 7.1. Changes in personality ratings were generally in the direction of greater maladjustment. He received lower ratings in mental awareness, concentration, interest in people, persistence, and behavioral consistency, but higher ratings in anxiety, moodiness, and impulsiveness. Two positive signs were noted on the retest, moreover. These were improved ratings in generalization ability and in tendency to conform.

Follow-up

Four weeks after Emmet graduated, he was interviewed again. He had been picking apples at $1.00 per hour. He had not as yet looked for a job as a welder, nor did he go through with his plan to move to Cleveland. He still wanted to be a welder, but he is also interested in auto mechanics. In retrospect, he said, "The program is a pretty good deal. Anybody that went through that will be more able to get a job. People will know that you know how to weld, that you have some experience."

In conclusion, Emmet was a capable welder and a good student in the academic class. He was not a consistent or independent worker. He made progress in arithmetic. He improved in manipulative skills. Although he had planned to look for a welding job, he did not follow through with it. Might his inconsistency have been a sign that he would not even look for a job? Contacts made with him for the next fifteen months revealed that he worked in a nickel plating plant for two to three weeks on three different occasions. At the time of the final contact he was unemployed.

KEY FEATURES OF THE CASE. Inconsistency. Improvement in arithmetic. Improvement in Performance Scale IQ. Non-training-related employment.

Dwight

Dwight is a 20-year-old boy who was registered in the upholstery class. He had been unemployed prior to entry into the course. His mother is the principal wage earner. She earns approximately $60 per week. His father had been a gas station attendant. After he was involved in an accident, he had become totally disabled.

Due to a fire in his former school, Dwight's school record was not available. A former teacher reported that Dwight was unable to read and left school when he turned sixteen in grade nine. Dwight admitted, "I couldn't learn much." Explaining further, he said, "I had two car accidents as a child. Since the accidents I could not learn. I thought I would get better but I never did."

Pretraining Tests

On the Wechsler Intelligence tests, his Verbal Scale IQ was 64; his Performance Scale IQ, 55, and his Full Scale IQ, 58. A marked deficit was noted in vocabulary. Scores on the Benton confirmed the classification of educable mental retardation. Scholastic achievement scores were grade 1.8 for reading; grade 3.1 for arithmetic, and grade 1.8 for spelling. Personality ratings on the Rorschach were low for generalization ability, empathy, social responsibility, cooperation, tact, and conformity. His mental functioning was made less efficient by his overreliance on minute detail.

Training Observations

During training he was interviewed several times. Often he misunderstood the interviewers' questions. The interviewer endeavored to simplify his questions by making them more concrete. Dwight liked the upholstery program. His immediate and long-range plans called for him living at home and working in an upholstery plant. He expected to earn $1.35 to $1.50 an hour. Salary, to him, was the most important factor to consider in taking a job.

Throughout the interview, he spoke disparagingly about the academic teacher. It was quite clear that he did not like her. The academic teacher had observed him to have poor work habits. In addition, she noted, "this is the only student I have ever caught cheating. I have tried several different methods but to no avail. He knows I have seen him and continues even when I stand beside him. . . . He thinks people have something against him if he is corrected. . . . Dwight wants you to think he is dumb, but he is sly and smarter than you think." Despite the fact that instructional materials were programmed and the correct answers were always available, rather than test his knowledge he would copy the correct answer without understanding it. He had not learned that he could master as much or as little as he set out to do. Rather he felt that he had to impress his teacher with high scores on a test.

One of his fellow students said he tries to make you think he is "an operator." Dwight claims to be organizing a rock-and-roll band. He expects to promote it throughout North Carolina. This, his buddy explained, is gas station talk. On Saturdays Dwight goes to the gas station and unfolds elaborate money-making schemes to any appreciative audience. What he does not know is that his audience urges him to fabricate for the entertainment of Dwight playing the fool.

His vocational instructor said, "Dwight wants to make it but couldn't. He can't grasp it. The others pick on him. It bothers him. If anyone could afford to spend the time with him, he'd be a steady worker. He needs a lot of attention but he is worth saving." He added that one day some of his classmates were fooling with him and stapled his fingers with the pneumatic stapler used in fastening cloth to the arms and backs of chairs.

Post-training Tests

At the completion of the program, the Wechsler Intelligence Test was readministered. His scores were essentially the same as on the pre-test. On tests of scholastic achievement, increase of .6 of a grade was noted for reading, of .3 grades in spelling, but no change in arithmetic. Personality test scores were the same as those on the pretest. A slight decrease in persistence and increases in cooperation, social responsibility and tact ratings were observed. Academics was distasteful to him. His negligible achievement is attributed to his wish to demonstrate failure to the test examiner. It was believed that in this way he could communicate his hostility to the academic teacher.

Follow-up

Four weeks after training he was interviewed again. He said he approached several upholstery factories but they would not hire him. He added, "no one helped me find a job." He finally got a job putting up machinery as a day laborer. What pleased him most about his work was people would know he had a job.

When asked how he felt about his job, he said that he was disappointed because he thought he had enough experience when he left the training program. The personnel managers told him that he could not learn upholstery in sixteen weeks. His long range plans still call for him becoming an upholsterer and living in his home town. When asked if he would like to continue his education and under what conditions, he said he would like to become a radio-TV announcer and would not want subsidization but if he had to take further work in upholstery he would want an allowance.

In conclusion, Dwight is a mentally retarded student who could not grasp the essentials of the vocational program and despised the academic program. Little change in academic achievement was noted. Two weeks after this interview, Dwight was fired. He went to work for an upholstery firm and was fired again. He took odd jobs mowing lawns in the community. For six months he was unemployed. He took a job as a short-order cook-clerk-waiter at an ice cream stand. He appeared to be quite popular with the customers. He earned eighty-five cents per hour. In retrospect,

OSC, he said, did little for him. He enjoys working the grill. With the money he earned, he bought a car. Girls, he emphasized, went for him now. When the opportunity to cook at another grill occurred, Dwight quit his job. Now he earns ninety-five cents per hour.

KEY FEATURES OF THE CASE. Mental retardation. Lowering of persistence. Dislike for academic program. Dissappointment with training-unrelated job. Difficulty in distinguishing between fantasy and reality.

Brad

Brad is a 17-year-old boy who was registered in the brick masonry class. He had been gainfully employed as a truck operator and porter for a concrete company. His father raises cotton in season and drives a truck during the winter. He earns approximately $30 per week. His mother accepts part-time housekeeping jobs.

The elementary school record was unavailable. In junior high school, Brad's marks were B in language and B– in arithmetic. He received an A in citizenship. In grade nine, all of his marks were failures. His eighth grade teacher wrote, "Brad is a very reserved boy. He reads a great deal and tests show his intellect to be good. With proper care he can make an excellent student." However, his ninth grade teacher wrote, "Needs special help and encouragement if he is to stay in school. Poor home life." In grade nine, his difficulty with some subjects made him study others harder. Soon he failed so much that he lost interest in school. He felt that "this is the way some things are," and he left school.

Pretraining Tests

Upon entry into the program, the Wechsler Intelligence Test was administered to him. His Verbal Score was 101; his Performance Scale, 98; and his Full Scale score, 100. All scores were categorized "average." On the Benton, however, all test scores were in the mental defective range. This discrepancy may be attributed to the memory factor involved in the Benton. Brad's scholastic achievement was grade 9.8 in reading; 9.8 in spelling; and 6.7 in arithmetic. Scores on the Rorschach suggested reasonably adequate personal and social adjustment. He was observed to be perfectionistic. Among other observations were that he was mentally alert, flexible, and very consistent.

Training Observations

During the program, he was interviewed several times. The academic program deeply impressed him. Brad said he learned quite a bit in general science. Reading became more enjoyable now that he got more meaning out of books. He frequented the town library.

His feelings about the vocational training were also positive. He believed he could learn enough to hold down a job as a brick mason anywhere he might go. Within five years, he estimated, he would be a first-class mason. He has talked with masons and watched them work. His hope was to begin as a brick layer rather than as a helper, anticipating an income of $1.50 to $2.50 an hour. He is willing to move out of town to get a job. His long-range goal was to be a brick mason somewhere in North Carolina.

The academic teacher evaluated Brad as a good student. She said he began his assignments promptly, followed directions, tried to exceed earlier accomplishments, and discussed applications of what he studied. She added, "Brad has to support his parents. He is a conscientious student and works very hard." Later she noted a change in him, she said, "Brad dyed his hair and lately has come to have the attitude that the world owes him a living."

His vocational teacher said, "I thought he'd be my best bricklayer, but he needs constant supervision or else he disrupts the other workers. If he were asked to sketch a house he would draw one. I would not want him on my crew. I cut his pay last week."

Post-training Tests

Retests at the end of the program revealed that Brad's Performance IQ rose fourteen points to 112 and Verbal IQ, eight points to 108. An increase of .9 of a grade in reading was observed. No change was seen in arithmetic, and there was a loss of one year in spelling achievement. Most errors were careless. There were few personality test score changes. The ones observed were quite significant. Brad became less perfectionistic, less persistent, socially responsible, tactful, and confident.

Follow-up

One month later during the follow-up interview he related that he returned to his old job of bagging cement at $1.25 an hour. He didn't look for another job. His brother got him the job with his former boss. The main reason for choosing this job was that it was close to home. He had to depend on others for transportation. In his dreams he wants to be a brick mason, but in his long range plans he expects to be bagging cement near home.

If he had it to do over again he said he would still like to study brick masonry and would want a larger subsidy. He felt the "breaks" between classes should be longer. In retrospect, he said the program did not do anything for him.

In conclusion, Brad is an overly precise student who exaggerated the importance of his assignments. His need for supervision precluded his becoming a mason. He improved in performance IQ and reading ability. His progress at first was greater than what it was later. He had built up a false image of his abilities. At the end of the program, he bitterly returned to his old job. On several occasions the writer tried to contact Brad but to no avail.

KEY FEATURES OF THE CASE. Improved performance IQ. Increase in reading ability. Decrease in spelling achievement. Undependable, lacking in persistence. Inconsistent achievement. Willing to move. Did not look for a job. Training unrelated employment.

Ike

Ike is a 16-year-old boy enrolled in the upholstery class. He had no employment history. His mother, a divorcee, is the principal wage earner. She works in a knitting mill.

In his first three years in school, his average language grade was C and his average arithmetic grade was D. He was retained in grade four. Thereafter, his average language grade became B; his average arithmetic grade became C. He was retained again in grade five. Again he improved his marks the year of retention. In grade seven, he declined in achieving, receiving D's in most subjects. His teachers frequently commented that he was lazy. Typical of such comments is that of his sixth grade teacher who said, "Ike's lazy but capable of doing work. He wants attention. He pretends to be sick. Is absent a great deal. . . . Mother says she can't control him." In grade seven, Ike quit school. He explained, "I just could not learn . . . they gave me too much home work."

Pretraining Tests

His intelligence test scores at the beginning of the program were Verbal Scale—92; Performance Scale—107; and Full Scale—98. He was reading on the grade 5.3 level, his spelling was grade 4.2; and his arithmetic was 5.6. Personality ratings were low for generalization ability, above average for perfectionism, below average in mental awareness, and concentration, below average in persistence, high drive, high impulsiveness and low conformity.

Training Observations

Ike was not enthusiastic about the academic program. He avoided discussing it. On the other hand, he spoke openly about his satisfaction with the upholstery program. He expected to become an upholsterer and to live at home. Leaving his home town to find a job did not interest him at all. He was depending upon his teacher to get him a job. Salaries upholsterers were earning interested him the most. Had he the opportunity, however, he would have liked to study welding. His long-range plans call for him becoming a welder and living at home. The training would have to be subsidized before he would consider entering a program. He felt his progress as an upholsterer proved to everybody that he is not lazy. "I *can* work," he concluded.

The academic teacher felt that Ike's work habits were adequate. She said he began assignments promptly, recorded his answers neatly, and tried to exceed his previous accomplishments. She found him to be very nervous but a speedy worker.

The vocational teacher said Ike was always "pecking" the other students with the air hammer. He was a quick worker and had grown in interest in upholstery. "He is too mouthy, though," was the teacher's final comment. He would stir up the class.

Post-training Tests

At the conclusion of the program, retests of intelligence revealed that Performance Scale IQ increased twenty-seven points and Full Scale IQ increased fourteen points to 112. His reading achievement improved a half year to grade 5.8; spelling grade declined a half year to 3.7; and arithmetic grade increased to .3 grades to 5.9. Some personality changes took place. Generalization ratings were higher as were those for mental awareness, concentration, interest in people, persistence, motivation, and conformity. He was observed to be less impulsive and less attentive to details.

Follow-up

Four weeks later he was interviewed again. He said he had gone to the employment office but he could not find a job in upholstery because he was too young. He looked for a job for two weeks. He then took a job as a cook at a hamburger house. He found the work interesting, and although disappointed at first, he added he would not change his job. He was not certain about what kind of work he will be doing in the next year, but was sure he would be living at home. In retrospect, he found the training program had not helped him.

In conclusion, Ike was a capable student who, at first, did not take his training seriously. Toward the end of the program he settled down. He made sizable gains in performance IQ and some improvement in reading. Although he felt he did not benefit from the program, he tended to become more accepting of social demands of a situation. He was too young to be employed as an upholsterer, so he took a job as a cook. Later he lost his job as a cook. Still later he worked as a dishwasher in the hospital. For seven months he scrubbed pots and pans for $23 a week. During this time his mother became quite ill. Ike worked during the day and prepared meals and cleaned house at night. He left the hospital job because he could not "make ends meet." He worried so much he could not sleep. At the same time he paid fines for four traffic violations, all incurred on the same day. When the writer visited the home, his mother was recuperating. She spoke highly of his virtues. He did not smoke, drink, or go out with girls. Ike was working as a shipping clerk for a warehouse. He earned $1.45 per hour.

KEY FEATURES OF THE CASE. Able student. Not serious at first. Gained in intelligence. Persistent. Motivated by money. Unsure of plans. Nonmobile. Training-unrelated employment.

Dan

Dan had three years of gainful employment as a helper in the construction industry. At the time of entry into the carpentry class he had been unemployed for less than a month. The principal wage earner was his mother who worked in a dry cleaning plant.

There was no record of Dan's achievement in elementary school. His marks in high school were all C– and D. The only comments on his school record were "average in class work, likes music, and is inclined toward the mechanical arts." His teachers noted he was absent often. Dan's account of his withdrawal from school was as follows, "I wasn't doing too poorly. All my friends were dropping out and living a life of leisure. I was terribly disappointed after quitting and regretted it." He added he wanted to return but he feared his friends would ostracize him.

Pretraining Tests

At the time of entry into the program, his Wechsler Verbal IQ was 84, Performance was 79, and Full Scale IQ was 81. His reading achievement was at grade 3.4, spelling at 2.6, and arithmetic at 4.2. The results of the personality tests indicated that he received low ratings in generalization ability, empathy, persistence and conformity. He received high ratings in interest in people, confidence, and motivation.

Training Observations

During the training he was interviewed several times. He said he would like to be a carpenter. He was especially interested in building frames for houses. His long-range plans call for him becoming a carpenter and living in Newark, N. J. He said he heard that a Negro carpenter does well in the North. His deep motivation for training is evidenced by his statement that he would like additional training without allowances. He doubted that he benefitted much from the academic program, but he didn't disapprove of it. In general, he said the program gave him a feeling of self-satisfaction because he now had a skill.

The academic teacher found him to be inconsistent. He would begin assignments promptly, try to exceed previous accomplishments, and follow directions but not all of the time. She found him to be consistently lazy. She said, "Dan is a sly fox. He's a perfect angel to your face and very sneaky behind your back. . . . He admitted drinking and was sent home. Absenteeism (sic) habit!"

The vocational instructor found him to be undependable. "He could learn tools," the instructor asserted, "but wasn't interested in class. You had to keep after him all of the time. He has skill, though. You had to get him interested in it. When he was out a lot, his mother said he was sick. We know he got work digging graves. He feels the world owes him a living."

Post-training Tests

Retests of intelligence revealed that his Verbal Scale IQ rose three points and his Performance Scale and Full Scale IQ's, eight points. There was no change in achievement. He may still be considered functionally illiterate. Ratings on the personality test changed somewhat. Although he was still rated low in generalization ability, he became more perfectionistic. He did become more persistent but less responsible, tactful, and confident.

Follow-up

One month after the completion of the program, he was interviewed again. He was working with a surveyor, helping to cut a "right of way." He wanted a job in carpentry. At the time he was not actively seeking one, though. A friend of his, he confided, was looking for him. What he liked most about his job was the people working there. His long range plan was to be a carpenter and to live at home. It should be noted that his attitude toward mobility has changed. He also changed his mind about the kind of training he would like to be in. He said he would like to be a welder. In retrospect, he said the school taught him a skill. "I don't have to work as a laborer," he added. He feels it put him two years ahead in experience.

In conclusion, Dan is a youth of low normal ability. He did not have good work habits in the program. Changes in intelligence and in achievement are slight. As a person he did change somewhat. He became more persistent but less responsive to social restrictions. Dan had been hired by a construction company. He was sent across town on a job. Because he did not know his way around town, he went home. The last contact revealed that he was running an elevator in a hotel in New Jersey.

KEY FEATURES OF THE CASE. Inconsistency. Persistence. Poor work habits. No progress in the course. Training-unrelated employment.

Ducky

Ducky was an 18-year-old boy enrolled in the brick masonry class. He had never been gainfully employed. His father, the principal wage earner, is a mill worker.

His school records reveal that from grades four through six his average marks were C−; in grades seven and eight, they were D; in grade nine they were F. The teachers rated his personal and social assets, below average. Typical of these ratings were those for dependability, industriousness, initiative, and leadership. In grade five, his teacher noted, "He is beginning to want to learn, *on his level* (one or two) grade. He writes beautifully." In grade nine, his teacher wrote, "Very slow. Cannot read." This was his last year in school. Ducky said, "I always wanted to go to school until I got into trouble with the principal. I thought about quitting but my father made me go back. One day the principal made me walk home to get an excuse, and I never returned. School was just like a prison camp. Every move you make they give you a blue slip. . . . I hardly ever stayed out but I just couldn't learn."

Pretraining Tests

Upon entering the program, the Wechsler Verbal Scale IQ was 64; Performance Scale, 82, and Full Scale IQ, 70. This placed him in the educable mentally retarded classification. His reading grade was 2.4; spelling 2.2 and arithmetic 3.9. Personality ratings were low for generalization ability, empathy, cooperation, and conformity. He was found to be very picayune and aggressive. His mental efficiency was reduced by his low generalization ability, perfectionism, poor emotional control, and compulsivity.

Training Observations

During the program he was interviewed several times. He said his parents made him go through the program. Neither the vocational nor the academic program interested him. Had it not been for the training allowances, he would never have consented to enter the program. His long-range plans call for him doing brick masonry or farming and living at home. He does not feel the program did anything for him.

His academic teacher said he had no consistent work patterns. One day he would begin his assignments promptly, on another day he would not. She concluded, "Ducky would love to be top man on the totem pole. When he is corrected he just sits and grins. He has improved a lot, but still has a long way to go."

The vocational teacher said that Ducky started off well. "He got a lazy streak. He could not work without supervision, doesn't pay attention; he can't plan. He lays brick well, but you have to be after him all the time. He'll not bother anyone, he just sits." These were the perceptions of his teacher.

Post-training Tests

Retests on Ducky indicated that he lost six points in Verbal Scale IQ, but gained twelve points in Performance Scale IQ. There was overall no change in Full Scale intelligence. No changes were noted in achievement either. Nor were there any significant changes in personality. The few changes which did take place were in the direction of greater persistence, cooperation, and tact.

Follow-up

The follow-up interview revealed that Ducky was digging basements and employed by his father at $1.00 per hour. His attraction to work was its closeness to home. He said he did not want to become a mason. His greatest disappointment was that the program did not offer diesel mechanics. He plans someday to work at a mill close to home. In retrospect, he felt he did not get much out of the program.

In conclusion, Ducky made little progress in the program. He was not dependable. He did not enter the program voluntarily, changes in Performance IQ were, however, noted.

KEY FEATURES OF THE CASE. Mental retardation. Persistence. Parent coercion. No progress. Training-unrelated employment.

SUMMARY

In summing up the last ten cases it is quite clear, that these graduates had few characteristics in common. Rather several clusters of possible explanations may be observed. Many of the graduates who entered nontraining employment were considered highly skilled by their vocational instructor. They were too young to pursue their calling but they did want to work. They were persistent. Perhaps because of the unavailability of positions to them, but not solely for this reason, they took the first job that came along. In some cases, the graduate did not look for a job, rather some relative or friend made the initial contact with an employer. There were other students who had such low mental ability that they could not benefit from the training. Consequently, they could not get training-related jobs. Finally, there were graduates who were not interested in training at all; they were more interested in the allowances. Although the vocational instructors judged them to be able workmen, a few trainees lacked the good work habits necessary to pursue their calling successfully.

From all of the data available thus far, there appears to be but two characteristics which distinguish this group from the unemployed and they are higher ratings in "persistence" and "motivational inconsistency."

Youth, little effort in looking for a job, antipathy to mobility, mental retardation, poor work habits, persistence, and inconsistency were the characteristics of the training unrelated employment group. One year after the program was over most of the mountain graduates were unemployed. The graduates from the Piedmont had been in and out of jobs. Not one, however, had been in training-related employment.

More than unemployed graduates, those with training-unrelated jobs condemned OSC. The images they had developed as skilled workmen were shattered. The unemployed, however, still had hopes.

EMPLOYED—TRAINED RELATED

Silas

Silas is a 19-year-old youth with no previous employment history. He lives with his parents, six sisters, and four brothers. His parents are both unemployed and the major source of family income is from the Welfare Department.

While attending public school, Silas was evaluated under two grading systems, the conventional literal marking system in grades one and two and the unsatisfactory-improving-satisfactory system in grades three and four. From grade five on he was again marked according to the A,B,C system. In grade seven, Silas left school. Although he was truant thirty-eight days in grade one and thirty-eight days in grade two, or 21 per cent of the time each year, his marks were B's and A's in language and in arithmetic. In grades three and four Silas read satisfactorily and improved in arithmetic. In grade five were the first indications of inadequate academic achievement. He earned D's in most subjects. He did, however, receive an A in citizenship. The two years he was in grade six he earned C's and D's. He was fourteen years old when he left school. The comment on his record was "too lazy to try."

All of the teachers who rated Silas as being below average in dependability, industriousness, and initiative, rated him as average in self control and courtesy. This may be the reason Silas consistently earned A's in citizenship.

The teachers made these statements regarding Silas: grade two —"a good student, very slow"; grade three—"agreeable but not very energetic (sic)"; grade five—"an irregular student—could be a good one if he tried—lacks interest and initiative—cannot be promoted." Silas was promoted, however. Grade six—"an irregular student—seems undernourished and needs medical attention—can do fair work when he tries—needs encouragement"; Grade seven—"student quit school; lacked initiative; did practically no work though he could have done better, poor home circumstances."

Although the school records indicated that he quit school in grade seven after repeating grade six, Silas stated that he quit in grade eight after repeating grade seven. There is further lack of agreement regarding age; Silas said he was seventeen when he quit but the school records indicate he was only fourteen years old at the time he severed his relationship with the school. No one could explain this inconsistency.

Pretraining Tests

Silas gave as his reason for leaving school that he had to work around the house. At the time of the pretest, however, Silas told the test administrator that he quit because he was failing in his courses. Generally, Silas did not respond freely. Rather he would say "don't know" almost automatically. He needed considerable prodding. On the Wechsler Adult Intelligence Scale (WAIS) Silas received the following scores: Verbal, 78; Performance, 94; and Full Scale intelligence score of 84. The full scale WAIS score of 84 places Silas in the dull normal category. However, on a culture free test (the Benton Visual Retention Test) from which two IQ scores were attained he was classified as borderline on correct response score and defective on error of response score. On the Wide Range Achievement Test, Silas failed to measure up to his sixth grade background. He was found to be functioning at the grade 4.9 level in reading; 3.8 in spelling; and 4.5 in arithmetic. The results of a personality test administered to Silas indicated that he is above average in his capacity to follow through on a planned course of action and that he was very willing to work. He did tend to be perfectionistic. Noted also were wide interests, mental alertness, and behavioral consistency.

Training Observations

During the three interviews with the research staff of Operation Second Chance, Silas continued to be uncommunicative. He was rather reluctant to give any opinions of his training. Therefore, it is difficult to determine what the training actually meant to him. From observing him in the welding class, the research staff concluded that he applied himself in the training program. He was seeking the work experience that would enable him to find employment. He applied himself despite being in a training program that was not among his stated preferences in pretraining counseling interviews. In an interview at the completion of the training program, Silas indicated he would rather become a mechanic or an upholsterer.

Silas apparently wants a job so much that just to have any kind of employment is his main goal in life. The training allowances, he explained, helped him meet transportation costs and meals.

At the end of the training program Silas was undecided about leaving or staying in the area. He stated; "I don't know if I will stay here or not. I haven't made up my mind." He has been out of the area only on rare occasions and appeared to be happy in the familiar environs of the mountains.

Silas did know what he was looking for in a job. The first thing was a good salary because, "I need the money," but he gave no reasons for needing money. Second, he wanted the kind of job that would interest him "so I can do my best work" and third, the job should be "close by" so he could return home frequently.

The academic instructor for the Operation Second Chance program indicated that Silas had a good attitude toward the academic work. She further indicated that in general Silas followed directions very well, began assignments promptly, and tried to get the general idea of the assignment. The vocational instructor indicated Silas had sufficient knowledge to become a welder who needed no supervision.

Despite being out of training for three consecutive weeks Silas made some gains in academic achievement, as indicated by test results. Through hard work he had made up a considerably large portion of the training he had missed during his period of absence.

Post-training Tests

The battery of tests administered at the conclusion of the program indicated that Silas had indeed made progress. On the Wechsler Intelligence Test the Verbal IQ score dropped three points. This is within the standard error of measurement. However, the Performance IQ score was raised by seventeen points. This is a highly significant gain. Also significant is the Full Scale IQ gain of seven points. On the Benton Visual Retention Test the IQ scores obtained indicate an increase. The number correct score went up from the seventy to seventy-nine range to the eighty to ninety-four range and the error score from the below seventy range to the ninety to ninety-four range. These are significant changes indicating that Silas did increase in measurable intelligence factors during the training program. The Wide Range Achievement Tests also indicated gains in arithmetic from 4.5 to 4.8, in reading from 4.7 to 5.1 and spelling from 3.8 to 4.6.

The personality test indicated that Silas improved in his ability to use a logical approach to solution of problems, as well as in his adaptability to life situations. He also indicated a greater recognition of his responsibility to society but indicated a lessening of his willingness to accept and be directed by social customs. He was still perfectionistic.

Follow-up

Silas accepted employment as a welder in his home area and has remained on the job for three months. Later he worked at a thread plant putting spools of the same size in proper racks. He was earning $15 per day. He said they got after him "right smart" and he quit. He had worked for nine months. At the last contact he had been jobless for six months.

KEY FEATURES OF THE CASE. No interest in public schools. Low socioeconomic background. More ability than was exploited by the schools. Sincere wish to find employment. Perfectionistic, confident, significant gains in IQ and achievement.

Sam

Sam is an 18-year-old who left school when he was in the tenth grade. He had been working intermittently as a farm hand since then. His father has silicosis and has not been employed for five years. He had been a mica miner. His mother has cancer and has not been employed for years. She had worked as a cook. Sam stated in an interview that he was the principal wage earner of the family.

Reviewing his school records, one notes that Sam had achieved unsatisfactorily in language and in arithmetic from the very beginning. In grade one he was absent twenty-seven days (15 per cent of the year). These absences coupled with an apparent slow learning ability and related disinterest in academic offerings began a cycle of failure-despair-lack of motivation for school. At the time he repeated grade one he earned four marks of B, three marks of C and one D. The second time Sam was in grade one he earned seven marks of B and one mark of C. His lowest marks both years were in reading. Might one speculate about the impact of the first set of marks on subsequent development. His marks belie the failure conferred upon him. The despair-school avoidance—failure sequence may very well have been established and henceforth functioned autonomously.

In grade two, all marks were satisfactory except for reading which was "unsatisfactory." Lack of reading ability became cumulative and by the third grade he performed unsatisfactorily in all of his subjects. With the exception of grade six, when he received a C in reading, Sam earned D's in arithmetic, reading, language and spelling through his school career. One may well ask how much punishment could Sam's ego take before he felt like running away. Stripped of his self esteem, the most effective way to guard against further smarting of his ego was to withdraw from the situation.

One teacher wrote, "I don't think he is capable of doing first grade work. Not interested in school." All teachers were in agreement that Sam had adequate self control but was below average in dependability, industriousness, initiative, and leadership. His defense was withdrawal from scholastic activities. It is important to note that he did not become a nuisance or attention seeker. Instead he avoided academic stimulation; at first by daydreaming; later by staying away from school. In the ninth grade he was absent sixty-four days or 36 per cent of the year. He thought about leaving school permanently at that time. However, he was promoted to grade ten and returned to school in the fall. Before Christmas, Sam decided to leave school for good. He said that he had been staying out a lot and knew he could not pass the work.

Pretraining Tests

After Sam contacted Operation Second Chance about the training programs offered he took a battery of tests. On the Wechsler Intelligence Test he received the following scores; Verbal IQ, 76; Performance IQ, 67; Full Scale IQ, 70. On the Benton Visual Retention Test the number correct IQ and the number errors IQ were below seventy. From these tests he was observed to be in the educable mentally retarded range.

Although Sam had reached the tenth grade his scores on the Wide Range Achievement Test indicated that he was functioning at the third grade level in reading, spelling and arithmetic. The Structured Objective Rorschach Test indicated that Sam was moody, impulsive, lacking in self confidence, perfectionistic, but tactful, persistent and practical.

Training Observations

After beginning the training Sam stated during an interview that the academic portion of the program was good for people who didn't know how to read and that the academic program should be three hours a day rather than two hours a day because it was possible to learn more in three hours than in two hours. In a subsequent interview Sam discussed the types of materials he was learning in the academic class stating that he learned more than in high school and on this occasion suggested that the academic class be extended by one half hour per day. With regard to the vocational program during the first interview Sam stated that it was a "good program for a boy that quit school" and told of some of the specific tasks he had performed. In the second interview he revealed that he liked to tack backs of chairs best of all. He felt he was improving in reading.

Sam stated during the course of three interviews over the sixteen week training period, where he planned to work after the completion of the training program but never mentioned any plans or goals beyond getting a job in Hickory, North Carolina. He was, however, willing to go anywhere in order to get a job. "Don't like it here in the mountains much—nothing to do," he summed things up.

Sam felt that the type of job he wanted to get would be one in which he would be doing something useful, would make a good salary, and would have his kind of people as co-workers.

Apparently the patterns of the past provided the clothing of the present for Sam in the academic class. His instructor averred that he consistently came to class late, failed to budget his time properly, and showed signs of boredom in the middle of assignments. She stated that Sam's attitude left much to be desired and that he did as little work as possible. She further stated: "He is one of the few upholstery students who has not tried to gain something from this school." Sam's vocational instructor felt that he had a fair grasp of upholstery work but needed additional training or experience in all phases of the work. Here we see Sam, then, apparently seeing positive changes in his behavior. Yet these changes were not noticed by the teachers. If anything, the teachers disagreed with Sam's self evaluations.

Post-training Tests

When the research staff administered tests at the conclusion of the training program, a slight loss, three points, was noted on the Wechsler Full Scale IQ. There were no changes on the Benton retest, both the number correct IQ and number of errors IQ were still below seventy. The post-training administration of the Wide Range Achievement Test indicated Sam changed from 3.7 to 4.4 in reading, 3.3 to 4.5 in arithmetic but 3.5 to 2.9 in spelling.

The Rorschach scores indicated Sam had become somewhat more aggressive, had gained confidence, and had improved his ability to concentrate. He also became less moody and less impulsive. He also became less perfectionistic. These scores suggest that Sam responded favorably to the program and most important began to view himself more favorably.

Three weeks after completing the training program Sam had a job with a manufacturing company in Thomasville, North Carolina. After nine months away from home he returned to the mountains. He was jobless until he affiliated with an antipoverty sanitation project.

KEY FEATURES OF THE CASE. Mental retardation; slow learning;

low reading skill; history of disinterest in academics; perfectionistic; no plans or goals beyond getting and keeping a job; interest in training; improvement in self confidence; training-related work.

Steve

At the time of entry into the pre-admission counseling phase of Operation Second Chance, Steve was eighteen years of age, married, and had twice dropped out of public school. The death of his father upset him emotionally. Through psychiatric therapy he gradually became readjusted. His mother, the principal wage earner, worked in a textile plant. Steve was not employed prior to entry into the Operation Second Chance program.

Steve appeared to be a student of some promise in grades one, two and three. He received twenty-three A's and seven B's. It was not until grade six that he received his first C. That year he had three C marks and six B marks. In the seventh grade he earned two B's, five C's and his first D. He pulled his average up in grade eight earning one A, eight B's and one C. In the ninth grade he received two F's and two D's. In the following year he repeated grade nine. He failed several subjects and decided to quit school. When the new high school was opened, Steve made another try at high school level work, but left again because "the rules were too strict." During his first eight years of schooling Steve received A's in reading for five consecutive years, then B's for the next three years. He received A's in spelling for five straight years, then a B, a C, and a B. In arithmetic it was A's for three years, a B in grade four, an A in grade five, a B in grade six, a C in grade seven, and a B in grade eight. In grade nine the English grade was D−, and the mathematics grade an F.

Pretraining Tests

Steve took the battery of pre-entrance tests with the following results: On the Wechsler Intelligence Test his Verbal IQ was 92, Performance IQ, 81, and Full Scale IQ, 86. On the Benton Visual Retention test, however, his scores placed him in the below-seventy category. Steve could read on the 7.3 grade level, spell on the 6.2 grade level, and do arithmetic on the 8.1 grade level. Mental efficiency, it was found on the Rorschach, was reduced by low generalization ability, perfectionism, worry and compulsivity. His range of interests was restricted. In addition he was neither ambitious nor flexible. He had little confidence in his behavior, was tactless and not socially responsible. Once he found a set of rules he would stick by them whether they were functional or not.

Training Observations

Interviews with Steve indicated that he became increasingly enthusiastic about the vocational training in which he was engaged. Initially, Steve's interest in academic training was quite high. Toward the middle of the program he felt he knew "the material being taught and further training on that level is worthless." His disenchantment with the program came about when he had some personal problems with the teacher. He felt she was "power crazy" and unjust in her punishments.

Steve felt that training allowances were necessary for him to stay in the program. He had no plans for future training. "With a wife and child there will be no room for any more education."

Although there is no record of previous mobility, Steve feels that he would go anywhere in the country to improve himself. He would, however, prefer to stay in his local area.

Despite the financial stress of the family situation Steve's major interests in a job were not of monetary nature. It was of primary importance that the job be interesting. He was also concerned about the kind of people working with him because he could not work with people who were not friendly.

Steve was a good student in the academic program. He began assignments promptly, followed directions, tried to exceed his previous accomplishments, tried to get the general idea of the assignment, and reviewed his work.

The vocational instructor stated that Steve is quick, a good worker who is very dependable and one who will "make it" on the job.

Post-training Tests

At the end of the training period another battery of tests was administered to the group. The Wechsler Intelligence Scores for

Steve indicated that his Verbal IQ score went up three points, his Performance IQ went up thirty-two points, and his Full Scale IQ score went up twenty points. Such sizeable gains as are indicated in the performance and full scale score could not be the result of chance factors. Steve made a significant gain in intelligence. The Benton IQ scores confirm the Wechsler scores. The Benton IQ's came up from below 70 to the 95-109 range. The Wide Range Achievement Test shows that the gain in intelligence was accompanied by a gain of one and one half years in reading level and two years in arithmetic level.

The Rorschach test showed that Steve was still quite perfectionistic and apprehensive. However he became less compulsive. This change in generalization ability is of particular significance.

Follow-up

Steve was hired for an upholstering job before the training program ended. He said that the program had helped him by teaching him the basic ideas of upholstery and the experience necessary in order to be hired. He also stated that Operation Second Chance had helped him to face up to his needs and responsibilities and to face life better. Now he entertained a better outlook on life. Steve stated in the follow-up interview that he quit public school on the advice of a doctor because of a nervous condition. Steve worked for six months, when his buddies left the plant to work elsewhere, Steve quit. He found a job in his home town and has been working there ever since.

KEY FEATURES OF THE CASE. Emotional factors interfering with academic achievement by reducing intellectual efficiency. Improved generalization ability. Training-related work.

Saxon

Saxon is a 19-year-old who left school in grade nine. He took a job in a textile mill. He worked in the mill about two years and then quit. He had been asked by his supervisor to perform some task during the lunch hour. Saxon walked off the job. When he applied for training in Operation Second Chance, he had been unemployed. He lives with his parents.

In September of 1951 Saxon entered public school. That first year he received four marks of C and four marks of B. Despite having passing marks, he repeated the first grade. The second year he was in grade one he earned four D's, two C's, and one B. These marks were much worse than those he received the preceding year but he was promoted to grade two. Saxon received two A marks in grade two along with three B's and four C's. In grade three he received nine B's and two C's. In contrast, in grade four he received two B's and nine C's. Grades five through eight found Saxon receiving marks of C and D in about equal numbers with an occasional B or A. His reading, spelling and arithmetic marks would each average to C for grades one through eight. Saxon first thought of leaving school in grade seven. He could not raise his marks. In grade nine, a teacher advised him to work or to quit. Saxon left.

His teachers felt that he was below average in dependability, industriousness, and initiative. The teachers also judged him to be a slow learner. Among the comments on his record are: "Is slow and a problem. Has improved some"; "Have to keep right after him," "Very slow child. Has improved in manners and in interest but incapable of competing with the group. Seems to have malnutrition"; "Lazy in work-conduct improved greatly—writing difficulty."

Pretraining Tests

The Wechsler Intelligence test of the pretraining test battery gave these scores for Saxon: Verbal IQ—77; Performance IQ—72; Full Scale IQ—73. The Benton Visual Retention Test gave two IQ scores for Saxon—number correct IQ—below seventy, number errors IQ—below seventy. Scores on the Wide Range Achievement test indicated that Saxon was functionally illiterate. He was reading at about the grade 4.9 level, spelling at the grade 4.0 level, and doing arithmetic at the 5.0 grade level.

The personality test indicated that Saxon was in the average range for the majority of the traits measured. There were, however, tendencies toward low generalization and perfectionism. There was a definite indication that poor control, i.e., thoughts not channeled readily into effective processes, lowered Saxon's intellectual performance. He was found to be cooperative, flexible, confident, and interested in people.

Training Observations

When Saxon was interviewed during the training program he indicated that he was going to try to get something out of the training program but that he was not definitely committed to carpentry. He seemed to feel that he had gained considerably from the academic training.

Saxon did not appear to have made any definite plans or to have established any definite goals. At the completion of the training program he stated a preference for training as a brick mason or a mechanic. He wanted to move away from the area but stated further that a year from now he would probably be living at home with his parents.

At the end of the training program, Saxon was asked what would be the most important things about a job. He wanted a "good boss man" to work for, to work with people who do not lie or cuss, to make a good salary.

The academic instructor reported that at various times Saxon distracted others, that he came to class late, that he did not budget his time properly, and that there were other times that he put forth extra effort in an attempt to do well in his work.

The vocational instructor reported that Saxon settled down after a couple of weeks and really applied himself. "He puts his heart in his work." This instructor believes that if Saxon is given a chance he will make good as a carpenter. During the training he became romantically involved with a trainee in another program. Without notice she jilted him. He became restive in class. When his father learned about it, he beat him. Thereafter, Saxon applied himself to the school tasks and became a model student.

Post-training Tests

Wechsler Intelligence scores upon completion of training were: Verbal IQ—76; Performance IQ—75; and Full Scale IQ—73. The differences in the pretraining and post-training tests were slight. There was no change in the Benton IQ scores, either. On the Wide Range Achievement Test, Saxon had gained almost one grade level in spelling and one and one half grade levels in arithmetic. Gains of this magnitude could not be due to chance alone. On the personality test indications again were noted that he had low generalization ability and tended to be perfectionistic. He did become more ambitious, flexible, confident, and consistent.

Follow-up

Saxon was interviewed four weeks after the completion of his training program. He had secured employment as a carpenter the day the program ended and was still working. He felt that the training he had received in Operation Second Chance was the causal factor in securing his job. He was earning $1.45 per hour. This seemed to impress him so much that he wanted more training—even forty weeks without training allowances in order to learn more about his trade. He apparently changed his value system regarding work. Now he felt the most important factor in work was that the job is interesting. Of secondary importance was the salary. He has been steadily employed for a year and a half.

KEY FEATURES OF THE CASE. Poor reading ability; low intellectual efficiency; low generalization; perfectionistic; no clearly defined goals, and training-related work.

Sarah

An older sister has been Sarah's guardian since their parents death. Six months after graduation from high school, Sarah, jobless, sought help from the Operation Second Chance office.

A review of her school record revealed that in the first eight grades of school her marks were A's and B's. In grades nine and ten she made C's and D's, in grade eleven she received all C marks and in grade twelve she received one D, two C's and two B's. Teachers rated her as being average or above average in cooperation, courtesy, dependability, initiative, industriousness, leadership, maturity, and personal appearance. One eighth grade teacher dissented from the generally favorable image which Sarah had established. He judged her to have a very poor attitude and to keep a scowl on her face almost all the time. In grade nine, no comment was made about attitude. In grade ten, one teacher stated, "She did have a bad disposition but has improved greatly." And, in grade eleven, "I have not seen a scowl or heard an ugly remark. Her grades have also improved." There is no explanation or statement of probable causes of such reversal of behavior contained in her record. It is important to recognize, however, that the years in which she received unfavorable teacher comments were not those in which she received low marks. On the other hand, in the years in which she received low marks she received more favorable personality ratings.

Pretraining Tests

Her pretraining Wechsler Intelligence scores were in the average range; Verbal IQ—94, Performance IQ—96; Full Scale IQ —94. The IQ scores obtained from the Benton Visual Retention test were essentially the same, namely in the eighty to ninety-four range. On the Wide Range Achievement Test she placed grade 9.5 in reading, 8.8 in spelling, and 5.9 in arithmetic. Several problem areas were noted on the Rorschach test. Her full intellectual capacities were lowered because of her inability to form concepts or generalizations, her perfectionism, and her persistence in following wrong courses. She was not in tune with what was popular. Tact, confidence, conformity, social responsibility, and ambition were all rated below average.

Training Observations

Sarah was quite interested in the nurses' aide program at first but as she learned more about hospital routine, laboratory and x-ray technology took on new fascinations. By performing all her duties effectively and efficiently, she was able to get the necessary recommendation to work part time as a nurses' aide and learn laboratory technology the remainder of the day. She therefore used the Operation Second Chance program as a stepping stone to somewhat higher occupational status. Sarah had, however, no interest in the academic program. She felt it was two hours per day wasted although she tried to stay busy and get something out of it. Despite a distaste for the general education program, Sarah's teacher made the following observations: "Good student. Works at all subjects. Quiet and puts forth best effort." "Good and capable student. Mature and accomplished much, I believe. She made good use of her time, though often tired." The weekly ratings in the academic class show that Sarah tried to exceed previous accomplishments and tried to get the general idea of the assignment.

The vocational instructor assigned Sarah the highest ratings of the class in all phases of performance of duties as a nurses' aide. She further described Sarah as "dependable, capable of learning and quick to learn, works fairly well with patients." The vocational and academic instructors agreed that Sarah made progress day by day throughout the training period.

Post-training Tests

The test battery was administered upon completion of the course. This time Sarah had a Verbal IQ score of 96, a Performance IQ score of 87, and a Full Scale IQ score of 91 on the Wechsler Intelligence test. Once again the Benton Visual test (form C) IQ's ranged from 80 to 94. On one form of the Benton her IQ went above 109. It appears that once she feels comfortable with a test her scores increase. It is possible, then, that many indices of her behavior are incorrect because inner dissatisfaction interferes with effective demonstration of abilities.

Sarah made significant scholastic gains. Her dislike of the academic portion of the course notwithstanding, she gained 1.5 grades in reading, and one full grade in both spelling and arithmetic. Motivation, however, plays an important role in her demonstration of skill. On a spelling test given a day or two before the post-training tests she made no gains in spelling.

Few changes were noted, moreover, on the Structured Objective Rorschach Test. Sarah was still so low in generalization ability, and so high in perfectionism and in compulsivity that she could not assert her full intellectual abilities. She became less interested in people, less ambitious, flexible and conforming, but more persistent, tactful and consistent. Despite many signs of maladjustment, Sarah became one of the best trainees in the program. Often plagued by her feeling that everything she did was wrong she nevertheless tried to master her environment. It is worthy of note that she preferred the world of test tubes and specimens to a world of people.

Follow-up

Four weeks after the program had ended Sarah was interviewed once again. At that time she felt that the training and experience she had received had enabled her to obtain her present part time nurses' aide position without which she could not afford to learn laboratory technology.

Sarah began work the day after the Operation Second Chance program was completed. She found the work interesting. Now she had a future. Not only that, but she had status. She put it like this, "People would like you (i.e., me), think a lot of you. You could have money and be independent." Sarah was still in her work-training program eighteen months after the completion of her training in Operation Second Chance. She said the "nurses' aide course helped me to land this chance to do what I want to do."

Watson

Watson is a 16-year-old boy who only recently dropped out of school. He was in the ninth grade at the time. Thoughts of dropping out recurred intermittently from the time he was in the seventh grade. All the times he had considered quitting he was sure he would graduate. When he reached his sixteenth birthday, he knew he was old enough to quit. He said, "it made you look good to quit. Thought I could get a job, buy a car and other things I needed. Got along with all the teachers except ninth grade. She would not let you know how you were doing. Fed up with teachers. My parents wanted me to go back but I wouldn't listen. The principal tried to talk me out of it. But I went to work full time preparing feed for a dairy farm."

Off to a good start in school, he earned all B's in grade one. He was improved in grade two, earning three A's and four B's. In grade three Watson slipped a bit; he received three C's, two B's and two A's. In grade four he earned one A, five B's, three C's, and one D. During the fifth grade, Watson earned one A, five B's, and four C's. The marks for grade six were the same as for grade five. Watson left the seventh grade with six C's, three B's and an A. In the eighth grade he earned six B's, three C's and one D. The downward trend accelerated in grade nine. That year he received two F's and two D's. The following year he returned on schedule to repeat grade nine but stayed in school only until his sixteenth birthday. On Watson's cumulative record, typical comments were:

"Slow student. Bad grades because of too many bad mistakes." "Slightly improved; bad grades due to too many absences."

Pretraining Tests

Tests administered prior to training revealed a Verbal IQ of 89; a Performance IQ of 90; and a Full Scale IQ of 88. On the Benton Visual Retention Test his IQ's were within the 70-79 range. Watson could read at grade level 5.7, spell at grade level 6.3, and perform arithmetic at grade level 8.5. On the Rorschach test the following was observed: average ratings in mental functioning, persistence, social responsibility, impulsiveness; above average in tact, ambition, and flexibility. He was, however, not concerned about mundane issues.

Training Observations

Watson stated that at the beginning of the training program he wanted to be a brick mason but later decided carpentry would be better. At the time of the second interview he stated that if a mechanic's course were offered he "would prefer that to a job." During the third interview, Watson indicated that if he were unable to get a carpentry job he would take the brick mason course. This suggested that Watson had no clearcut image of himself as a worker. Interest was shown in the academic portion of the course, especially the arithmetic. Arithmetic was perceived as quite useful to carpenters. He felt that the same material was being taught as in public school but he could "learn it better like it is here." Watson felt that he had gained something by being in Operation Second Chance.

Although there had been little mobility in the family, Watson stated he would prefer to live in Florida or California. He further stated he would be willing to "move up North to find a job." In discussing jobs, what interested Watson most is a job which he could do learning interesting things. A job would also have to provide an opportunity to do something useful. He would also take a look at the other workers. He explained, "because if you cannot get along you might lose your job."

The academic instructor rated Watson as one of the better students in her class. He had good work habits and a motive to learn especially mathematics. During the sixteen weeks he studied basic geometry texts, and beginning algebra and arithmetic texts.

The vocational instructor felt that Watson was one of his best. He was at the top of the class. He also said Watson was dependable, had the skill and understood the work. He anticipated Watson would become a foreman.

Watson appeared to have the willingness and the capacity to learn to benefit from the training program. Allowances were withdrawn but one week. One afternoon he had returned to school intoxicated.

Post-training Tests

At the conclusion of the training a battery of tests was administered. The Wechsler Intelligence test indicated a change in IQ that was a significant change. The Verbal IQ changed from 89 to 90, the Performance IQ changed from 90 to 109. The Full Scale IQ changed from 88 to 101, the performance and full scale IQ could not have been caused by chance factors alone. The Benton Visual Retention Tests IQ's changed from 70 to 79 to 95 to 109. This is another indication of Watson's gains. The Wide Range Achievement test results indicate a gain in achievement that is significant. The reading level was increased from grade 5.7 to grade 6.8. The spelling achievement increased from grade 6.3 to grade 6.5. The arithmetic grade level was increased from grade 8.5 to 10.6.

Retests on the S-O Rorschach test indicated few changes in his personality attributes. He tended to become more perfectionistic and to become highly anxious. He became less persistent. He did become more conforming and more able to grasp principles.

Follow-up

Four weeks after completing the training, Watson was interviewed once again. He had obtained a carpentry job three days after the training program ended and was still working at the time of the interview. Watson felt deeply interested in his work. He was also pleased with the kind of people working there and that he was doing something useful. He was earning $1.45 an hour. He felt quite important. His earnings allowed him to feel secure enough to marry. He recommended the Operation Second Chance program to his wife. She, in turn, became one of the more competent trainees in the sewing for upholstery course.

The Operation Second Chance training program had proven to be valuable to Watson in many ways. He embarked on the world of work with good pay. He felt he could do the job better as a result of the training. Understanding other's problems as well as his own problems was an unanticipated outcome. He said that "he feels better about working now." He has been employed steadily since graduation.

KEY FEATURES OF THE CASE. Mobility, willingness, significant gains in IQ's, anxiety, perfectionism, significant gains in achievement, training-related job.

Sadie

At the time of her entry into Operation Second Chance for pretraining counseling and testing, Sadie was nineteen years old. She was living at home with her parents and an older sister. Her father, the principal wage earner, was a compressor operator for a feldspar mining corporation. He earned $65 per week. Sadie was a newcomer to the world of work.

Sadie failed in her first year in public school. She received C in reading and in arithmetic. Her other marks were C's. Thereafter, her marks were good. She received B's in all of her subjects the year she repeated grade one. In grades two and three she received thirteen A's and five B's. In grade four she earned one A, one C, and ten B's. In grade five her marks were two A's and ten B's. In grade six she had as many A's as B's. Achievement began to decline in the seventh grade. She earned five C's, Three B's and one A. In grade nine she received three F's and two D's. In grade ten her marks sunk even lower. One F, three D's and one C closed her scholastic career.

Generally, the teachers rated Sadie as average or above on all personal assets. However in grades nine and ten her teachers noted that Sadie became undependable, lacked industriousness, initiative and leadership. One teacher commented ". . . needs to put forth more effort and have more confidence in herself." "Quiet and cooperative but could do better work. She is absent too much."

Many girls think of dropping out of school. Sadie was no exception. She could not recall when it was that she first thought of leaving but she reminisced, "I couldn't get it off my mind." One day, after three weeks in the eleventh grade she left school at the regular hour and thought she would go back the next day. The next morning she decided that today would be a good time to quit and she never went back. Her teachers asked her to return; her parents asked her to return. Life without school, however, looked so easy that Sadie refused to go back.

Pretraining Tests

Sadie took the pretraining battery of tests the December before the program started. The Wechsler Intelligence test results indicated that Sadie had a Verbal IQ of 90, a Performance IQ of 80, and a Full Scale IQ of 85. The Benton Visual Retention Tests suggested, however, retarded mental development. The Wide Range Achievement Test indicated Sadie was reading at the grade 7.6 level, was doing arithmetic at the grade 5.5 level, and was spelling at the grade 7.9 level.

Personality tests indicated at least two areas in which mental ability was reduced in efficiency. She was unable to grasp main ideas or principles. In addition she was perfectionistic. Her interests were quite narrow. She was not in tune with everyday events. Although she was highly motivated and quite confident of her abilities, she was not persistent. She was a flexible girl who had a strong feeling of responsibility. Yet she found following rules and regulations quite distasteful.

Training Observations

Sadie had an interest in nursing before she came into the program. She would have come into the program without a training allowance and would have preferred sixteen weeks of training. She knew that she wanted to stay in nursing service in some capacity but had not made definite plans regarding just how she would do it. The nurses' aide training appeared to give Sadie some part of what she wanted from life. She stated in one interview that her family was pleased with the program because they knew what Sadie "put everything she had into it." Sadie enjoyed the academic phases although she could not understand how it would help with nursing but, "It must help or they would not have it—I just can't see how it helps."

The nurses' aide instructor rated Sadie very high in all areas. She found Sadie quick to learn, alert to patients' signals, treating patients sympathetically, responding to instructions well, and observant of all hospital procedures.

The academic instructor reported that Sadie was one of the best of the students. She followed directions, tried to exceed her previous accomplishments and tried to get the general idea of the assignments.

Once having had the taste of nursing, she wanted to continue learning. She said she would be willing to move anywhere to get the type of training that she wants or the type of job that she wants. She likes the mountains but realizes that the opportunities for advancement are so much better elsewhere.

Sadie is looking for a job in which she knows she could help others. The work would also have to be interesting. Through nursing she felt that she could become someone important. Sadie was deeply involved in her training. Serving humanity was deeply satisfying. When discussing the class, however, she frequently became angry about the insincere students who were collecting their government allowances on Friday but who disrupted the class all week. Sadie felt they were cheating her of good learning time.

Post-training Tests

When the post-training battery of tests were administered it was found that Sadie had gained in Verbal IQ by one point from 90 to 91, had gained in Performance IQ by nine points from 80 to 89, and had gained in Full Scale IQ by three points from 85 to 88. Only the gain in performance IQ was significant. Scores on the Benton were in the retarded range, still in disagreement on the Wechsler.

On the achievement tests, Sadie improved slightly in reading.

She was now reading on the grade 7.8 level. Her greatest gain was in arithmetic, one year, to the 6.5 level. There was a slight decrease in spelling of a half year to the grade 7.4 level. Slight changes in personality were noted. She became more interested in people, less self centered and less socially responsible. She was still quite perfectionistic. She pursued the letter of the law without grasping its principle.

Follow-up

Four weeks after the completion of the course Sadie was interviewed again. A representative of Operation Second Chance had taken her to a nearby hospital for an interview. She was offered the job and accepted it. Asked again what she felt was most important to her work, she replied, it had to be interesting. She added that she had to be doing something useful. She wanted very much to become someone. With the $100 per month she was earning plus room and board, she felt she had made it this time. Nurses' aide was but one step in her long range goal of becoming a practical nurse. Dedication and curiosity were the two characteristics which she felt would help her move forward in her new calling. She feels the program has been the high point of her life. Without it, her life had no direction. Sadie worked for five months. She quit her job to get married. After her marriage, she relocated in South Carolina. There is a tuberculosis sanatorium near her home. She has filed an application to work there. Her hope is to become a teaching practical nurse.

KEY FEATURES OF THE CASE. Low generalization, perfectionism, willingness to work hard for what she wants. Working in a training-related job.

Dolly

Dolly is a 21-year-old girl who was registered in the nurses' aide program. She had never been gainfully employed. Her father was the principal wage earner. He fired boilers at a mining plant. His earnings were approximately $50 per week.

Her scholastic history was quite uneven. Her first year in grade one she received D's in language and in arithmetic. Her next year she received B's in these subjects. In grade two she received A's. In grade three, B's; in grade four, C, in grade six, A in language but D in arithmetic. This fluctuation between B and D continued through the eleventh grade. Her teachers rated her average in personal and social assets throughout her school experience. They rated her a good reader, but felt she needed more encouragement and time than they were willing to give. The events surrounding her withdrawal from school are unclear. In the tenth grade she thought of leaving school at least once a month. The thoughts were associated with scholastic failure. While in the eleventh grade her mother was involved in an accident. She was blinded. Dolly stayed at home to care for her. The reason she gave for leaving, though, was that she did not have money to pay for books, clothes or lunches. At another time she said that she left school because her mother had a heart attack. She added, moreover, that she did not like the idea of going to school everyday.

Pretraining Tests

Upon entering the training program, her Wechsler IQ's were Verbal—86; Performance—82, and Full Scale—83. She was reading on the grade 9.2 level. Her spelling was grade 6.9, her arithmetic 5.2. On the personality tests her mental efficiency was found to be reduced because of her inability to categorize and poor emotional control. She was also observed to be lacking in tact, persistence, social responsibility, and interest in people. She was, however, able to concentrate, to conform, and to cooperate.

Training Observations

During training, she enjoyed both the academic and vocational programs. She would have preferred to become a secretary. Taking temperatures and blood pressure interested her the most. Her plan was to get a job in a hospital and earn $82 per month after deductions. She did not want to have to leave her home town, though. Being near home was especially important to her. Her long-range plan, however, was to be a nurses' aide in Minneapolis, North Carolina.

Her academic teacher found her to be a conscientious student.

Dolly began her assignments promptly, selected additional assignments during her free period, and tried to exceed her previous accomplishments. No statement was available from the nurses' aide instructor.

Post-training Tests

Retests of intelligence indicated no rise in Verbal IQ but an increase of twenty points in Performance IQ and one of eleven points in Full Scale IQ. She improved three years in reading to grade 12.2, .6 of a year in spelling to 7.5, but not at all in arithmetic. Personality retests showed slight but noteworthy changes. She still had difficulty developing concepts. She was still lacking in persistence. She had become more aware of people. As a result, scores on human relationships, social responsibility and tact increased. She became better controlled emotionally. She was able to give the most minute of details her attention.

Follow-up

Four weeks after training she said that she had been an aide for three weeks. A representative of the training program brought her to the hospital and introduced her to the personnel manager. Dolly enjoys helping sick people. When asked what her salary was, she replied to the interviewer that she was not sure how much money she was earning as no one ever discussed salary with her. Her long range plans were to remain at the local hospital. Her supervisor confided that Dolly has a good chance to continue. Dolly's lack of responsiveness and her inability to communicate spontaneously gave the appearance that Dolly was performing like a robot on the ward. The supervisor hoped she would be friendlier. The interviewer believed Dolly to be a very frightened girl, unsure of where she wanted to go in life. Her happiest moments were in reading books. Though a competent nurses' aide, she lacked the spirit necessary to buoy up the patients.

In conclusion, Dolly made great strides through the program. She was gainfully employed in a training-related field. Eighteen months later Dolly was contacted again. She was still working at the same hospital. She was receiving $145 per month. Without her training, she insisted, she could not have gotten a job. In retrospect, she wished Operation Second Chance had given her more training in arithmetic and English.

Biddy

Biddy is an 18-year-old girl who had never worked full time. She wanted to become an auto mechanic, but was placed in the sewing for upholstery class. Her father is the principal wage earner of the family. He is employed in a cotton mill and is earning $67 per week.

In her first eight grades in school, Biddy received B grades in language and B− grades in arithmetic. In the ninth grade, however, she failed all of her subjects. Ratings of her personal and social assets were average. She left school in grade ten. Her reason was, "I just didn't like the idea of people telling me what to do, but if I had it to do over again I wouldn't quit."

Pretraining Tests

The Wechsler Intelligence Scale was administered to her upon entry into the program. Verbal Scale IQ was 83, Performance Scale IQ 85, and Full Scale IQ, 83. Scholastically she placed at the grade 7.9 level in reading, 7.6 in spelling, and 5.4 in arithmetic. Interference with mental efficiency was observed to be due to low generalization ability, perfectionism, high anxiety and poor emotional control. She may be described as being unable to concentrate, disinterested in people, lacking in persistence, no social responsibility, without tact, lacking in confidence, and lacking in ambition. She was noted to be a practical person who was cooperative and conforming.

Training Observations

Initially she was quite excited about the program. She enjoyed making sofa backs, tea cushions, and chair covers. She believed the academic portion of the program had been helping her. Later in the training program, she felt she was not being stimulated. She enjoyed repairing the sewing machines more than sewing itself. She demonstrated that she was quite adept with tools. Although she would have preferred becoming an upholsterer, she found sewing somewhat satisfying. She planned to become a sewer and live at home. In retrospect, she feels the program helped her become more communicative. "I am not as backwards or shy as I used to be," she summed things up at the last interview. Biddy was one of the most bouyant students in the class. She raised student morale to a very high level.

The academic teacher said that Biddy began assignments promptly, followed directions, and discussed applications of what she studied. "She is a good student," her teacher wrote, "but too much of a clown. Biddy is a very consistent, hard worker. She has personal problems." The nature of the problems cited was mixed feelings about becoming romantically involved. Her sex role was further confused when her sister ran off with a married man. Distrusting herself, Biddy rejected male companionship.

The vocational teacher said, "She could sew, but had to be in the sewing mood. Just a very happy-go-lucky person with no responsibility." Despite personal disappointments and self doubts, Biddy did her work, although with no degree of consistency.

Post-training Tests

On the retest, Biddy declined eight points in Verbal IQ but increased thirteen points in Performance IQ to 98. These changes did not increase the original Full Scale IQ, however, by more than two points. Scholastic improvements were noted, too. Biddy improved 1.5 grades in reading to 8.8, .5 grades in spelling to 8.1, and .7 grades in arithmetic to 6.1. The personality changes were in the direction of better adjustment. Although still rated high in anxiety, ratings on generalization ability, perfectionism, interest in people, persistence, social responsibility, tact, ambition, and confidence improved. Difficulty in concentration and in controlling impulses were still noted. Decline in aggressiveness appeared, too. The concession she made for her improved social adjustment was becoming less dominant.

Follow-up

Four weeks after she graduated, she was interviewed again. She said she started to look for a job on her own immediately after graduation. She was turned down by an upholstery firm. She did get a job sewing draperies at $1.25 per hour. What was most attractive about the job was that she could become someone. She hated to sit at home doing nothing. Her long-range plans called for her sewing draperies or shirt collars. She did not want to work with cushions. She complained, though, as she improved, the supervisor would change her job. She was nearing production at the plant. She did not want to leave her home town at all; not even for a better job. In retrospect, she found the academic part of the course more useful to her on the job than the sewing.

In conclusion, Biddy was an alert student with much nervous energy. She was not a steady sewer. The program did stimulate her to change mental and personality patterns of behavior. Two months later she quit and then went to work sewing for upholstery at a plant closer to home. She was contacted once again eighteen months after graduation. She was still employed at the upholstery plant.

KEY FEATURES OF THE CASE. Disinterested in sewing; a good sewer; progress in both phases of the course. Increased persistence and generalization ability. Training-related employment.

Abe

Orphaned at age thirteen, Abe, his mother and seven siblings had for several years lived only on widow's benefits and social security. After he quit school, he worked in an upholstery plant. During the second year of work, he began to feel that his supervisor was exploiting him, so he quit. More recently he had been employed as a bagger in a grocery store. He has three years of gainful employment. At the time of entry in the brick masonry class, he was twenty years old.

In his first three years in school, Abe had been a good student. He received B's in language and in arithmetic. In grades four through six he received C's. In grades seven through nine, he received D's. He was retained in grade seven. At age seventeen, he left school. He was in the tenth grade. He said he saw no connection between school and training for work. He admitted that he would like to have gone to college. His teachers found him conscientious, easy to get along with, but unable to do the work.

Pretraining Tests

Upon entering the program his Verbal IQ was found to be 111, Performance IQ 98, and Full Scale IQ 106. Scholastically, he was considered a fair student. His reading grade was 8.0, spelling 5.6, and arithmetic 7.5. This is approximately what his status was in grade seven. On the personality test he was found to be perfectionistic. Except for below average interest in people, his adjustment was rated as resembling the average adult. He was viewed, then, as a responsible, motivated, flexible, confident, persistent, conforming worker.

Training Observations

The research staff found Abe to be the most perceptive, honest, and mature student in the program. Brick laying was a challenge to him. He was quite confident that he would "make" a good mason. He expected to start at $1.50 an hour. He added that if he had to move to get a job, he would. He saw more opportunities in the big cities than in the small towns. His long-range plans, however, called for him to be laying bricks and living at home. He found the academic portion of the program very helpful. He felt the teacher was making the students too dependent upon her rather than letting them grow up. He disapproved of her constantly chastizing the class. His opinion was that the teacher meant well but she was not giving the students a chance to prove to themselves that they were grown-up.

His academic teacher judged him to be a good student. He began his assignments promptly, selected additional assignments during free period, followed directions, tried to exceed previous accomplishments, and drove himself to improve. She noted, "he is a hard worker and tries to keep the other boys straight. . . . A consistent worker."

His vocational teacher said, "Abe is one of the best. He studies anything given. Works on problems. He'll be a supervisor in no time at all."

Post-training Tests

Retests revealed that Abe increased three points in Verbal Scale IQ, fifteen points in Performance Scale IQ and ten points in Full Scale IQ to 116. Abe was particularly anxious to learn if he had improved. In reading he went up .2 of a grade; in spelling .6, but in arithmetic he improved 3.7 grades to grade 11.0. Personality changes were in the direction of better adjustment. He received higher ratings in persistence, mental awareness, and he became less picayune, too. He was, moreover, more demanding of himself.

Follow-up

At the completion of training he was interviewed again. He had been working as a mason since his graduation. When he spoke of his job he was suffused with excitement. He had found a place for himself in the world of work. His earnings were $1.35 an hour. He did not want to leave the area because he was satisfied with his work. A contact was made with his supervisor who said few workers accept tasks as gracefully or work as dependably as Abe. In retrospect, the training program taught him to work hard and like it. He said he also learned the give and take of working with people. A contact made eighteen months after graduation revealed that he had worked for the same boss for twelve months. He received two raises. He quit to go to work for another construction firm at fifty cents per hour more than he had earned previously. Within three weeks he received a twenty-five cent per hour raise.

In conclusion, Abe was an able student, highly motivated to succeed. He made great strides in the program. His IQ and scholastic achievement improved. "A consistent worker" was the evaluation his Operation Second Chance teachers gave him. One might only speculate that had he perceived his public school training as relevant that he might have gone to college as he had hoped.

KEY FEATURES OF THE CASE. A hard worker. Class leader. Consistent. Persistent. Great progress in the program. Training-related work.

SUMMARY

This group of graduates differed from those unemployed and those employed in training-unrelated jobs in several ways. They seemed to be older, had better personality adjustment, made greater progress in the training course, had better work habits, were more persistent, and were more consistent. They were more willing to travel to take a job. They looked more favorably upon employers. In addition, their willingness to work made them more attractive to employers. It should be noted, though, that these observations hold for the Piedmont dropouts. Most of the mountain graduates who had been employed in training related jobs one month after graduation often quit their jobs and were jobless up to six months of the eighteen month period in which the writer maintained continuous contact with them. The impact of the training program may only be temporary. After the novelty of work wears off, the graduate has to look for encouragement from friends or from his conscience. Such "blood" transfusions spells the difference between the anemic and the self actualizing worker.

CONCLUSIONS

The purpose of presenting thirty randomly drawn case studies was to demonstrate how vastly different from one another each school dropout is. School histories were unlike. Some students had been good students until the day they left school; others had been good students until the last year or two of school; others had been poor students until junior high school and then they improved; others had been good students until junior high school and then their achievement declined; and still others had been poor students from the very beginning. As for personal and social patterns, there were as many different ones as there were students. Most dropouts, moreover, had received quite favorable teacher ratings.

The focus of this study was predicting training outcomes. There was no single factor which could be used to predict which trainee would become employed.

Several clusters of traits which are reliable harbingers of training outcomes suggested themselves from the case studies. These are an ability-achievement factor and a persistence-drive-conformity factor. Both contribute to the attractability of an applicant to an employer. Not only that but both contribute to an applicant's view of himself as acceptable to an employer. In those cases of unemployed trainees who *anticipated* rejection by the employer, it was often observed that such apprehensions were rarely based on experienced rejection.

Ability-achievement

The average intelligence quotients of the three groups were very similar. (See Appendices A and B.) For training-related students it was eighty-four; training-unrelated, eighty-one, and unemployed, eighty-two. It is apparent, moreover, from Table XXII that the training-related employment group had the highest pretraining achievement test scores.

TABLE XXII

AVERAGE PRE-TRAINING ACHIEVEMENT TEST SCORES OF TRAINEES

Employment Group/Achievement	*Reading*	*Spelling*	*Arithmetic*
Training related	7.3	6.2	5.5
Training unrelated	4.7	4.2	4.5
Unemployed	5.7	4.4	4.1

Though not different in intelligence, the training-related employment group appears to have exploited their ability to learn more than did the other groups. This is more poignantly shown in Table XXIII which contains the general achievements of each IQ group.

TABLE XXIII

AVERAGE ACHIEVEMENT SCORES OF INTELLIGENCE GROUPS

Employment Group/IQ Group	*70-79*	*80-85*	*86-100*
Training related	3.7	6.9	7.3
Training unrelated	2.7	—	6.5
Unemployed	2.8	4.5	6.9

What distinguishes the training related-employment group from the others is their achievements relative to their ability. Therefore, it should be clear that the ability of school dropouts does not in and of itself determine what a trainee will accomplish in his retraining. Since all trainees were exposed to the same program, it is not likely that the program alone caused these changes. If we look at the motivations and goals of the trainees, traits which were a part of the trainee prior to his entry into the program, we see a possible explanation for the different achievements.

Persistence-drive-conformity

Among the many attributes measured by the structured objective Rorschach test are *persistence, activity potential, and conformity.* The persistence measure reveals how much "stick-to-itiveness" a person has. Certainly few people will disagree that the capricious student is too erratic to absorb what he is being taught and too slipshod to work with any degree of precision. Persistence also connotes dependability.

Activity potential or "drive" is human energy directed toward attaining some goal. In some instances energy is diffuse and hints at the internal tempest which draws energy from the seething currents of human frustration. This energy, unlike goal directed drive, is confined primarily to the removal or dissipation of a troublesome situation. "Anxiety" is the name which psychologists have called it. While the anxious person does have abundant energy it is used primarily in maintaining equilibrium. The high drive person directs his energy toward self improvement. Torpor is the opposite of a high drive level.

Conformity is the receptivity to direction by social rules, traditions, or customs. Setting aside one's self-centered and sovereign impulses for the good of the group is assurance that a trainee or a worker will not obstruct the productivity of his co-workers or threaten the administrative cadre.

Table XXIV illustrates that the combined ratings for persistence, drive and conformity were, prior to training, highest in

TABLE XXIV
FREQUENCY OF PRE-TRAINING PERSISTENCE-DRIVE-CONFORMITY RATINGS

Employment Group/Ratings	*Below Average*	*Average*	*Above Average*
Training related	11	14	5
Training unrelated	13	11	6
Unemployed	17	7	6

the training-related employment group, lower in the training-unrelated employment group, and lowest in the unemployed group. Initially, then, there was a group of trainees who had ambition, who persisted at their activities and who were willing to work under a set of rules. Several students were stimulated by the program to change their motivational patterns. This is reflected in the post-training persistence-drive-conformity ratings. These appear in Table XXV. These data suggest that the training-related group achieved essentially the same ratings. On the pretraining tests, they received 63 per cent average or above ratings; on the post-training tests, 70 per cent. Fifty-seven per cent of the pretraining ratings of the training unrelated group were average or above. On the post-training tests, 67 per cent of these ratings were that high. Prior to training, 43 per cent of the ratings of the subsequently unemployed group were favorable; on the post-training tests 57 per cent of the ratings were average or above. For both sets of tests then, the training-related group is more highly motivated than the other two groups and the training-unrelated group is more highly motivated than the unemployed group. Some further evidence for this view is offered here.

Some evidence has been adduced by some psychologists indicating that perceptual levelers, that is people who characteristically blunt the stimulus they view, are not as highly motivated as perceptual sharpeners, the characteristically acute observers. The Benton Visual Retention Test was the only perceptual task which could be scored for perceptual blunting and sharpening. In Appendix A are these evaluations. Eighty per cent of the unemployed group tended to "dedifferentiate" and blunt their reproductions. Ninety per cent of the training related graduates tended

TABLE XXV

FREQUENCY OF POST-TRAINING PERSISTENCE-DRIVE-CONFORMITY RATINGS

Employment Group/Ratings	*Below Average*	*Average*	*Above Average*
Training related	9	17	4
Training unrelated	10	9	11
Unemployed	13	11	6

to have sharp perception. The training-unrelated group revealed no clear cut perceptual tendency on the Benton. If the theory of motivated behavior based on sharpness with which people perceive stimuli is correct, the high percentage of sharpeners in the TR group and the high percentage of blunters in the UN group suggest that prior to training the motivations of these two groups were unlike.

Together, the achievement-ability factor and the persistence-drive-conformity-factor suggest that employed trainees were those who, prior to training, most resembled in mental activities and ambition the middle class image of the industrious, stable worker. The more they resembled it, the greater the likelihood they would become employed in training-related work.

Such workers are attractive to employers. They are able to adjust to the demands of the job. Trainees lacking in these traits may sense this deficit in themselves and, anticipating rejection, may not even try to look for a job. On the other hand, they may not be aware of their inadequacies, so they do seek employment. If given an opportunity to work, they often fail to adjust and are fired.

The implication for training programs such as Operation Second Chance are clearly in the direction of more careful assessment of the job opportunities in an area. The employers must be willing to give the graduates a chance to work. In addition, the job requirements must be known and integrated into the admissions policy as well as the curriculum. More careful attention needs to be given the inconsistent trainee. Work habits often can be improved through programming the instruction to insure their development. Occasionally, psychological guidance is needed for faltering students. Among the traits to be alert to are achievement relative to ability, persistence, drive and conformity. Finally, placement practices need to be reexamined. Qualified workers should be granted employment. The despair experienced by skilled workers unable to obtain employment not only degrades them as individuals but denies the economy the benefits of their talents. Program planners need to be alert to the "goldbrick." If they cannot remotivate him, any retraining program is of questionable value. There were students who did not believe they had to earn their reputation. They were mostly from the area known as Appalachia. Prior to any retraining a program in occupational information is needed in order to permit such students to examine their faulty occupational reasoning. Without such an examination, the program cannot be expected to "soak" in.

As for optimum length of a training program, it is not reasonable to assume that all students will attain the same level of skill in a trade at the end of a sixteen week training program. Some students require more than sixteen weeks to learn to perform even minimally on the job. To them, sixteen weeks merely whets the appetite. They are more disappointed than ever, because their hopes of achieving self respect die with the closing of the program. The question need not be whether their disillusionment is offset by the victories of those trainees who succeeded; rather, the question has to be, How can we build a vocational training program that will prepare each youth for gainful employment?

A second chance program should extend as long as it takes the last trainee to become skilled enough and industrious enough a worker to succeed on the job!

There is a destiny that makes us brothers
None goes his way alone:
All that we send into the lives of others
Comes back into our own.

EDWIN MARKHAM

APPENDIX A

PRE-TRAINING SCORES UNEMPLOYMENT GROUP NO. 1-10

Trainee	*IQ*	*R*	*S*	*A*	*Per*	*Coop*	*Tact*	*Cfd*	*Act*	*Cty*
Greg	45	0.7	1.0	0.9	H	A	BA	BA	A	L
Jill	94	8.5	9.9	9.6	L	A	A	A	AA	AA
Herb	81	3.9	3.1	4.1	BA	A	A	A	BA	BA
Chip	92	5.3	4.4	4.1	BA	BA	BA	BA	BA	BA
George	70	3.4	2.8	2.7	H	A	A	A	A	L
Ronnie	60	0.0	1.3	2.2	A	L	A	A	A	L
Ed	93	9.5	6.9	5.6	A	A	A	A	H	A
Deke	83	5.7	3.6	3.9	AA	A	A	A	BA	BA
Georgia	82	9.8	8.2	5.2	BA	A	A	A	BA	L
Cindy	82	7.1	6.2	4.5	L	AA	A	BA	BA	A

Coded as:

R = Reading
S = Spelling
A = Arithmetic
Per = Persistence
Coop = Cooperation
Tact = Tact
Cfd = Confidence
Act = Activity Potential
Cty = Conformity
L = Low
BA = Below Average
A = Average
AA = Above Average
H = High

PRE-TRAINING SCORES TRAINING UNRELATED EMPLOYMENT GROUP NO. 11-20

Trainee	*IQ*	*R*	*S*	*A*	*Per*	*Coop*	*Tact*	*Cfd*	*Act*	*Cty*
Jay	70	1.7	1.9	2.7	BA	A	A	A	A	BA
Al	70	4.7	4.2	4.5	BA	A	BA	BA	A	BA
Mary	109	12.4	9.5	9.3	BA	A	A	A	AA	AA
Len	103	10.7	8.2	4.8	A	A	A	A	A	AA
Emmet	93	9.2	6.5	4.8	A	A	A	A	BA	BA
Dwight	58	1.8	1.8	3.1	AA	BA	BA	A	A	L
Brad	100	9.8	9.8	6.7	AA	A	A	A	A	A
Ike	98	5.3	4.2	5.6	BA	A	AA	H	AA	BA
Dan	81	3.4	2.6	4.2	BA	A	A	AA	AA	L
Ducky	70	2.4	2.2	3.9	A	L	BA	A	A	L

PRE-TRAINING SCORES TRAINING RELATED
EMPLOYMENT GROUP NO. 21-30

Trainee	*IQ*	*R*	*S*	*A*	*Per*	*Coop*	*Tact*	*Cfd*	*Act*	*Cty*
Silas	84	4.9	3.8	4.5	A	A	A	A	AA	A
Sam	70	3.7	3.5	3.3	A	A	AA	L	A	L
Steve	86	7.3	6.2	8.1	AA	A	BA	L	L	A
Saxon	73	4.7	5.1	6.7	A	A	A	AA	H	L
Sarah	94	9.5	8.8	5.9	BA	A	BA	BA	BA	BA
Watson	8.8	5.7	6.3	8.5	BA	A	A	A	A	A
Sadie	85	7.6	7.9	5.5	BA	A	A	H	H	L
Dolly	83	9.2	6.9	5.2	H	A	BA	A	A	A
Biddy	83	7.9	7.6	5.4	L	A	BA	BA	L	A
Abe	106	8.0	5.6	7.5	A	A	A	A	A	A

APPENDIX B

POST-TRAINING SCORES UNEMPLOYMENT GROUP NO. 1-10

Trainee	*IQ*	*R*	*S*	*A*	*Per*	*Coop*	*Tact*	*Cfd*	*Act*	*Cty*
Greg	42	1.1	1.6	2.5	A	A	A	A	A	L
Jill	105	10.0	9.1	8.1	BA	BA	A	A	AA	BA
Herb	83	5.2	3.2	4.5	AA	BA	AA	AA	AA	L
Chip	92	7.4	5.4	5.5	A	A	A	A	A	A
George	64	3.9	2.8	2.7	A	A	A	A	A	L
Ronnie	49	1.4	0.7	2.0	A	A	BA	A	A	BA
Ed	99	9.7	5.6	11.0	A	A	BA	A	H	BA
Deke	78	5.6	4.2	5.4	A	A	A	A	BA	L
Georgia	92	9.4	9.1	4.9	L	A	BA	A	AA	L
Cindy	86	8.3	6.4	6.2	L	AA	A	A	AA	A

POST-TRAINING SCORES TRAINING UNRELATED EMPLOYMENT GROUP NO. 11-20

Trainee	*IQ*	*R*	*S*	*A*	*Per*	*Coop*	*Tact*	*Cfd*	*Act*	*Cty*
Jay	61	2.3	1.0	3.8	AA	BA	BA	A	A	L
Al	60	5.2	4.2	4.8	BA	AA	BA	BA	A	AA
Mary	125	14.2	10.6	12.3	BA	A	BA	BA	BA	AA
Len	96	9.2	9.1	5.6	AA	AA	A	A	A	AA
Emmet	96	8.8	7.1	5.6	BA	A	A	A	BA	AA
Dwight	54	2.4	2.1	1.2	A	A	A	A	AA	L
Brad	108	10.7	7.2	6.5	BA	A	BA	BA	A	A
Ike	112	5.8	3.7	5.9	A	A	AA	H	H	AA
Dan	86	3.5	2.9	4.2	AA	A	BA	BA	A	BA
Ducky	72	2.1	2.2	3.6	AA	A	A	A	A	L

POST-TRAINING SCORES TRAINING RELATED EMPLOYMENT GROUP NO. 21-30

Trainee	*IQ*	*R*	*S*	*A*	*Per*	*Coop*	*Tact*	*Cfd*	*Act*	*Cty*
Silas	91	5.1	4.6	4.8	AA	A	A	A	AA	BA
Sam	73	4.7	5.1	6.7	A	A	A	AA	H	L
Steve	106	9.0	6.1	10.2	A	A	AA	A	A	A
Saxon	73	4.7	5.1	6.7	A	A	A	AA	H	L
Sarah	91	10.3	8.7	6.7	A	A	A	BA	L	L
Watson	101	6.8	6.3	10.6	BA	A	A	A	A	A
Sadie	88	7.8	6.8	6.5	BA	A	A	A	A	BA
Dolly	94	12.2	7.5	5.3	L	A	A	A	A	A
Biddy	85	8.8	8.1	6.1	A	A	A	A	BA	A
Abe	116	8.2	6.2	11.2	AA	BA	A	A	A	A

AUTHOR INDEX

Allen, D., 33
Aller, C., 51
Archer, E., 14
Asher, E., 61

Battle, H., 35
Bell, H., 48
Benney, C., 54, 55
Bienstalk, H., 10
Bledsoe, J., 21, 33
Borrie, C., 14
Bowman, P., 32, 35
Buck, R., 13
Burchill, G., 41

Cantoni, L., 12
Chang, T., 17
Coleman, J., 135
Collins, M., 34
Cook, E., Jr., 35
Craigo, R., 27

Davie, J., 12
Davis, A., 14, 15
Deck, J., 52
DeLaurier, E., 34
Dillon, H., 21, 23, 24, 29, 35, 47, 48
Dresher, R., 27

Fillmore, E., 61
Fine, T., 26
Forlano, G., 42
Freeman, F., 62

Gill, G., 39
Gillingham, J., 34
Grittner, K., 22, 30

Havinghurst, R., 14
Hollingshead, A., 12
Holzinger, K., 62
Hoyt, K., 34

Jeffries, A., 34
Johnson, E., 35

Katz, A., 11
Kitch, D., 21

Legg, C., 35
Lichter, S., 40

Matthews, C., 32, 35
McCreary, W., 21
Merachnik, P., 45
Miller, H., 11
Miller, L., 17, 18, 21, 29
Mitchell, B., 62
Mitchell, N., 38
Moore, P., 36
Morrison, W., 14
Morrow, R., 39

Nelson, L., 22
Neugarten, B., 13
Nienstedt, C., 23

Penty, R., 36
Perrella, V., 11
Plunkett, M., 22, 35, 47
Powers, E., 39

Rapien, E., 40
Riches, N., 22, 35, 47
Roe, A., 95
Roens, V., 39
Rothney, J., 39

Savitzky, C., 29, 49
Schwarn, O., 20
Segal, D., 20
Seibert, F., 40
Sibley, E., 12
Skeels, H., 61

Sklansky, M., 40
Slotkin, H., 42
Silberman, C., 16
Smith, H., 29
Somerset, H., 14
Sorenson, M., 33

Teuber, N., 39

U. S. Department of Labor, 10

Van Dyke, L., 34

Wheeler, L., 61
Wills, C., 28
Wilson, P., 13
Wirtz, W., 41
Wolfbein, S., 35
Wolfe, D., 22

Young, J., 39

SUBJECT INDEX

A

Accomplishment, 147
Adjustment, 33, 54, 61, 253. *See* Trainee characteristics
Advisory board, vii, viii, 115, 116, 128, 133, 159
Agency jealousy, 130
American Samoa, 17
Appalachia, 121, 124
Arizona, 18
Atlanta, 30
Attendance, 27
Automation, 6, 8
Avery County, North Carolina, 62, 63, 108

B

Basic literacy, 150
Benton Visual Retention Test, 65, 160

C

California, 17
Calipatria, California, 40
Canada, 17
Case studies, 157 ff
Chicago, 43
Colorado, 18
Community, ix, x, 55-58, 85, 102, 117-122, 126, 127, 154
Competition, 6, 32, 101
Conflict, 35, 103
Connecticut, 23, 25
Continuing education, 49, 50, 55
Counseling, 38, 39, 40, 42, 44, 132
Curriculum, 7, 139, 160

D

Dade County, Florida, 22, 34
Demography, 23
Demonstration programs
  aims, 25
  project, ix, 51
Department of Community Colleges, 129, 130
Diploma, 6, 8
Disadvantaged, 56, 136
Disenfranchisement, 14
Dropout
  age, 24, 25, 92
  decision, 31
  definition, 17, 19, 20
  prevalence, 16, 24, 25, 30
  rates, 6, 16, 22, 33, 34
  reasons, 35, 37, 53, 92, 101
  stereotype, 5
  symptoms, 6, 26, 27
  world, 124
Dropout theory, 36

E

Economics, x, 10, 44
Education-earnings, 12, 101
Educators, x
Ellerbe, James, vii, 64, 159
El Mirage, Arizona, 56
Employability, 93, 195
Employment, viii, 47, 49, 55, 57, 59, 60, 89, 91, 99, 127
Employment Security Commission, 64, 100, 114, 129, 130, 131, 138
Equipment, 144, 153
Everett, Massachusetts, 46
Extracurricular, 26, 36

F

Family, 27, 34, 38, 92
Fast learners, 155
Flint, Michigan, 41
Follow up, 165, 169, 173, 176, 181, 184, 186, 189, 191, 193, 199, 202, 205,

208, 210, 213, 216, 218, 220, 222, 227, 230, 233, 236, 238, 241, 245, 247, 249, 252

G

GATB, 64
Generalist training, 143, 149
Greensboro, North Carolina, 36

H

Hawaii, 17
Hiring practices, 135, 136
Holding power, 22, 24
Holland, 17

I

Idaho, 33
Illinois, 26
Incentive, 145, 148
Income, 11, 12, 101
Individual differences, 7
Indonesia, 17
Industry, 8, 34, 113, 114
Isolation, 13

J

Jones, J. B., 157, 162
Jordan, 17
Juvenile delinquency, 15

K

Kennedy's dropout campaign, 29, 31
Kentucky, 22

L

Laymen, x
Leadership, 128-130
Lincoln County, North Carolina, 62, 63
Lincolnton, North Carolina, 19, 125
Los Angeles, 22, 55

M

Manpower training, 93, 125
Markham, E., 10, 258
Maryland, 25, 32, 36
Mental ability, 12, 13, 27, 31, 61, 86, 139. *See* Trainee characteristics
Michigan, 27
Mitchell County, North Carolina, 62, 63, 108
Mobility, 95, 100, 102
Mobility network, 124, 125
Motivation, 125, 126, 223

N

Needs, 7, 9
Negroes, 11, 119, 132, 195
Nevada, 18
New Mexico, 18
Newspapers, 5
New York, 23-25, 28
New Zealand, 14
North Carolina, 18, 19

O

Occupational information, 141
Oregon, 19

P

Pasadena, 45
Pennsylvania, 47
Personal styles, 86-88, 93, 95, 100
Philadelphia, 44, 55, 56
Poverty, 9, 13, 19
Pregnancy, 36
Profit motive, 6
Programmed instruction, 67, 151
Psychodynamics, 40
Psychologist, x, 110, 132

R

Recruitment, 144
Responsibility, 95
Roads, 129
Rochester, 21
Reading ability, 27, 36
Rural-urban, 13, 18, 19, 25, 34

S

Sanford, Terry, vii
School failure, 27-30, 36, 101

School promotion, 22, 32
Self view, 14, 32, 146, 149
Senter, M., 17
Slow learners, 152
Social caste, 128
Social class, 9, 12-14, 21, 33, 128
Society, 8, 9, 88
Sociologist, x
South Carolina, 18, 19
St. Louis, 44, 55, 56
St. Paul, 22, 30
STEP, 46, 47
Structured Objective Rorschach Test, 65, 160
Syracuse, 21

T

Tacoma, 21
Talent, 14
Tasmania, 17
Teacher evaluation, 8, 35, 106, 107
Teacher preference, 7
Tennessee, 15, 37, 61
Trainee characteristics
  achievement, 69-77, 83-93
  mental ability, 73-93
  personality, 71-79, 87-93, 124, 140, 254
Trainee evaluations, 94, 96, 98, 105, 150
Training, viii, 61
  aims, ix, 59
  length, 112
  observations, 164, 167, 171, 174, 178, 183, 185, 188, 190, 193, 198, 201, 204, 207, 209, 212, 215, 217, 219, 222, 225, 229, 232, 235, 237, 240, 243, 246, 248, 251
  programs, 66
    automechanics, 67
    bricklaying, 66
    carpentry, 66
    nurse aide, 67
    upholstery, 66
    welding, 66
Tucson, 21
Tyrell County, North Carolina, 62, 63

U

Underachievement, 11, 40
Unemployment, 23, 51, 62, 64, 91, 100
Union County, New Jersey, 45
United States Department of
  Commerce, 11, 24, 48
  Health, Education, Welfare, 17, 18, 43
  Labor, vii, 51, 52, 55, 129
Utah, 18

V

Values, 32, 35
Verbal facade, 52
Vermont, 24, 25
Virginia, 48
Vocational interests, 64

W

Washington County, North Carolina, 62, 63
Washington, 17
Washington, D. C., 43
Wechsler Adult Intelligence Scale, 65, 160
Welfare, 108
West Virginia, 18, 19
Western Electric Club, 49
Wide Range Achievement Test, 65, 160
Winston-Salem, North Carolina, 36
Wisconsin, 17
Work habits, 253
Work-Study programs, 41, 42, 43, 44, 45, 46, 50, 51, 53, 54
Worker traits, 6
Workers
  blue collar, 10
  skilled, 12
  unskilled: 12
  white collar, 10
Wyoming, 18

Y

Yancey County, North Carolina, 62, 63,